KHAMS PA HISTORIES

BRILL'S TIBETAN STUDIES LIBRARY

EDITED BY

HENK BLEZER
ALEX MCKAY
CHARLES RAMBLE

VOLUME 2/4

KHAMS PA HISTORIES

Visions of People, Place and Authority

PIATS 2000: Tibetan Studies: Proceedings of the Ninth Seminar
of the International Association for Tibetan Studies, Leiden 2000.
Managing Editor: Henk Blezer.

EDITED BY

LAWRENCE EPSTEIN

BRILL
LEIDEN · BOSTON · KÖLN
2002

Publication of the Proceedings of the Ninth Seminar of the IATS was made possible through financial support from the Gonda Foundation (Royal Dutch Academy of Sciences—KNAW) and was facilitated by the International Institute for Asian Studies (IIAS)

Die Deutsche Bibliothek - CIP-Einheitsaufnahme

Epstein, Lawrence:
Khams Pa Histories : Visions of People, Place and Autority. PIATS 2000: Tibetan Studies: Proceedings of the Ninth Seminar of the International Association for Tibetan Studies, Leiden 2000. Managing Editor: Henk Blezer / edited by Lawrence Epstein.
Leiden ; Boston ; Köln : Brill, 2002
(Brill's Tibetan studies library ; Vol 2/4)
ISBN 90-04-12423-3

Library of Congress Cataloging-in-Publication Data

Library of Congress Cataloging-in-Publication Data is also available

ISSN   1568-6183
ISBN   90 04 12123 4

Cover design: Cédilles / Studio Cursief, Amsterdam.

PRINTED IN THE NETHERLANDS

TABLE OF CONTENTS

INTRODUCTION

LAWRENCE EPSTEIN (UNIVERSITY OF WASHINGTON)

This volume contains five of the six papers presented at the panel on 'Khams pa Local History' at the Ninth Seminar of the International Association of Tibetan Studies, in addition to two papers presented elsewhere at that meeting. To various degrees these papers address politics, history and agency, as well as their historiographical representations on the Khams frontiers.

Recent historiography has trended in three major directions. Once preeminent metanarratives of nation-states are under critical scrutiny with concern over local voices and events in history-making, rather than their being submerged by grand narratives. At the same time, while it is axiomatic that "all history is local," the essays included here are also concerned with larger historical forces, attitudes and ideas which construct the local, dissolving its boundaries in the very process, and tying it to regional, national and global narratives. Simultaneously, once-standard operating concepts of historical analysis have themselves become subjects of reflexive inquiry. Concepts like the local and the global do not merely constitute an analytic frame to work with, but are also sites to work upon through critical interventions in them as loci of power.

Khams is a particularly apt field of inquiry to assess these discursive concepts. Situated between two power centers, China and Tibet, particularly during the times which the papers address—from the late nineteenth to the mid-twentieth century—when imperial, colonial and local forces clashed and intersected in the process of place-making and nation-building. Khams became an unsettled and unsettling meeting ground for diverging forces, but rife with historical possibilities. Too often latter-day Chinese, Tibetan and Western accounts have ignored these, and peripheralized local concerns. The multiplex conditions that constituted the Khampa geopolity have received little attention.

The papers in this volume address aspects of the axes of power, space and identity in this frontier zone and the often discordant visions of various parties who wished to transform it. Likewise, they discuss ways those visions were themselves transformed by Khampa agencies. Traditional historiography characterizes the frontier as an incorporating and civilizing zone flowing outwards in a single direction from centers of power; it thus ignores almost entirely the frontier as discursive process. Hence, while the essays herein are concerned with Khams, it is conceived neither as a unitary object, nor a place to be known merely for its own sake; it is also a site for the critical reassessment of historiographies. In traditional studies of frontier places, the people who inhabit them have been portrayed as passive objects, and their responses to forces beyond their immediate control simply ignored. When viewed from the centers of power, frontier zones like Khams were easily relegated to the margins of history. This position has been interrogated increasingly in recent scholarship of the Qing frontier and elsewhere and has led to a "recentering of the local." The essays here discuss as well how Khampas employed political strategies, which appropriated both local and inflowing resources, thus turning them into power sources and establishing their sense of centrality.

Unfortunately our historical, geographical and ethnographic knowledge of Khams is still tenuous. Like much of the Tibetan national cultural area, there is a dearth of first-hand ethnographic studies from traditional times, and, to a large extent, historical studies have taken Central Tibet as their axial focus. Basically Khams seems to have erupted most strongly into Tibetan and Chinese consciousness only in the mid-nineteenth century with Nyag rong Mgon po rnam rgyal and late Qing and Tibetan activities in the border regions. Yet there are strong indications that even before this period there was an emergent ethno-national consciousness among Khampas, of which Mgon po rnam rgyal was only a part. We still lack, for instance, fine-grained studies of the relationship among such nineteenth century Khampa movements as Mgon rnam's attempt to restructure society and build a Khampa state, the religio-philosophical union propounded by the *Ris med* synthesis, and the revival of the Gesar cult, as the foundational saga for unification. Certainly, taken together, these movements seem to signal an already nascent sense of a unique Khampa national identity.

One cannot but agree with Wim van Spengen's observation that "one would also like to know more about the nineteenth century" in Khams. Indeed we would, and more. What underlies this quest is a critique of historiographic claims that the modern nation-state evolves as the sole "subject" of History and wellspring for identification, superseding all other existing identities. We still lack detailed knowledge of the highly diverse locales that constituted the Khams region, in terms of their basic economic, family, social and political structures and the relationships of these local polities to one another, let alone the complex discourse of Khams' relationships to Central Tibet and China. Perhaps, with increased availability of and access to Tibetan and Chinese archival materials, and more ethnographic field research, these serious lacunae will be filled.

The papers in this volume have been arranged to reflect the themes that they share in common. The papers of Wim van Spengen, William Coleman and Peng Wenbin locate Khams in a broader political history. They explore the fluidity of the frontier and its turbulent dislocations, as Khampas encountered and responded to Tibetan and Chinese national projects in the early part of the twentieth century. Fabienne Jagou and Carole McGranahan shift their gaze to individual figures and their engagement with Chinese and Tibetan social politics. Peter Schwieger's analysis of history as oral narrative takes up several of the same themes as Carole McGranahan's preceding paper. Both position Khams in relation to Central Tibet, as does the subject of Tsering Thar's paper, which brings us to religious innovation in contemporary times.

Wim van Spengen discusses the social and political chaos which reigned along the ethnically complex frontiers in southern Khams from the turn of the century on. His deep structural analysis urges us to consider both the rapid shifts in human space-time, and the slower tempos of geographical time, which aid in understanding the long-standing political instability—wars, lesser conflicts and, in particular, the frequent banditry—of this region, where different ecological, cultural and political zones intersect.

William Coleman employs Duara's concept, the cultural nexus of power, to analyze the seminal events at Batang in 1905 and their aftermath, calling attention to the ways bodies of power fluctuate and shift across time. He shows that a crucial shift diminished the authority of the local *tusi,* and increased the power of the local monasteries and other players. This destabilized a long-standing regional balance of power, thereby changing Khams and increasing the probability of conflict between Tibet and China. He discusses Zhou Erfeng as an agent of modernity, whose actions changed both Chinese and Tibetan understandings of modernity, nationalism, and empire, bringing Khams into Tibetan and Chinese consciousness in their own nation building projects.

Peng Wenbin explores the intricacies of three Khampa "self-rule" movements in the 1930s, which have been largely written out of standard Tibetan and Chinese histories. He discusses the "empowerment and predicament" of the local and the fluidity and ambiguity of local identity politics, concentrating on the traffic in "modern" political ideologies into the frontier region which were appropriated and strategically deployed by Khampas. He shows how new social visions for Khampa political actions were mapped in response to political exigencies in Central Tibet and China, whereby Khampas attempted to maneuver into existence new forms of regional autonomy while engaging and coping with the Chinese and Tibetan nation-building projects.

Fabienne Jagou's paper takes up a similar theme of how modern ideas of nation-building were adapted and changed over time. She discusses the political symbolism underlying the titles granted to the Sixth Panchen Lama in Republican China. The Republicans hoped Panchen Lama would play a pivotal role in "civilizing" the peoples of the Tibetan and Inner Mongolian frontiers. But, as she notes, due to the "inherent ambiguity of the chaplain-donor relationship in a Republican environment," his activities and efforts to institute Nationalist ideologies eventually conflicted with the interests and agendas of different parties.

Carole McGranahan writes about one of the best-known, wealthiest, and certainly the most controversial, Khampa families, the Pondatsangs. Focusing on the unsolved murder of its patriarch, Nyigyal, in 1921 Lhasa, she probes the social milieu of wealth, status, regional origins and politics among the Lhasa elite. She subtly explores the mutually constituting interplay of facts and meanings, the role of memory and interpretive devices through which histories are produced, that reveal more about culture and social conditions than the events themselves.

Peter Schwieger analyzes the text of a traditional oral history. He also finds that history, as a valorized and authorized description of events, fades into inconsequence. In contrast to Tibetan scholastic literary models, the meaning of such *lo rgyus* abides in how these narratives amalgamate several text types, such as local legends, descriptions of places and episodes from the lives of culture heroes. Analogously, the significance of these texts lies in their essential role in the formation and maintenance of social identities for people on the margins, in resistance to the authority of cultural centers.

Tsering Thar investigates the life and works of Shar rdza Bkra shis rgyal mtshan, the most important twentieth century Bonpo *ris med* lama of Khams. He analyzes the specific Khampa contexts for his continuing legacy, and the influence of his intellectual life and activities on Khampa religious thought and institutions, which turned a small hermitage into a center of practice for certain Bonpo traditions.

These essays eschew either a Tibet- or China-centered point of view and recover a multiplicity of voices from the frontier. The volume brings together different disciplines, styles of research, and resources, ranging from oral history, Tibetan and Chinese archival materials, family histories, travelers' records, and field interviews and observations by authors of diverse academic backgrounds in anthropology, history, geography and religious studies. It is encouraging to see the contributors transgress conventional disciplinary boundaries, reflecting not only new trends in contemporary scholarship, but also the essential complexities of frontier areas such as Khams. Khams is conceived here not only as a geopolitical and historical terrain of contacts and conflicts, but also as a contact zone in the conceptual sense, where new ideas can be spawned, tested and negotiated.

FRONTIER HISTORY OF SOUTHERN KHAM: BANDITRY AND WAR IN THE MULTI-ETHNIC FRINGE LANDS OF CHATRING, MILI, AND GYETHANG, 1890-1940

WIM VAN SPENGEN (UNIVERSITY OF AMSTERDAM)

On 19 June 1906, Chinese soldiers under the command of Chao Erh-feng, entered the Tibetan monastery of Sangpiling in the southern Kham district of Chatring or Hsiangcheng.[1] It had taken a full seven-month siege to take the monastery-fort, leaving the besiegers utterly exhausted and the besieged utterly defeated. Local feelings, for many years after the event, are perhaps best summed up in the words of an American missionary living in the area at the time: "And to this day every Shangchen Tibetan hates a Chinaman."[2] The story is too well known to be repeated here, yet to gain an impression of the scale of the event, it may be well to remember that several thousand monk-defenders and laymen inside and several thousand heavily-armed Chinese soldiers outside the monastery were involved.[3] The district

---

[1] Sperling 1976:17-18.

[2] Shelton 1923:96.

[3] As far as European-language sources about the siege of Sangpiling are concerned, it might be wise to distinguish between sources written during or shortly after the event and told to passers-by not too long afterwards, and later compilations. In the first category, we have an eye witness report by Chao's interpreter Wei, as found in John Huston Edgar's report about his journey in the Hsiangcheng region together with the Reverend J.R. Muir in September 1907. See Edgar 1935:13-22 which refers in effect back to Muir's diary as published in *The North China Herald* twenty-seven years earlier. Muir's 'Diary' apparently also served as the basis for a Foreign Office report under the title of *Siege of Hsiang-Cheng* [from the diary of Revd. J. Muir, Encl.2 in No.55, Jordan to Grey, 7 January 1908 in *F O 535/11*, referred to by Mehra 1974:69, note 5]. Primary information on the siege may also be filtered from Bacot 1909:178-182 [from a journey in a neighboring area in the first half of 1907], retold with some additional information in Bacot 1988:134-139 [the narrative of his second journey when he actually visited Sangpiling in October 1910]. Moreover, Bacot 1912:140 features two rare photographs taken from different angles from the monastic complex of Sangpiling. Another narrative is by Tafel 1914(2):207-209 (extensive note 1), based on his journey to Eastern Tibet, which brought him to Tachienlu in May 1907, where he saw the Chinese military activity in the area and obtained firsthand information on the siege of Sangpiling the year before. His story contains a few details not to be found in other root stories on the event. Then there is the fictional narrative written by Filchner 1924:158-189. Attractive and apparently well researched as it is, this book is sometimes taken as a scien-

was located in southeastern Tibet where the pale of Tibetan civilization intermingled with the multi-ethnic fringe lands of northern Yunnan. Chatring, or Hsiangcheng by which name it was commonly
known to the Chinese, was divided into Upper Hsiangcheng, governed by an indigenous chief who answered to the jurisdiction of the
Deba of Litang, and the Lower Hsiangcheng lands which paid allegiance to the monastery of Sangpiling. However, both Upper and
Lower Hsiangcheng were considered an integral part of the principality of Litang.[4] To the south and west lay the plateau of Derong,
the most southern part of the neighboring principality of Ba,[5] and to
the east and southeast, the lands of Do[6] and Gangkarling, better
known as Konkaling.[7] Further southeast, already within Yunnan jurisdiction, lay the 'Lama Kingdom of Muli', headed by a hereditary
lama and his entourage, governing a mixed population of Tibeto-
Burman stock.[8] Further westward was Gyethang, or Chungtien as it is

---

tific history, a fact noticed already by Snelling 1993:39 (esp. note 18, p.276). In his
autobiography, Filchner 1950:166 explicitly states that *Sturm über Asien*, though to
be trusted in outline, is political fiction after all. A good example of this debatable
reliability is the Plan of Sangpiling shown on p.160 of his 1924 book. Filchner cannot have had any firsthand knowledge of the monastery and its surroundings, as he
never visited this part of Tibet and certainly nowhere around 1906. It is my informed
guess that he drew the Plan after the two photographs of Sangpiling in Bacot
1912:140. Imperceptibly we have moved toward the second category, later compilations on the siege of Sangpiling. But some of them were probably well informed.
Such is the case with the contribution of the missionary F. Goré (1923:349). Useful
compilations too, probably based on British intelligence sources, are Younghusband
1910:371, and Teichman 1922:21-22. W.D. Shakabpa's account of the siege
(1967:225) is largely based on Younghusband 1910 and Teichman 1922. Dhondup's
short reference to the event (1986:25-26) is seemingly based on Shakabpa, but contains some added contextual information. I should very much like to know whether
there are any genuine eye witness or firsthand Tibetan reports of the Siege of Sangpiling.
    [4] Soulié 1897:59-60. For a short journey to Upper Hsiancheng (1915), see
Shelton 1923:143-156 [diary].
    [5] Soulié 1904:92, 97.
    [6] Soulié 1897:54-55; Bacot 1912:116, and photos facing pp.112, 114, 120, and
130.
    [7] Bacot 1912:125-130, photos facing pp.126, 130; see also the well-illustrated ar-
ticle by Rock 1931:1-65. Though Rock did not visit 'Konkaling' [Gangkarling]
Monastery personally, he did visit the bandit-ridden eastern part of the district centering on the Konkaling snow peaks. For a photographic impression, see Rock 1947:
plates 55-59.
    [8] By and large, the Muli area, like the other areas mentioned, has been little trav-
eled, but see Amundsen 1900:620-625 [map, p.623]; Johnston 1908:213-233, also
notes on pp.428-433; Davies 1970:235-252; Kingdon Ward 1924:122-147 [journey

often named in the literature at the time, a district under Chinese suzerainty since 1724, but with a powerful clerical opposition ever since that date.[9] Just like Muli, Chungtien formed a transitional zone between the Tibetan culture world to the north and the only partially sinicized tribal lands to the south.

It is within the wider geo-historical context of these Sino-Tibetan frontier lands that I want to assess the historical importance of the siege of Sangpiling, as well as the following period of unprecedented growth of banditry and general lawlessness in the area. According to Kristof, a frontier is an outward-oriented marchland, a border area in which the effective territorial control of the central state is limited. It is also an area of potential expansion, one of a forward moving culture, bent on occupying the whole belt in front.[10] Historically speaking, the Sino-Tibetan multi-ethnic fringe lands display all the characteristics of a frontier region, and that so in a double sense. Whereas the local border populations in varying degrees had experienced a cultural, but less so political, integration into the Tibetan mold, the Chinese at different periods had tried to subdue areas of rebellious incidence, which in their definition were 'tributary' to China, but over which they had only nominal control. Especially in the years after 1904, in what may be interpreted as a direct response to the Younghusband Expedition, the Chinese launched an outright forward policy in their Western fringe lands, intent on establishing a firmer political, and in effect military, control.[11] Although the history of Kham, mainly on the basis of Tibetan and Chinese sources, is increasingly in the process of being unraveled, I propose here to highlight the contribution the older European-language literature can make to this attempt at reconstruction. After all, travelers, missionaries, and political agents had a chance to see and hear things, which, when put in their proper context, provide us with an additional perspective on the frontier history under review.

1921]; Kingdon Ward 1931:11-31 [journey 1913]; Rock 1925:447-492 [the most accessible account]; see also Rock 1930:385-437; Roosevelt and Roosevelt 1929:93-126; Schäfer 1933:208-242; Stevens 1934:57-88; Potts 1940:222-233; and, of course, Kessler 1986 [which had the great virtue, amongst many others, of providing the initial stimulus for my interest in the area]. See also McKhann 1998:23-45.

[9] Siguret 1937:14-44 [Tchong-Tien (Chungtien), but beware of the KMT point of view]; Wiens 1967:321-327.

[10] Kristof 1959:270-271.

[11] Sperling 1976:10-36.

It is precisely against the above background that a discussion of
historical events on the Sino-Tibetan frontier should be set, because
it gives a structural framework from which to start our analysis. First,
it is necessary to discuss the historical events surrounding the Sangpiling siege in terms of the transitional historical period covering the
demise of the Ch'ing Empire, the geopolitical contest for Tibet, as
well as the Chinese Revolution of 1911. Second, a structural discussion of regional characteristics is needed, preferably in terms of the
explanatory power of the geographical setting, the multi-ethnic background of the region, and the territorial structure of its local political
power holders. Finally, by way of conclusion, it will perhaps be possible to shed some theoretical light on the structural developments
within the wider setting of southern Kham frontier history.

Frontier History Between the Yangtse and the Yalung

An historical event like the siege of Sangpiling in 1906 did not occur
out of the blue. There are related events before and after, just as these
events were geographically situated in the lands of Hsiangcheng,
Gyethang, and Mili, as well as within the wider frontier settings of
the Tibetan principalities of Litang and Ba, and the Yunnan-
Szechuan provincial border divide. Although we cannot pursue it in
detail here, an important question concerns political unrest in the area
under review regarding the influence of possible disturbances in the
Chatring-Hsiangcheng region resulting from the campaigns of Nyag
rong Mgon po rnam rgyal, the nineteenth century Khampa warlord
who tried to establish a personal state in Eastern Tibet in the years
1835-1865.[12] According to one map,[13] Chatring was part of Nyag
rong Mgon rnam's territorial and military exploits, although reports
disagree on whether Chatring felt the full reverberations of war.[14] If it
did, it may have planted the seeds of political unrest in the region
later in the nineteenth century. In any case, when Father Soulié, a
French missionary, visited the Hsiangcheng region in October,

---

[12] See Tsering 1985:196-214.
[13] Tsering 1985, map facing p.198.
[14] Tsering 1985:203, esp. note 32. Cf. Soulié 1897:51-52, who noticed in the sub-
districts of Molashog and Do on the eastern boundary with Hsiangcheng quite a few
material remains which showed the area had once been more thickly populated and
that the area under settled agriculture must have been rather more extended.

1894,[15] he heard of recent friction in the area.[16] It seems at that time the monastery of Sangpiling was growing in political power. Though entitled to an annual payment by the Deba of Litang, to which they nominally belonged, the monks, or at least the abbot, had the impertinence or the courage to ask for a larger amount which the Deba refused. This put the monks of Sangpiling in a spirit of revolt, causing them to rend the Litang Deba's authority.[17] At this point there is the intervening story of a Chinese military officer from Litang and his son visiting the Hsiangcheng area, but who unfortunately were killed, possibly at the instigation of the abbot of Sangpiling. A party of Chinese troops was sent to punish the offenders, but they were defeated.[18] Perhaps as a corollary to the latter event, the Deba of Litang decided to wage war on Sangpiling, asking for reinforcements in early November 1894, from the inhabitants of Molashog and Do.[19] Under the circumstances it proved impossible for Soulié to visit Sangpiling. Chao Erh-feng's interpreter, Wei, in his account of the siege of Sangpiling more than a decade later, wants us to believe that Sangpiling's allegiance had shifted to the Dalai Lama, and that the abbot of Sangpiling became ruler of Hsiangcheng allegedly on the former's behalf.[20] Chinese influence in the area for the next ten years was reduced to almost nothing, and an occasional Chinese casualty or misfortune proved this point.[21] In the meantime, Sangpiling Monastery fortified its position as a center of illegal traffic, partly in slaves hailing from Menkong in Tsarong, westwards across the Yangtse and the Mekong.[22]

But it is at a higher level of geopolitical inquiry that the conditions are to be found for a radically altered Sino-Tibetan frontier history after the turn of the century. It was the Younghusband Expedition of 1904 that made the Chinese fundamentally reassess their Eastern

---

[15] Soulié 1897:36-80.

[16] Soulié 1897:55.

[17] Soulié 1897:60; cf. Adshead 1984:57.

[18] Sperling 1976:17.

[19] Soulié 1897:66.

[20] Wei's 'Account', as to be found in Edgar 1935:16; Adshead 1984:68.

[21] Edgar 1935:15 refers to a Chinese military officer flayed alive by the 'Hsiangcheng lamas' in 1902; and in the winter of 1905, a company of Chinese soldiers, who had come to summon the abbot of Sangpiling to swear allegiance to China, was "treated with contumely" (Younghusband 1910:372).

[22] Edgar 1935:17; cf. Kingdon Ward 1923:178ff. [slave-dealing of the Tsa-rong Tibetans].

Tibetan frontier position. The eighteenth century boundary line, just west of the Yangtse near Batang,[23] had never been translated into an effective territorial and political control in the outlying areas east of the Yangtse and west of the Yalung. Hence, the British thrust into Central Tibet was seen as a direct threat to Eastern Tibet by the Chinese. It is not the place here to repeat everything that has been written about the Chinese reaction in the east.[24] Suffice it to say that political and military measures taken under Chao Erh-feng were both radical and bloody. In the course of events at Batang in 1905, the principal monastery was razed to the ground, after which its surviving monks fled southward to the Sangpiling Monastery in the *de facto* independent Hsiangcheng district. They were joined by their co-religionists from the great monasteries of northwestern Yunnan which had been looted by Chinese troops and had risen in turn.[25] The result was that thousands of angry monks and frightened laymen flocked together in the Sangpiling Monastery, which eventually led to its siege and fall.[26] In the neighboring district of Do, the main monastery of Chongtang, thought to have harbored some six hundred monks at one time,[27] initially succeeded in defending itself, but in June 1906, had to surrender, after which forty-eight monks were beheaded.[28] The monastery of Konkaling too fell into Chinese hands.[29]

In the years after the 1905-1906 revolt had been crushed, Chao introduced a program of political and social reform, meant to establish tighter Chinese administrative control. The *tussu* structure of indirect rule, by which Chinese officials were sometimes attached to local chiefs, was now abolished, though its effectiveness had already been questioned in 1902. Political power, by that time already, seems

---

[23] Cf. Lamb 1989:49, note 73.

[24] But see Teichman 1922:19-34; Goré 1923:348-351; Mehra 1974:67-79; and in particular Sperling 1976:10-36.

[25] Younghusband 1910:370-371; Teichman 1922:21.

[26] For the relevant sources, see note 3.

[27] Soulié 1897:54 ["5 à 600 lamas"]; the end map of Soulié's article shows a figure of 600.

[28] Dhondup 1986:26. Bacot (1912:115, 117) found the monastery a couple of years later occupied by the Chinese, but apparently their presence went not uncontested. For an impression of Chongtang, see p.114 (photo facing).

[29] Goré 1923:349. For photos of the Konkaling region and its monastery, see Bacot 1912:124, 126, and 130 (*infra*).

to have shifted into the hands of the Tibetan Buddhist clergy.[30] By 1908, Chao had established a number of Chinese magistracies (*hsien*), amongst them Ting-hsiang hsien, the former Chatring or Hsiangcheng,[31] by which he hoped to establish tighter control in the area. Stringent measures were taken to curb the power of the monastic establishment,[32] and some modern education was introduced.[33] But the Chinese-Tibetan contest for local power was by no means yet over. As Louis King, British consul in Tachienlu, was to write a few years later: "Had it not been for the lamas, Chao's work would undoubtedly have met with lasting success."[34] Teichman too had realized the historical depth of the Sino-Tibetan encounter when he wrote that "the feud between the Chinese and the people of Hsiangcheng, which had begun long before, was not to an end."[35] By the end of 1910, only a couple of months after Jacques Bacot had paid a visit to a relatively quiet, Chinese-occupied Sangpiling,[36] the neglected Chinese garrison at the monastery made common cause with the local Tibetans against the central Chinese government.[37] Chao again was forced to send troops to Hsiangcheng, which, with the usual severity, put an end to the rising.[38] Even before the 1910 mutiny, Bacot had found a Hsiangcheng district in ruins, despite signs of repopulation.[39] No wonder that after a second thrashing within a few years "the inhabitants of this turbulent district were more than ever irreconcilable to Chinese rule."[40] The fact that a Chinese force had taken Lhasa on 12 February of the same year, may have contributed to their stance.

But the fall of the Ch'ing dynasty was near. The revolution of 1911 meant a temporary weakening of Chinese authority and military

---

[30] Soulié 1904:92, 94.
[31] Rock 1947:342; Sperling 1976:23.
[32] Younghusband 1910:33; cf. Siguret 1937:18-22.
[33] Cf. Shelton 1923:147 ["First Chinese school – no good"].
[34] Mehra 1979:183.
[35] Teichman 1922:22; cf. Soulié 1897.
[36] Bacot 1912:140-151.
[37] Teichman 1922:30; Goré 1923:149.
[38] Teichman 1922:30-31; Goré 1923:149 ["Le général Fong Chan fut chargé de réprimer (la révolte de Hiang-tch'eng) et s'en acquitta à la satisfaction de son maître, en fusillant tous les soldats de la compagnie mutinée"].
[39] Bacot 1912:140; cf. the ruined countryside as seen by Edgar (1935:19) in Upper Hsiangcheng in 1907.
[40] Teichman 1922:31.

power. Chao Erh-feng, the 'Warden of the Marches', was treacher-
ously murdered by Szechuan revolutionaries in December 1911, and
by mid-1912, the Chinese had lost control of most of their frontier
districts.[41] The outlying garrisons in southern Litang and Ba had to
retreat to Batang, where on two occasions they were besieged by the
Tibetans, one time by troops from Lhasa, and a second time by
Hsiangcheng venturers.[42] From October 1912 onwards, Chinese republican troops tried to reestablish their military presence in the
southern Kham region, especially with an eye to the strategic but
vulnerable Yunnan-Burma border area further south.[43] In February
1913, a special army unit was sent to force Hsiangcheng to capitu-
late. It made slow progress, but in the end the fight against heavy
odds made the rebel monks and their followers retreat across the
Yunnan provincial boundary. In June 1913, the Sangpiling Monastery was reoccupied.[44] China emphasized its renewed presence in the
area by explicitly stating at the Simla Conference that Batang and
Litang would *not* be part of Inner Tibet but of China proper. This
proposal was rejected by the British and the Tibetans, which in the
end made the Chinese refuse to ratify the April 1914 Convention. In
the summer of 1914, Hsiangcheng again became the scene of frontier
fighting and pillaging, this time through the complex interaction
between Hsiangcheng rebels and deserting soldiers under a Chinese
commander.[45] The recurrent fighting in Hsiangcheng during the better part of 1914 brought new devastation to a country district already
suffering from local warfare for more than eight years. Many villages
and monasteries were destroyed,[46] but already one year later Dr.
Shelton could report that many people were building new houses in
the Hsiangcheng area,[47] possibly tempted to do so by the prevailing
truce between China and Tibet after the close of the Simla Conference. But peace did not reign long in Hsiangcheng. In March 1915,
the newly concocted rebel-*cum*-soldier bands even posed a threat to
Tachienlu, but they were dispelled from the town by loyal Chinese

---

[41] Teichman 1922:38; Goré 1939:163-164.
[42] Teichman 1922:165.
[43] Teichman 1922:166-167.
[44] Teichman 1922:42; and especially Goré 1939:168.
[45] Shelton 1923:96; Goré 1939:175.
[46] Teichman 1922:43.
[47] Shelton 1923:149.

troops from Litang.[48] From 1915 onwards, the theatre of Sino-Tibetan frontier hostilities shifted westward towards Chamdo and
northward into Kham.[49] Southern Kham, except for scattered bandit
activity,[50] remained relatively peaceful. Unfortunately, civil war
erupted between Szechuan and Yunnan in 1916-1917. When the
Yunnanese finally had to retreat from a Szechuan-besieged Tachienlu, they did so with great difficulty through the wild mountainous
country of Muli.[51] The first half of 1918 saw the Tibetans regain
much frontier land in Eastern Tibet, but the truce of Rongbatsa, en-
acted by Teichman, once more assured relative peace for a number of
years.[52] In southern Kham, however, rebellion continued to plague
the Hsiangcheng district and surroundings well into the 1920s, but as
the district was located at a strategic position,[53] it continued to enjoy
China's geopolitical interest.[54]

Banditry and the State

One of the most conspicuous developments in the frontier region
under review is the growth of brigandage and banditry, especially
after the beginning of Chao's forward policy in 1905. This is not to
say that brigandage in the area did not occur before that time.
Amundsen refers to the country around Chungtien (Gyethang) as a
notorious robber haunt,[55] and that already so in 1899. Father J.-A.
Soulié, in his description of the situation in southern Ba in 1902,
mentions the robber country of 'Tomarong',[56] which is probably the
same as 'Tonguarong' as marked on the map accompanying Goré's

---

[48] Goré 1939:175; cf. Lamb 1989:36.

[49] Teichman 1922:51-58.

[50] Handel-Mazzetti 1927:156 [Konkaling robbery in the Muli area], p.160 [Threat
of Konkaling robbery along the Muli-Chungtien road, July 1915; the robbers appear
to have been deserted Chinese soldiers], p.160 [Impossibility of travel in the area
between Muli and Tachienlu], p.173 [Hsiangcheng robber threat against Chungtien,
August 1915].

[51] Teichman 1922:50.

[52] Teichman 1922:52-58; Richardson 1984:120.

[53] On the one hand overlooking the main southern China-Tibet road from Tachienlu to Batang, and on the other guarding a major through-route from Batang to
the Yunnan-Burmese frontier region south of Atuntze.

[54] Lamb 1989:48, note 60.

[55] Amundsen 1900:533.

[56] Soulié 1904:97.

study of the Tibetan marches of Szechuan and Yunnan.[57] Tomarong or Tonguarong probably refers to the area where the dreaded Tongwa were living,[58] which is in fact the southwestern part of Konkaling. If the terms brigandage and banditry refer to robbery in bands, in contrast to individual acts of crime committed in isolation, the question immediately arises as to what social and political circumstances gave rise to these early forms of communal robbery.

First, we may think of the social setup of many of the petty principalities and monastic estates in the Sino-Tibetan marchlands. Generally speaking, taxes were not high, but the labor corvée was more often than not a heavy burden to the local population.[59] The 'Lama Kingdom' of Muli in particular is mentioned time after time in the literature as a land of forced labor and corvée.[60] Consequently, the common people in Muli have been described as poor and oppressed.[61] Under such circumstances, youngsters, in search of a better life, may have run away to known haunts of brigandage such as the neighboring district of Konkaling.

Second, and undoubtedly the more important reason even before 1905, must have been the growing pressure of Chinese administration in the areas south of Litang and Batang. As referred to in the previous section, minor Chinese officials were sometimes attached to the more important *tussu* with the object of knowing what was going on in and around the local courts.[62] In addition, small Chinese military frontier posts were found pushing into areas of lesser control, as for example the military post at the village of Nainda, south of Litang.[63] But only after 1905, the year in which Chao Erh-feng started his forward policy in the marches, brigandage seems to have developed into larger-scale banditry. At first, it was primarily the monks that were hunted from their monasteries, as they were seen as the main instigators of trouble. But where opposition developed into

---

[57] Goré 1923, endmap.

[58] See Rock 1931:50, 64; Rock 1947:251; Siguret 1937:30; Goullart 1955:90, 94.

[59] Bodard 1921:368, but see Legendre 1913:185-186 ["Les lamas prélèvent une large dîme sur les troupaux, sur les champs, sur tous les produits"].

[60] Soulié 1897:50; Kingdon Ward 1924:135; Rock 1925:467; Roosevelt and Roosevelt 1929:96 ["Muli is an Oriental Despotism"]; Schäfer 1933:216-217; Stevens 1934:70-71.

[61] Amundsen 1900:621 ["The Milians are poor and oppressed"]; Davies 1909:233 ["Eastern Mili country is very poor"]; Rock 1925:467.

[62] Soulié 1904:92.

[63] Soulié 1904:102.

full-blown revolt, the Chinese did not hesitate to burn whole villages, to destroy crops and herds, and to starve the population.[64] The result was an increased floating population which plundered for sheer survival.

Then there were the Chinese deserters. At times, whole garrisons in outlying areas were neglected and perhaps forgotten in times of political upheaval. Already in 1907, during his first journey, Bacot heard several times of soldiers in revolt.[65] Towards the end of 1910, the Chinese garrison at Sangpiling mutinied.[66] Five hundred soldiers with modern rifles murdered their officers and fled southward to the district of Chungtien in Yunnanese territory.[67] In the summer of 1914, the Austrian botanist Handel-Mazzetti, on his journey in southern Gyethang, heard a batch of Chinese deserters had attacked a Tibetan caravan.[68] With more Chinese soldiers deserting and more displaced Tibetans around, new leagues were formed, turning against provincial and central Chinese authority alike. Shelton even heard that the Hsiangcheng rebellion of 1914 stood under the command of a runaway Chinese, who with his Tibetan rebels destroyed the German-built bridge near Ho-kou on the Yalung.[69] But most bands of bandits were thoroughly Tibetan, sometimes headed by formerly high-placed persons, as in the case of Drashetsongpen, the bandit chief of Konkaling,[70] who had been a lama of Chungtien Monastery (Tsongtsanling).[71]

The dynamics of rebel band formation and disintegration is a little understood process. One tends to agree with E.J. Hobsbawm that how long a band lasted depended on "how tense the social situation, or how complex the international situation, was."[72] But one also wonders whether a monopoly of force actively sustained by a local warlord of strong personality may have served the purpose of perpetuating a group of outlaws equally well. The question to be answered therefore with regard to southern Kham is why banditry in the

---

[64] Teichman 1922:43; Shelton 1923:96.

[65] Bacot 1912:148.

[66] Teichman 1922:30.

[67] Bacot 1912:149.

[68] [July 30 1914, near Mount Beshui]: Handel-Mazzetti 1927:82, see also p.160.

[69] Shelton 1923:96-97.

[70] Rock 1930:402, Rock 1931:18, 43, 50.

[71] Rock 1931:17.

[72] Hobsbawm 1978:19.

Konkaling and Hsiangcheng regions continued to grow in the 1920s,[73] despite a relatively quiet international frontier situation, as pointed out at the end of the previous section. From about 1920 onwards, frontier robbery developed into a more professional activity of greater scale, reach and ferocity. Better armed[74] and better organized, robber expeditions by hundreds of outlaws from the Hsiangcheng and especially the Konkaling area played havoc near places as far away as Tachienlu, Chungtien, and Likiang. Modern arms were increasingly carried by bandits. In fact, the advance of the Chinese military in their home areas offered an opportunity for bandits to arm themselves, by attacking and looting the garrisons and carrying off rifles, pistols, and artillery.[75] The Muli King later bought two field pieces from the outlaws.[76] According to Joseph Rock, a long-time resident in a neighboring area, and one of the very few Europeans actually to have visited the Konkaling area, arms were also *sold* by the Chinese, mainly by generals residing in the Kienchang valley at Ning-yuan fu. As they were first and foremost interested in money, old and surplus rifles went to the highest bidders. The raiding 'Lolo' (Yi) and Tibetans of the Szechuan-Yunnan border often became the happy new owners.[77] The weapons thus bought made larger-scale robbing expeditions possible, of which we have several reports.

The years 1921-1923 were bandit-ridden. In the spring of 1921, a robber band from Hsiangcheng pillaged the Minyag region east of the Yalung.[78] The next winter, a group from Hsiangcheng appeared in the Yangtse valley west of Chatring. Villages in the area were sacked, and the whole population made for the other side of the Yangtse after which the boats that had brought them across were burned. For several months people lived under arms on the west side

---

[73] Rock 1931:17-18. Cf. Kapp 1973:54.

[74] The question as to where these arms came from is worth an investigation of its own. There seems to have been an increased availability of all sorts of arms hailing from Europe after the armistice of World War One. See Jowe 1925:198. The disturbed state of China in these years with its rampant warlordism can at least be partly related to the large-scale smuggling of arms into China by several European countries. Cf. Jowe 1925; see also Ch'i 1976:116ff., 120 note [arms trade]; Chan 1982. According to Handel-Mazzetti 1927:172, arms reached the multi-ethnic fringe lands of Eastern Tibet also via Tibet.

[75] Rock 1931:14, 17.

[76] Rock 1931:14, 17.

[77] Rock in his magisterial study, 1947:251-252.

[78] Goré 1923:351.

of the river.[79] The general disturbance of the country was so great that the Dalai Lama wrote to the people of Hsiangcheng not to cause any further trouble, despite the fact that Chatring was nominally under Chinese rule.[80] In the early spring of 1922, Joseph Rock was refused a visit to the Muli King on the grounds that Hsiangcheng robbers were too numerous that year.[81] Over the summer, the botanist Kingdon Ward managed to spend five months in Muli, but work was difficult, owing to "the unusually disturbed conditions of the country."[82] In the same year, Chungtien fell to the Tongwa from Konkaling.[83] It had already fallen into the hands of regular Tibetan troops in 1917,[84] but had been handed over again to the Chinese in 1918. The Tongwa drove out the Chinese officials and robbed the Chinese soldiers of their rifles.[85] Then they went further southwards, into the Na-khi districts of Ha-ba and Bber-dder in the Yangtse loop, where the local population was no match for them. They proceeded to loot and burn their villages.[86] Just across the Yangtse, they destroyed the little town of Taku and terrorized its population.[87] Afterwards, they occupied the Atsanko Gorge and entrenched themselves near the village of Noyü on the west side of the Yangtse River. Regular Chinese soldiers were dispatched from Tali to chase the Tongwa with machine guns. But, according to one source, "they stood their ground and kept up their fire."[88] Towards the end of 1923, an even bigger force of Tibetan bandits crossed the Yangtse, and came to within thirty kilometers of Likiang, where the 'Battle of the Peshwe Bridge' was fought, apparently killing many Chinese soldiers.[89]

It should come as no surprise that trade under such disturbed conditions suffered accordingly. In the early years, the little trading,

---

[79] Goré 1923:369-370.
[80] Richardson 1998.
[81] Rock 1925:447.
[82] Gregory and Gregory 1923:241.
[83] Rock 1947:251, 257.
[84] Kingdon Ward 1923:29.
[85] Rock 1947:257.
[86] Rock 1947:250.
[87] Rock 1947:251.
[88] Rock 1947:257.
[89] Rock 1925:453; to what extent the perhaps hyperbolic number of 1200 Tibetans is true, of which reportedly only one was killed, remains a problem.

consisting of wool, pottery, and locks,[90] that was done by the Hsiang-cheng themselves was effected at the market of Ho Chu and respected by both Chinese and Tibetans.[91] However, long-distance trade passing through and along the outskirts of the troubled region, especially during the disturbed years of 1910-1917, received a severe blow.[92] Long-distance trade, which passed through the area immediately to the south, as was for instance the case along the Tachienlu-Muli-Likiang and the Muli-Chungtien roads, remained threatened for many years to come. After the difficult 1921-23 years, banditry, although by no means subsided, occasionally appears to have been low enough to let some traffic pass, but the roads remained insecure.[93] Finally Joseph Rock was officially invited by the King of Muli; on his way to the 'Land of the Lamas' he met a Tibetan caravan from Tachienlu, and was told that the road ahead was free of brigands and that he had nothing to fear.[94]

This was not so in Gyethang and the Likiang area, where the Tongwa, who had taken Chungtien in 1922, went on the rampage again. At first united under a Chinese commander (1924), they proceeded to Yungbe to chase rebellious 'Lolo' (Yi) from the area, but afterwards bolted and went on the warpath for themselves. They crossed the Yangtse to Hoking, south of Likiang, where they beat the local militia. In the end they reached Cheku, a small trading town not far from Likiang. It was severely looted and burned, and its population terrorized.[95] The next year, a couple of hundred Chungtien Tibetans devastated the Chinese village of Wuchou in the Yangtse valley,[96] and in mid-October 1926, a mixed band of Hsiangcheng and Tongwa, about 600 strong, again crossed the Yangtse and destroyed the village of Kiu-tien.[97]

The Hsiangcheng remained a serious threat to the Batang-Litang road too. In 1927, two hundred Hsiangcheng ambushed a hundred

---

[90] Duncan 1952:129.
[91] As Edgar (1935:14) has observed, "Ho Chu, always loyal to China, was apparently also scrupulously fair to Hsiangcheng, and when the crisis came (Sangpiling 1905-1906) her neutrality was respected by both."
[92] Edgar 1930-1931:6-7.
[93] Siguret 1937:30.
[94] Rock 1947:455.
[95] Siguret 1937:29; cf. Rock 1947:251.
[96] Siguret 1937:29.
[97] Siguret 1937:30.

Chinese soldiers and slaughtered over twenty of them.[98] Rock, on his visit to the mountains of Konkaling in 1928, was warned by the King of Muli *not* to visit the monastery of Konkaling proper, as its 400 monks were always on the alert to rob.[99] On his visit to the Minya Konka area in early spring 1929, he was informed at the village of Mudju that the bandit chief of Konkaling, Drashetsongpen, had arrived at the Yalung with his 'horde' of 800 outlaws.[100] On that river, the ferry and rope bridges near the large village of Baurong had always been of strategic importance, and, next to their agriculture, the local population could make some extra money in helping parties cross the river. Johnston, on his journey in 1906, described the place as relatively large and prosperous, though vulnerable to mountain robbers.[101] But in the 1920s, it became a consistent target of Konkaling robbers, until it was found by Rock to have been reduced to a heap of ruins when he visited the place in the spring of 1929.[102] Other travelers too have commented on Baurong's wretched appearance.[103] The village of Gendschü, on the opposite side of the river, was generally spared because it was in Muli territory, and as the outlaws were on friendly terms with the Muli King, it was passed by. Baurong, on the other side, however, was considered Chinese territory, as indeed was the Minyag region.[104] Chungtien was again occupied by the Tongwa in 1933, from which place they raided surrounding areas.[105] Only one year later, the Muli King was murdered on 10 September 1934,[106] not by Hsiangcheng or Konkaling outlaws, but by a Chinese militarist, bent on the gold of Muli. That was a sure loss to the stability of the area, as the Chinese knew very well; by allowing the Lama-King to continue to rule, they could keep the Konkaling robbers at bay.[107] By the late 1930s, the situation had not

---

[98] Duncan 1952:105.

[99] Rock 1931:27.

[100] Rock 1930:411 [The Minya Tibetans had been the victim of Konkaling robbery several times, but they had now armed themselves and were prepared to make a fight].

[101] Johnston 1908:181-182.

[102] Rock 1930:435.

[103] Schäfer 1933:209 ["Baurong ist ein fürchterlich ärmliches Drecknest"]; Potts 1940:222 ["Baurong was a rather decrepit place"].

[104] Rock 1930:435.

[105] Rock 1947:251.

[106] Rock 1947:357.

[107] Weigold 1935:390 ["Das war kluge Taktik auf beiden Seiten"].

improved, travel in the country being regarded as far from safe. The
American Potts, who traveled through Muli in 1938, was accompanied by two Chinese gun-runners with a number of Mauser pistols,
and seven young monks on pilgrimage to Lhasa, all armed with long
lances.[108] He ended up in Yungning, where the abbot of the local
monastery showed him his collection of loaded firearms, including
Brownings, Mausers, and a magazine shotgun of Belgian manufac-
ture.[109]

From the above section it is easy to see that southern Kham between the Yangtse and the Yalung was for decades an utterly disturbed country with an unusually unruly population. According to the
King of Muli, the Chinese were solely to blame for the current state
of affairs.[110] They had destroyed a Tibetan administrative setup, in
which the districts of Hsiangcheng and Konkaling were subject to the
princely state of Litang, but by their haughty imperialistic policies
had failed to establish an accepted authoritative administration. It
seems all very clear: before Chao's advent *peace* was the prevailing
mode, and afterwards there was *anarchy*.[111] Or is it that clear after
all? By way of conclusion, I will now try to shed a more multi-di-
mensional light on this vexed problem of frontier agitation.

Into the Deep

The history of events, which may refer in a Tibetan application to the
siege of Sangpiling, the truce of Rongbatsa, or to the murder of the
Muli King, is regarded by historians of more structuralist persuasion
as rather superficial. The latter believe in deeper levels of historical
understanding, showing the explanatory power of slowly changing
social and economic structures, or even the semi-permanent structures of a particular geographical milieu in which human action takes
shape.[112]

Geographically speaking, the districts of Chatring, Mili, and Gyethang are located at a major ecological divide, where the higher pla-

---

[108] Potts 1940:224.
[109] Potts 1940:231.
[110] Rock 1931:14.
[111] Rock 1931:14.
[112] For an application of Braudel's ideas within a Tibetan setting, see van Spengen 2000.

teau lands of the north slowly give way to the more subtropical plains and river valleys of the south. Without wanting to be deterministic, and only speaking history-wise, Tibetan civilization has always been associated with upland areas, well above and beyond warmer climes. Kingdon Ward once even stated that the frontier of Tibetan civilization is the verge of the grassland and the fringe of the pine forest. If a Tibetan crosses this barrier, he must revolutionize its life.[113] For all its deterministic overtones, this observation seems important to me, because it implies that there is a major ecological divide in southern Kham, which historically speaking separated peoples of different material culture.[114] It was a world of limited circulation, and its frontier inhabitants had only intermittent contacts. It is my argument that, speaking for the southern Kham region, we have so far insufficiently taken into account the historical effects of this deep-seated north-south ecological frontier divide.

As a corollary to this ecological frontier there is a long-standing cultural frontier as well. This is the one between Tibetan ethnic groupings and Tibeto-Burman ones, interspersed with pockets of so-called 'Hsifan', a term which as far as I have been able to ascertain, refers to all shades of Tibetan and Tibeto-Burman *métissage*. This cultural frontier should not be conceived of as a fixed geometrical line, but as a transitional zone, in which Tibetan, Hsifan and Tibeto-Burman villages were coexistent at different altitudes in the deeply eroded river valleys of southern Kham. At the same time, groups found it sometimes expedient to shift their local ethnic identity when opportune. Nevertheless, such a cultural-ecological frontier, under certain historical circumstances, could assume the character of a political border. This may already have been the case in Nan-chao times, when the latter kingdom contested a border zone in northern Yunnan with the Old Tibetan Empire.[115] Many centuries later, the

---

[113] Kingdon Ward 1932:469.

[114] Cf. Jeffrey 1974:60: "Geographically speaking, we may consider that the people of Muli, Hsiangcheng, and Konkaling occupy a region where the shallow grassland valleys of the Tibetan plateaux of the North, are beginning to cut deeper and deeper, until on the South at lower altitudes they form the deeply cut valleys of Yunnan. The people are farmers and housedwellers."

[115] Cf. Backus 1981:40-45, 52-63, 69-100. See also Rock 1963:13 ["In A.D. 755, the territory was captured by the Tibetans, but afterwards it became part of the Nan-chao kingdom. There seem to have been many skirmishes between the various tribes and the land changed hands for short periods"].

'Ancient Nakhi Kingdom', centering on the Likiang area, reached its greatest power around the year 1600.[116] It offered shelter to fugitive Karmapa Lamas from Tibet, who were under pressure from the Gelukpa. In neighboring Muli too, the power of Karmapa monasteries was being curtailed.[117] At that time, however, the Nakhi Mu kings felt strong enough to make incursions *into* Tibetan territory, and as a result there was recurrent fighting on the southern Kham cultural-ecological frontier. It made the Tibetans build watch and defense towers all along a line crossing southern Kham from east to west, separating the Tibetans from the Tibeto-Burmans.[118] The seventeenth century saw a major eastward expansion of Central Tibetan authority into Kham under the fifth Dalai Lama.[119] In the wake of Gushri Khan's military exploits, several administrative functionaries were appointed and many Gelukpa monasteries founded by the Central Tibetan administration, sometimes literally on the ruins of Nyingma and Kadgyu ones. An example is the Galdan Sumtsen Ling Monastery in the Gyethang area.[120]

Historically speaking, there seems to have been a lot of strife in southern Kham, pre-dating the Chinese-Tibetan encounter of late Ch'ing and early republican times. One wonders how socially and economically stable these multi-ethnic fringe lands on both sides of the cultural-ecological boundary in fact were, and whether the local populations were able to establish some permanency of existence and social integration over the years in these apparently war-torn frontier lands. In this connection, perhaps the greatest tragedy that befell the southern Kham region was *not* to have profited from a stable central political administration at any time during its centuries-long history. The Sino-Tibetan border of 1727, which brought territory east of the Yangtse under nominal Chinese control, did in fact create another political-territorial vacuum, in which neither the Chinese nor the

---

[116] Rock 1947; see also Jackson 1979:9-22, 275-296.

[117] Dorje 1996:192.

[118] Rock 1947:318 ["These towers are common north in Muli, on the Zho Chu, on the hills in the Litang valley, on the Yalung, and in the region of Chiu-lung hsien, south of Tachienlu. They form in fact, an ethnic boundary line from the Mekong to the Tatu Ho"], see also plate 169, facing p.330; cf. Johnston 1908:197; Legendre 1913:236-237; Handel-Mazzetti 1927:155; Roosevelt and Roosevelt 1929:117-119 (see photo of Chiulung facing p.116); Rock 1930:401; Schäfer 1933:207.

[119] See in particular Ahmad 1970.

[120] Ahmad 1970:221.

Central Tibetan polity had much influence. From a structuralist historian's point of view, it is the combination of—historically speaking—an unstable *cultural-ecological* frontier with—administratively speaking—a non-effective *geopolitical* frontier that in the final analysis may contribute to an explanation of strife and lawlessness in the southern Kham districts of Hsiangcheng and Konkaling. In the light of such a perspective, the 'event' of the siege of Sangpiling fades in importance, and even Chao's forward policy after 1905 loses in explanatory power. In this connection, one would also like to know more about the nineteenth century: How stable was socio-economic development in the area at the time, were there conditions of lawlessness, were there perhaps outlaws or bandits already? There are some indications that there were.[121] We also need to know more about the dynamics of *tussu* rule, as a link between the peasantry and Empire. These are but a few examples of historical conceptualization within a wider structuralist perspective. It shows that the bare historical event may be better understood within a more elaborate analytical framework combining geographical, political and cultural factors. Perhaps such an added perspective will give us a sounder understanding of frontier history at large.

---

[121] Soulié 1897:55; Soulié 1904:97.

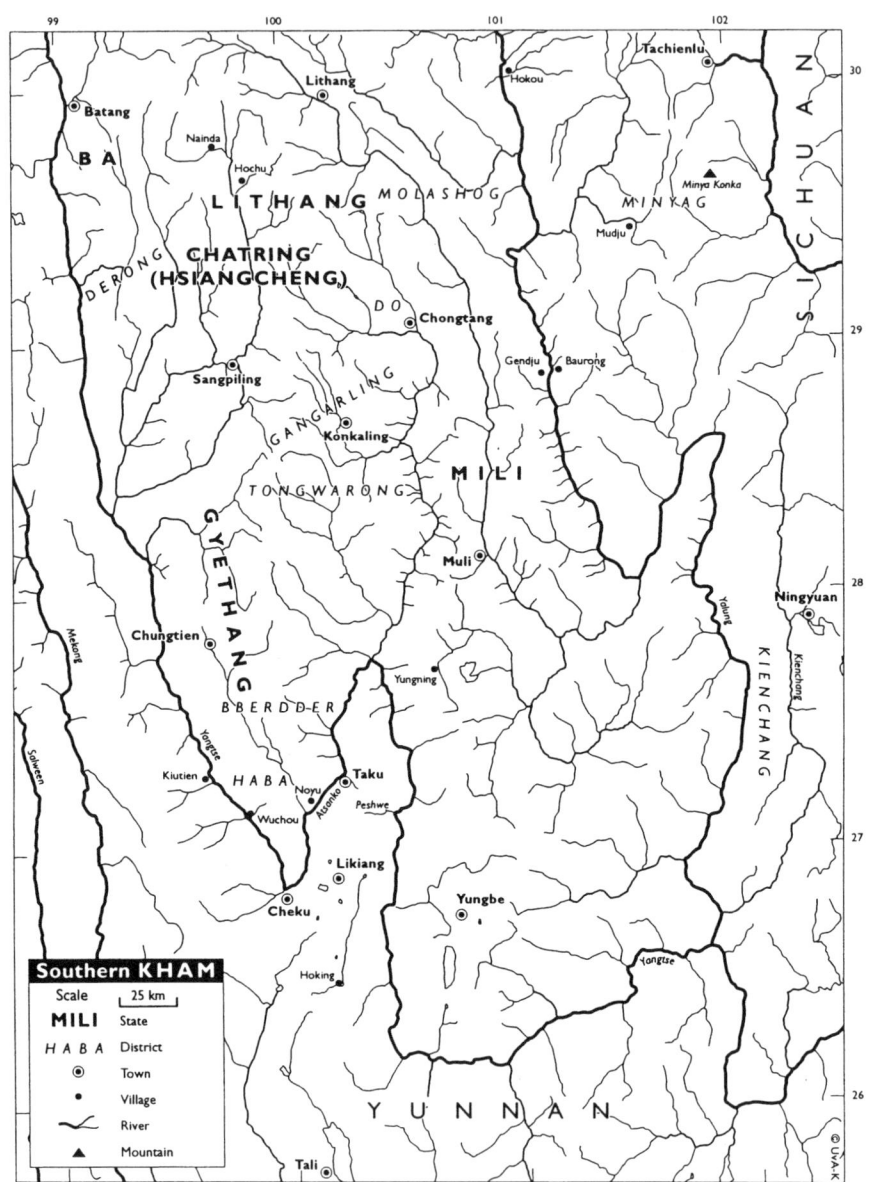

Southern Khams

BIBLIOGRAPHY

Adshead, S.A.M. *Province and Politics in Late Imperial China. Vice-regal Government in Szechwan, 1898-1911.* London: Curzon Press, 1984.

Ahmad, Z. *Sino-Tibetan Relations in the Seventeenth Century.* Roma: Istituto Italiano per il Medio ed Estremo Oriente, 1970.

Amundsen, E. "A Journey Through South-West Sechuan." *The Geographical Journal* 15, (June) 1900.

Bacot, J. *Dans les marches tibétaines*, Paris: Plon-Nourrit et Cie, 1909.

——*Le Tibet révolté. Vers Népémakö, la terre promise des tibétains*, Paris: Librairie Hachette et Cie, 1912. Reprinted Paris: Éditions Raymond Chabaud–Peuples du Monde, 1988.

Backus, C. *The Nan-chao Kingdom and T'ang China's Southwestern Frontier.* Cambridge: Cambridge University Press, 1981.

Bodard, A. "La propriété, l'impôt et les corvées dans les marches thibétaines." *L'Asie Française*, 1921.

Chan, A.B. *Arming the Chinese. The Western Armaments Trade in Warlord China.* Vancouver: University of British Columbia Press, 1982.

Ch'i Hsi-sheng. *Warlord Politics in China 1916-1928.* Stanford: Stanford University Press, 1976.

Davies, H.R. *Yün-nan. The Link Between India and the Yangtze.* Cambridge: Cambridge University Press, 1909. Reprinted Taipei: Ch'eng Wen Publishing Company, 1970.

Dhondup, K. *The Water-bird and Other Years. A History of the Thirteenth Dalai Lama and After.* New Delhi: Rangwang Publishers, 1986.

Dorje, G. *Tibet Handbook.* Lincolnwood, Il.: Passport Books, 1996.

Duncan, M.H. *The Yangtse and the Yak. Adventurous Trails In and Out of Tibet.* Ann Arbor, Mich.: Edwards Brothers, 1952.

Edgar, J.H. "Notes on Trade Routes Converging at Tachienlu." *Journal of the West China Border Research Society* 4, 1930-1931.

——"Hsiang Ch'eng or Du Halde's Land of the Lamas." *Journal of the West China Border Research Society* 7, 1935.

Filchner, Wilhelm. *Sturm über Asien. Erlebnisse eines diplomatischen Geheimagenten.* Berlin: Verlag Neufeld & Henius, 1924.

——*Ein Forscherleben.* Wiesbaden: Eberhard Brockhaus, 1950.

Goré, F. "Notes sur les marches tibétaines du Sseu-tch'ouan et du Yun-nan." *Bulletin de l'École Française d'Extrême-Orient* 23, 1923.

——*Trente ans aux portes du Thibet interdit.* Hongkong: Maison de Nazareth, 1939.

Gregory J.W. and C.J. Gregory. *To the Alps of Chinese Tibet. An Account of a Journey of Exploration up to and Among the Snow-clad Mountains of the Tibetan Frontier.* London: Seeley Service & Co., 1923.

Handel-Mazzetti, H. *Naturbilder aus Südwest-China. Erlebnisse und Eindrücke eines österreichischen Forschers während des Weltkrieges.* Wien und Leipzig: Oesterreichischer Bundesverlag, 1927.

Hobsbawm, E.J. *Primitive Rebels. Studies in Archaic Forms of Social Movement in the 19th and 20th Centuries.* Manchester: Manchester University Press, 1978.

Jackson, A. *Na-khi Religion.* The Hague: Mouton Publishers, 1979.

Johnston, R.F. *From Peking to Mandalay. A Journey from North China to Burma through Tibetan Ssuch'uan and Yunnan.* London: John Murray, 1908.

Jowe, P.S. "Who Sells the Guns to China's War Leaders?" *The China Weekly Review*, (April 18) 1925.

Jeffrey, J.H. *Kham or Eastern Tibet*. Elms Court, Ilfracombe: Arthur H. Stockwell, 1974.

Kapp, R.A. *Szechwan and the Chinese Republic. Provincial Militarism and Central Power 1911-1938*. New Haven: Yale University Press, 1973.

Kessler, P. *The Historical Kingdom of Mili*. Rikon: Tibetan Institute, 1986.

Kingdon Ward, F. *Mystery Rivers of Tibet*, London: Seeley Service & Co., 1923.

——*The Romance of Plant Hunting*. London: Edward Arnold, 1924.

——*Plant Hunting in the Wilds*. London: Figurehead, 1931.

——"Explorations on the Burma-Tibet Frontier." *The Geographical Journal* 80(6), (December) 1932.

Kristof, L.K.D. "The Nature of Frontiers and Boundaries." *Annals of the Association of American Geographers* 49, 1959.

Lamb, A. *Tibet, China & India 1914-1950. A History of Imperial Diplomacy*. Hertingfordbury: Roxford Books, 1989.

Legendre, A.-F. *Au Yunnan et dans le massif du Kin-ho*. Paris: Librairie Plon, 1913.

McKhann, C.F. "Naxi, Rerkua, Moso, Meng: Kinship, Politics and Ritual on the Yunnan-Sichuan Frontier." In M. Oppitz and E. Hsu, eds. *Naxi and Moso Ethnography. Kin, Rites, Pictographs*. Zürich: Völkerkundemuseum Zürich, 1998.

Mehra, P. *The McMahon Line and After. A Study of the Triangular Contest on India's Northern Frontier between Britain, China and Tibet, 1904-1907*. Delhi: Macmillan, 1974.

——*The North-Eastern Frontier. A Documentary Study of the Internecine Rivalry between India, Tibet and China*. Vol. I, 1906-14. Delhi: Oxford University Press, 1979.

Potts, W.H. *Wind from the East*. London: Blackie and Son, 1940.

Richardson, H.E. *Tibet and its History*. Second revised and updated edition. Boulder and London: Shambhala, 1984.

——*Tibetan précis*. Calcutta: The Manager Government of India Press. (origo 1945). Reprinted in M. Aris, ed. *High Peaks, Pure Earth. Collected Writings on Tibetan History and Culture*. London: Serindia Publications, 1998.

Rock, J.F. "The Land of the Yellow Lama." *The National Geographic Magazine* 47(4), (April) 1925.

——"The Glories of Minya Konka." *The National Geographic Magazine* 58(4), (October) 1930.

——"Konka Risumgongba, Holy Mountain of the Outlaws." *The National Geographic Magazine* 60(1), (July) 1931.

——*The Ancient Na-khi Kingdom*. Volume I. Cambridge, Mass.: Harvard University Press, 1947.

——*The Life and Culture of the Na-khi Tribe of the China-Tibet Borderland*. Wiesbaden: Franz Steiner Verlag, 1963.

Roosevelt, T. and K. Roosevelt. *Trailing the Giant Panda*. New York: Charles Scribner's Sons, 1929.

Schäfer, E. *Berge, Buddhas und Bären. Forschung und Jagd in geheimnisvollen Tibet*. Berlin: Verlag von Paul Parey, 1933.

Shakabpa W.D. *Tibet. A Political History*. New Haven: Yale University Press, 1967.

Shelton, F.B. *Shelton of Tibet*. New York: George H. Doran, 1923.

Siguret J., ed. and transl. *Territoires et populations des confins du Yunnan*. Peiping: Éditions Henri Vetch, 1937.

Snelling, J. *Buddhism in Russia. The Story of Agvan Dorzhiev, Lhasa's Emissary to the Tsar*. Shaftesbury, Dorset: Element Books, 1993.

Soulié, J-A. "Géographie de la principauté de Bathang." *La Géographie* 9, 1904.

Soulié, R.P.J. "De Ta-tsien-loû à Tsekou (rive droite du Mékong)." *Bulletin de la Société de Géographie*, 1897.

Spengen, W. van. *Tibetan Border Worlds. A Geohistorical Analysis of Trade and Traders*. London and New York: Kegan Paul International, 2000.

Sperling, E. "The Chinese Venture in K'am, 1904-1911, and the Role of Chao Erh-feng." *The Tibet Journal* 1(2), 1976.

Stevens, H. *Through Deep Defiles to Tibetan Uplands. The Travels of a Naturalist from the Irrawady to the Yangtse*. London: H.F.& G. Witherby, 1934.

Tafel, A. *Meine Tibetreise. Eine Studienfahrt durch das nordwestliche China und durch die innere Mongolei in das östliche Tibet*. Vol. 2. Stuttgart: Union Deutsche Verlagsgesellschaft, 1914.

Teichman, E. *Travels of a Consular Officer in Eastern Tibet*. Cambridge: Cambridge University Press, 1922.

Tsering, T. "Ñag-ron Mgon-po rnam-rgyal: A 19th Century Khams-pa Warrior." In B.N. Aziz and M. Kapstein, eds. *Soundings in Tibetan Civilization*. New Delhi: Manohar, 1985.

Weigold, H. "Ein 'Lebender Gott', sein Gold und sein Ende." *Atlantis* 7, (Juli) 1935.

Wiens, H.J. *Han Chinese Expansion in South China*. Hamden, Conn.: The Shoe String Press, 1967.

Younghusband, F. *India and Tibet*. London: John Murray, 1910.

THE UPRISING AT BATANG: KHAMS AND ITS SIGNIFICANCE IN CHINESE AND TIBETAN HISTORY

WILLIAM M. COLEMAN, IV (COLUMBIA UNIVERSITY)

Introduction

In *The Records of the Establishment of Xikang Province*, Fu Songmu writes:

> In Guangxu 30 (1904), the Assistant High Commissioner to Tibet, Feng Quan, went from Sichuan to Tibet, and he made it as far as Batang.[122] He saw the soil there was rich and fertile, and immediately he recruited Han people to open up the land. But according to the barbarian peoples' superstition, they thought the mountain god should not be disturbed, so they went out and obstructed them. Feng Quan would not listen, and at Cililong he tilled a field.... Then all the troops Feng Quan had brought with him practiced foreign drilling techniques using foreign drum calls. The barbarian people wondered if they were foreign officials, and so they obstructed the tilling of the field with more force. The indigenous official (*tusi*) and *mkhan po* (*kanbu*, abbot) exhorted Feng Quan to enter Tibet quickly, and thereby avoid something from happening in Batang.[123] Feng Quan swore at them, and increasingly aroused the hatred of the barbarian people.
>
> Thereupon the people of Qicungou plundered the field, killed the field manager, and then rose up and chased after Feng Quan. As for the Han troops, the few could not withstand the many, and they were killed.... The foreigner's church was moreover burnt down, and two Catholic missionaries were violently killed. Feng Quan escaped and entered the indigenous official's fort and negotiated peace with the barbarian people. The barbarian people deceitfully promised to [let] Feng Quan return to Sichuan. He led his retinue of soldiers and scholars and went east.... He traveled several *li*, but when he arrived at

---

[122] Tibetan: 'Ba' thang.

[123] Upon the first appearance of Chinese official titles, the original Chinese will follow the English translation. When authors transliterate a Tibetan official title in Chinese characters, the original Tibetan will be given first, followed by the original Chinese transliteration, and then the English translation.

The primary indigenous official of Batang at this time was Luo Jinbao, also known as Zhaxi Jicun. The assistant indigenous official was Guozong Zhabao, also known as Zhaba Jicun.

Yinggezui the barbarian people ambushed and attacked him.[124] The officials and soldiers died difficult deaths. Only Wu, the provisions officer, was spared because he had not yet gone. Among the soldiers and officials who had escaped, the barbarians protected all the virtuous ones.[125]

Through the critical examination of a variety of Chinese primary source materials like this one, in combination with a select number of secondary sources, I intend to accomplish two things in this paper. First, I will outline the political, cultural, social, and economic landscapes of the Khams region in the late nineteenth century. I will then trace several of the important changes these landscapes underwent in response to the events surrounding the 1905 uprising at Batang, the beginning of which is narrated above. Second, I will critique Western and Chinese historiography of Khams history during the late nineteenth and early twentieth centuries. In so doing, I will highlight the significance of Khams in Qing, Chinese, and Tibetan history.

The Cultural Nexus of Power in Batang

With the above narrative in mind, I want first to discuss the polity, broadly defined, of Khams civilization. The "cultural nexus of power," is a loosely defined concept that facilitates the abstract mapping of the political, cultural, social, and economic milieu of a region. It is fundamental to this discussion.[126] As an organizational category, "the cultural nexus serves as a framework that structures access to power and resources in local society. It also serves as the arena in which politics is contested and leadership developed in a society." The cultural nexus therefore allows one to analyze a region's "culture and legitimacy within the organizational context in which power is wielded."[127] In other words, the cultural nexus provides an organizational structure around which to identify fluctuating bodies of power across time. Discussion of these bodies in Batang and Khams in general will shed light on their positions in

---

[124] 1 *li*=.576 km, or approximately .33 miles.

[125] Fu 1912:5. Also quoted in Wu 1937:46. Complete citations are found in the Bibliography.

[126] The cultural nexus of power was first outlined by Prasenjit Duara in his book on rural north China (1988). See pp.1-41 for an extended discussion of this concept.

[127] Duara 1988:15.

the cultural nexus prior to the uprising, their roles in the events surrounding the uprising, and how their positions within the cultural nexus of power changed following it.

There are four primary players within Batang's cultural nexus of power: indigenous leaders, monasteries and their representatives, representatives of the Qing empire, and merchants.

Before the nominal conquest of Khams by Qing armies in 1719 (Kangxi 58), Batang was administered by two *sde pa* (*diba*, indigenous leaders), the principal *sde pa* (*'Ba' sde pa*) and the assistant *sde pa* (*gnya ngan sde pa*).[128] Both of Batang's original *sde pa* were sent from central Tibet in 1703 (Kangxi 42).[129] Their primary responsibilities were to appoint local elite (*sku tshab*) to assist them in managing local granaries, to supervise the *'u lag* system of corvée labor, and to collect taxes to support themselves.[130] After the two original *sde pa* died of illness, Batang's indigenous leaders assumed their titles, later passing on these titles and the responsibilities accompanying them to their descendents. *Sde pa*, to the extent that powerful monastic officials did not encroach upon their position within the cultural nexus, ruled Batang independently as the secular elite of society.

Following his father's military conquests, the Yongzheng Emperor began expanding nominal Qing control in Khams. In 1728 (Yongzheng 6), representatives of the Qing empire arrived in Batang and granted seals and charters of investitures to Batang's current *sde pa*.[131] Zhaxi Pingcuo was granted the title Primary Mollification Commissioner (*zheng xuanwushi*), and Awang Renqing was granted the title Vice Mollification Commissioner (*fu xuanwushi*). In Chinese official discourse, *sde pa* became *tusi*, and Batang was thereby incorporated into the Qing imperial system. With their new titles, Batang's indigenous leaders were able to maintain their positions in the cultural nexus by drawing on the legitimizing power of their

---

[128] Carrasco 1959:142. According to the *Dictionnaire Thibétain-Latin-Française* (p.384), the assistant *sde pa* in Batang had the family name Gnya ngan tshang. No other sources corroborate the Tibetan orthography.

[129] *Ganzi Zangzu zizhizhou minzu zhi*, p.35. See also Niu 1993:343. Indigenous leaders in other parts of Khams were sometimes known as *sde pa*, other times as *rgyal po*.

[130] Carrasco 1959:142-43.

[131] For a thorough discussion of the Yongzheng Emperor's efforts to incorporate Khams' indigenous leaders into the Qing empire, see Herman 1993.

status as both hereditary Tibetan *sde pa* and invested representatives
of the Qing empire. Evincing this dual legitimacy, Batang's *sde pa*
continued to carry out the activities they had undertaken before the
arrival of Qing armies. Moreover, they began to monitor trade and
collect taxes for the Qing empire. Significantly, Batang's *sde pa*
received a salary for the services they rendered for the Qing
empire.[132]

Monastic officials, as both individual actors and representatives of
larger religious institutions, constitute the second group of players in
Batang's cultural nexus of power. Their positions of power were
based on a variety of factors. Religion was an important part of life
for most Tibetans, and they looked to monasteries to support their
everyday religious practice and instruction. With their central role in
Tibetan religion, monasteries therefore maintained a unique source of
ideological power in the cultural nexus. Monasteries in Khams also
derived their power from their material wealth. Like indigenous leaders, most monastic officials in Khams collected taxes from the local
population.[133] Many monasteries, including Dinglin Monastery
outside Batang, also maintained vast estates with plentiful natural
resources across large areas. Important markets for Sichuan tea,
monasteries increased their financial and material wealth by
engaging in trade and serving as distribution centers for smaller local
markets. Monasteries also frequently loaned money to local people,
thereby further increasing their resources and power in the cultural
nexus.[134] As one late nineteenth century observer writes:

> The Lamas, keeping in their hands the retail...by this means reduce the
> people to absolute dependence upon them, exacting in return for the
> precious article (tea), labour and produce. Grain, yaks, sheep, horses,
> and even children, are given to the rapacious priesthood in return for
> tea.[135]

Finally, monasteries maintained military power. As we shall see
shortly, monasteries did not hesitate to use this power to protect their
exclusive interests. With access to and control over rich sources of
ideological, financial, material, and military power in Khams, mon-

---

[132] *Ganzi Zangzu zizhizhou minzu zhi*, p.35.
[133] See, for example, Cassinelli and Ekvall 1969:250.
[134] Tsering Thar 1995:981-85.
[135] Cooper (1871:409), as quoted in Gardella 1992:109-10.

asteries and their representatives maintained strong and influential voices in the cultural nexus.

Representatives of the Qing empire constitute the third and most diverse group of players in the cultural nexus of power in Batang. Mentioned above in the context of indigenous leaders, indigenous officials (*tusi*, indigenous leaders incorporated into the Qing administrative system) are the first manifestation of Qing representatives in the cultural nexus. As we have seen, in return for collecting taxes and monitoring trade for the Qing empire, these indigenous officials received a salary. Moreover, they used this imperially endowed authority to bolster their own legitimacy on the local level, and thereby strengthened their position within the cultural nexus. However, the granting of official titles and responsibilities to indigenous leaders in Khams does not necessarily mean that the Qing empire was able to exert direct influence through them. In his study of Qing expansionism in the seventeenth and eighteenth centuries, John Herman argues that *sde pa* and *rgyal po* were forced to grant the Qing empire many concessions in return for receiving the empire's support. He suggests that estates were divided, Confucian schools were established, periodic tribute was demanded, and inheritance (including the inheritance of the *tusi* office itself) came to be regulated by the Qing empire in Khams.[136] However, careful examination of later historical records suggests that the imperial policies Herman discusses were not successful. For example, the omission of references to Confucian schools in late Qing local records from Khams indicates that such schools had not existed in Khams for a significant period of time, if at all. Moreover, the Qing empire not only frequently exempted Khams' indigenous officials from tribute missions, but they also provided their territories with annual subsidies.[137] Intermarriage and polygynous marriages within relatively small elite populations also allowed indigenous officials to thwart Confucian inheritance restrictions. Given these observations, as well as the fact that Ma Weiqi and Zhao Erfeng (discussed in depth below) encountered serious resistance from local Tibetans on their way from Dajianlu to Batang (supposedly the territory under greatest Qing control) in 1905 (Guangxu 31), we may conclude that while indigenous

---

[136] Herman 1993:15-109.
[137] Fu 1912:4. Also quoted in Wu 1937:45.

officials in Khams did use their status as Qing representatives to increase their personal power, Qing control over these officials and the territories they administered was extremely weak.

The second manifestation of Qing representatives in Khams is posted Qing officials. Rarely noted by scholars,[138] three Qing provisions officers (*liangtai*) were stationed in Khams beginning in 1748 (Qianlong 13). Under the High Commissioner in Lhasa (*zhu Zang dachen*), these officials were charged with supplying Qing soldiers stationed in Tibet and Khams with provisions and salaries.[139] One of these provisions officers was stationed in Batang, and several lower ranking officials were stationed with him on rotating three year terms to provide assistance. Posted with these officials were also a number of soldiers, whose presence increased the power of Qing officials in the cultural nexus.[140] It is important to note that these officials did not necessarily exploit their military supremacy in Batang. Different from often arrogant higher ranking officials and soldiers merely travelling through the region, these civil and military officials were stationed there for extended periods of time, and evidence suggests that at least some (but certainly not all) of them maintained amiable relations with local Tibetans. For example, by the early twentieth century, a class of people of mixed ethnic background resulting from intimate relations between Qing officials and local Tibetans had emerged not only in Batang, but also throughout Khams. Known as *lo tsā ba* or *a bu lags* in local Tibetan, *tongshi* in Chinese, such people served as interpreters for Qing officials stationed in the region.[141] The narrative of the uprising quoted in the introduction also evinces the amiable relations between Tibetans and posted Qing officials. Despite the murder of Assistant High Commissioner Feng Quan and most of the members of his retinue, the Batang Provisions Officer, Wu Xizhen, was spared.

---

[138] Scholars often overlook the significance of Qing officials stationed in Khams. Ignoring their very presence, Adshead (1983:56) states, "Except for a few gold prospectors, Chinese trade...stopped at Dachienlu (Kangding); so did regular bureaucratic administration; and only diplomats and soldiers went beyond it, and then always in transit." Moreover, in his important article on early twentieth century Khams history, Sperling (1976) merely mentions the presence of Qing officials in Khams prior to the twentieth century, and does not discuss their significance.

[139] Hucker 1985:310.

[140] Wu 1937:45.

[141] Teichman 1922:147.

Merchants make up the final player in Batang's cultural nexus of power. While the longer but less demanding northern route supported most of the trade through the region, Batang, located on the shorter southern route, with its lower elevation, fertile soil, and temperate climate, was also an important trading post in the region.[142] Both local residents and itinerant entrepreneurs carried on trade in Batang, and their financial and material resources gave them influence in the cultural nexus of power. As early as the Yongzheng period, Chinese traders had established a sedentary presence in Batang. In 1727 (Yongzheng 5), Han merchants founded the Han Commercial Society (*Han shang gonghui*) to "manage business, offer financial assistance, and take care of societal affairs...[as well as] to provide relief for orphans and widows, help the poor, and support the weak."[143] This Society was still extant in the late nineteenth century. Following a devastating earthquake in 1874 (Tongzhi 13), it rebuilt the local Guandi temple and established a tri-provincial native place association (*sansheng tongxianghui*) in Batang.[144] Early twentieth-century western observers also note the presence of permanent Chinese settlers in other areas of Khams working as merchants. Teichman, for instance, writes about a community of Chinese merchants living in northern Ganzi who traded regularly with local Tibetans.[145]

Tea and salt made up the bulk of material traded in Khams. Because the value of tea rose twenty-fold between Dajianlu and Lhasa, *yin* permits for transporting and selling tea were in high demand. The provincial government was therefore able to sell the permits at high profits, and the Sichuan-Tibetan tea trade was an important source of revenue for provincial coffers. In the late nineteenth century, the sale of tea permits for export to Tibet accounted for two-thirds of the annual tea revenues for Sichuan province.[146] Salt tax revenues from Khams (which were administered in Batang) were another profitable source of income for the Qing government. Because of the large revenue they supplied the province, particularly in the late nineteenth and early twentieth centuries, the Qing government considered the success of the tea and salt trade very important. To facilitate this

[142] Guo 1996:71-77.
[143] *Batang xianzhi*, p.10.
[144] *Batang xianzhi*, p.11.
[145] Teichman 1922:77.
[146] Gardella 1992:107-10.

trade, the government worked hard to keep trade routes open in Khams and protect the merchants. With provincial backing and access to large profits from their trade, it is clear that merchants maintained significant influence in the cultural nexus of power.

With this background in mind, I will now turn to a discussion of a critical instance of unrest in Batang, the effects of which drastically altered the cultural nexus of power throughout Khams.

The Uprising at Batang

Beginning in the mid-nineteenth century, a series of events in Khams and Tibet compelled the Qing court to increase the empire's influence in the cultural nexus of power in Khams. The first of these events began in 1860 (Xianfeng 9). In that year Gompo Namgyal, an ambitious indigenous leader in Nyarong,[147] invaded several neighboring territories controlled by different indigenous leaders. Wanting to maintain stability in the region, the indigenous leaders of Derge and the Hor principalities appealed to both the Qing empire and Tibet for military assistance in expelling Gompo Namgyal from their territories and controlling his future behavior. The Qing empire was unable to offer any support at that time because their armies were preoccupied with the suppression of larger rebellions throughout China proper. The central Tibetan government in Lhasa, however, was able to provide assistance. In 1863 (Tongzhi 2), they sent in troops, and after two years of fighting their army defeated Gompo Namgyal. The central Tibetan government then appointed a resident commissioner to rule Nyarong and superintend Derge and the Hor principalities. Still focusing on their internal rebellions, the Qing court did not contest Lhasa's activities in Nyarong, and they quietly accepted the incorporation of these areas into the central Tibetan administrative system.[148]

In 1895 (Guangxu 21), indigenous leaders in Nyarong and the surrounding region rebelled against direct rule by Lhasa. They appealed to the Qing empire for support, and the Sichuan Governor-General, Lu Chuanlin, responded by sending soldiers to Nyarong who quickly

---

[147] Nyag rong. In Chinese, this principality is known as Zhandui, Sanzhan, and Jiaya. Gompo Namgyal's name is written in Chinese as Gongbu Lanjian.

[148] Teichman 1922:5; Shakabpa 1984:187.

pacified the region, thereby bringing Nyarong back under nominal Qing control. Lu Chuanlin, however, favored more than mere nominal control in Nyarong. Taking advantage of the empire's renewed strength in western Khams, he drafted an extensive proposal to bring the region under direct Qing administration by implementing *gaitu guiliu*, a process of administrative reform in which indigenous leaders were removed from their official positions and replaced with Qing civil and military officials.[149] Fearful of direct Qing influence in western Khams, the Lhasa government presented their objections to Lu's proposal to the Qing court, and the Guangxu emperor allowed Nyarong to return to the control of the Lhasa government. Lu's proposal had been rejected, but his authority had not. In 1903, he resigned as Governor-General and took a more influential position on the Qing Grand Council (*junji chu*). He did not forget his failure in Nyarong.

In 1904 (Guangxu 30), not long after the Nyarong affair, imperial policy in Khams was further complicated by the British invasion of Tibet. Hoping to facilitate negotiations between the British and the Tibetans for the withdrawal of British soldiers from Tibet, the Qing court dispatched You Tai as the new High Commissioner. Upon his arrival in Lhasa, You Tai attempted to persuade the Dalai Lama to negotiate with the British. The Dalai Lama, however, was unwilling to do so. You Tai then quickly sent a request to the newly appointed Sichuan Governor-General, Xi Liang, to dispatch 4,000 soldiers to Lhasa. He hoped the presence of these soldiers would press the Dalai Lama into negotiations with the British. Xi Liang, however, was strongly opposed to increasing the Qing military presence in Tibet, and he refused. Without further resources to bolster his bargaining position, You Tai was left with no choice but to grant concessions to the British.

The new British threat from the west and the lack of cooperation between Xi Liang and You Tai greatly angered the Qing Grand Council. In response the Grand Council, on the recommendation of its new member, Lu Chuanlin, began to advocate a more aggressive Tibet policy in late 1904. The Council first demanded Xi Liang work more closely with You Tai to strengthen their position in Tibet. Xi Liang therefore proposed to transfer the official residence of the As-

---

[149] Lu 1974.

sistant High Commissioner to Tibet (*zhu Zang banshi dachen*) from Lhasa to Chamdo. He hoped this action would restore social order in Khams and allow merchants to pass through the region uninterrupted. You Tai, however, took Xi Liang's proposal further:

> Litang and Batang were originally under the jurisdiction of Sichuan. The indigenous officials of these two areas are rather deferential and pliant. Already I have enlightened them with great principles, making these things known in order to glorify your righteousness. There are none that do not show their gratitude and respect. However, among those born and raised in the barbarian areas, it is not that there are none that have tyrannical and arrogant behavior. In the event there is a trifle, strife will flare up. If local officials were able to render substantial supervision, then peace would prevail and there would be no incidents. The monks in all the monasteries are proliferating, and the power of the *mkhan po* occasionally emerges from their midst. As for these monks, they exploit the people by stripping them, and they use all means to coerce the people. If debts are not repaid, then they resort to every form of search and repossession. Even when rogue barbarian Buddhists plunder and rob on the roads, if victims make an accusation to the authorities, the victimizers will in turn demand a *guili* (a kind of bribe).
>
> Because the region of Jiaya forms the border between Batang and Chamdo (Chamuduo), cases of robbery number as many as the trees in a forest, and travelling merchants dare not go forward. My humble opinion is that these barbarian monks are all our people, and...so it is certainly not that our country's laws do not cover them. Moreover, as for the intervention of the monks in these areas, they have been rampant and without inhibition. If we do not force them into submission quickly, I fear suddenly the tail will begin to wag the dog, and putting things back in order will be more difficult.
>
> I have consulted by letter with the acting Governor of Sichuan, Xi Liang, on this matter many times, and also with the Assistant High Commissioner Gui Lin. I propose to establish a substantial garrison in the Chamuduo area, and also to settle the stationing of a high official there, preparing provisions for emergencies, and drilling troops.... By living in the center he (the Assistant High Commissioner) can respond appropriately to problems. These are truly urgent matters, and your servant is working day and night...on them.[150]

Several points in this memorial suggest further reasons behind the Qing court's re-evaluation of its Tibet policy. You Tai criticizes not only the inability of indigenous officials to suppress ubiquitous brigandage in the region, but also the oppressive practices of monaster-

---

[150] You Tai, *Zouyi*, as quoted in Wu 1937:43.

ies. Fearing that further hesitation on the part of empire will allow conditions in Khams to escalate to uncontrollable levels, You Tai proposes to increase Qing presence in the region by stationing not only the Assistant High Commissioner to Tibet in Chamdo, but also a garrison of soldiers there.

In contrast to You Tai and the Grand Council, Xi Liang advocated a moderate policy toward Tibet. While he accepted the transfer of the Assistant High Commissioner's post to Chamdo, he remained strongly opposed to increasing Qing military presence in either Tibet or Khams. He therefore refused to provide the Assistant High Commissioner with a garrison of soldiers. Evincing a cultural sensitivity rare in the late Qing, Xi Liang also established a Tibetan school in Chengdu to teach Chinese officials Tibetan language, culture, and history. Xi Liang argued that "to govern barbarians, we must first conquer their hearts," and that "the important thing in frontier matters is to understand the native's mentality, and this can be done only through his written and spoken language."[151]

Despite Xi Liang's good intentions, the Qing court remained unsatisfied with his programs. The court's growing pressure ultimately convinced Xi Liang of the necessity for action, and he therefore initiated a series of reforms in Khams. Xi Liang reduced provincial taxes, laid the groundwork for a mining project, and established a small (two hundred *mou*) experimental project to develop agriculture, commerce, and mining in Batang.[152] However, still reluctant to increase Qing military presence in the region, he refused the Assistant High Commissioner Gui Lin's request for 10,000 soldiers to escort him to his new post in Chamdo. Complaining of an eye illness, Gui Lin resigned his position before embarking for Chamdo. The Emperor then tapped Feng Quan as Assistant High Commissioner to Tibet. Xi Liang provided him with an escort of only one hundred fifty policemen.[153]

Feng Quan was known for his aggressiveness, and his appointment to this position reveals the Qing court's desire to increase its influence in the cultural nexus of power in Khams. Upon receiving his appointment, Feng Quan immediately requested permission to

---

[151] Xi 1959:490, no.452, and pp.651-52, no.581, as quoted in Des Forges 1973:72-80.

[152] Sperling 1976:12. 1 *mou*=.16 acres.

[153] Des Forges 1973:74.

recruit and train local irregulars in Khams. The Emperor responded, "Conscientiously train them. I earnestly hope that it will be effective."[154] Travelling through Khams en route to his new position in Chamdo, Feng Quan memorialized:

> The indigenous official of Litang is deficient. All day he does things by exploiting the barbarian people. Of ten houses, nine are empty. The monks are many and the people are few. In large monasteries, monks can number as many as 4,000-5,000. By these means they subjugate the indigenous officials and exploit the barbarian people. They have had this long-standing habit for too many years. Our garrisons and outposts are weak and meager. Civil and military officials [just] stare at each other, and no one dares to do anything. They (the monks) plunder as frequently as before, and half of them (the civil and military officials) consider the monastery to be a refuge for criminals. As a result, traveling merchants who come and go quarrel about giving bribes to monasteries for insurance. Even if [the local officials] catch a *jag pa* (*jiaba*, bandit), invariably the monks will receive a bribe and allow him to escape....
>
> When your servant passed through Litang, I strictly ordered the indigenous officials and *mkhan po* to be just and to respect the laws. I also ordered them to investigate, purge, apprehend, and punish the *jag pa* severely. Moreover, I instructed the garrison commander, Zhang Shiyan, to recruit one hundred local braves from the indigenous officials to drill and aid our defenses....
>
> But to eradicate totally the problems, we cannot do without setting limits on monasteries. If we do not do this, then harmful practices will proliferate, and I fear that taking care of affairs will be more difficult in the future. I request that the number of monks in large monasteries in indigenous official areas not be allowed to exceed three hundred, and that for a period of twenty years the tonsuring of monks be stopped. Hereafter, limits should be set on the number of monks, and no permission should be granted for the private registering of even one monk. As for monks who are under the age of thirteen, their families should be ordered to take custody of them, and they should return to the laity. I will not only strictly command the indigenous officials and *mkhan po* to take the monks of large monasteries and order them all to return to their native tribes, but I will also establish small monasteries to accommodate the remaining monks. By these means I will divide their power. I request that you set aside an order to the Lifanyuan (Ministry Ruling the Outer Provinces) to decide to implement these suggestions. If we employ these methods, then after twenty years the monks will decrease daily and the people will increase daily, so why

---

[154] *Dezong shilu*, as quoted in Wu 1937:44.

would every family wander about and the monks be lazy? Now we can see that there will be land (in Khams) and people to work it.[155]

Fulfilling Feng Quan's request, the Emperor forwarded his proposal to the Lifanyuan for further consideration.

While local Tibetans were most likely unaware of Feng Quan's official memorials, they did witness his activities on the ground. En route to Chamdo, Feng Quan stopped in Batang. Here he quickly punished alleged bandits and treated the principal indigenous official, Luo Jinbao, with disrespect. On his own initiative Feng Quan also expanded Xi Liang's modest land reclamation project in Batang to 50,000 *mou*, granted a tract of land to the French Catholic mission in Batang, and encouraged Han migration to the fertile valley surrounding the village. Finally, he recruited two hundred local Tibetan men to serve in his army, training them in western field techniques. Angered by Feng Quan's radical actions, the monks of Dinglin Monastery led a crowd of monks and Batang residents numbering almost 3,600 to Feng Quan's compound, where they attacked him and his retinue.[156] The passage from *The Records of the Establishment of Xikang Province* quoted in the introduction picks up the narrative here, and it is not necessary to repeat it again. It is sufficient to state that Feng Quan had so disturbed the cultural nexus that the people of Batang rose up and killed him and his retinue, thereby marking the critical point in this uprising.

The rapid suppression of this uprising was crucial for Xi Liang and the Qing empire. Located mid-way on the southern road between Dajianlu and Lhasa, Batang was an important base from which Qing officials kept this route open for official travel and communication, as well as for trade. Xi Liang knew that if he lost control of Batang and the southern road then the province would lose substantial profits from the sale of tea permits and revenues from salt taxes. Because the Qing government (itself suffering a severe financial crisis) had recently begun requiring provincial governors like Xi Liang to support their provinces without national revenue, Xi Liang was extremely concerned about the effects of instability in Khams on provincial finances. He writes:

---

[155] Zhu 1958:5307, Doc.28. Also quoted in Wu 1937:44.
[156] You Tai, *Zougao*, as quoted in Wu 1937:47.

> By burning churches and killing officials, the lamas (of Batang) have committed great crimes.... We must extend the command of Heaven in order to suppress the rebellion and restore order.... The finances of Szechwan are in bad straits, but we must increase our troops in order to maintain control.[157]

Xi Liang knew he could not afford to lose revenues from trade going through Khams, and he therefore compromised his policy of moderation by dispatching Ma Weiqi and Zhao Erfeng with 4,000 troops to quell the unrest at Batang.

Writing from the Khams frontier in 1905 (Guangxu 31), Commander-in-Chief Ma Weiqi and his second in command Zhao Erfeng sent the following telegram to Xi Liang:

> On the eighteenth day of this month, I (Ma Weiqi) went to Sanba and seized a spy who reported: 'The Songlin pass has rebels, and a ramparted fort under guard.' Thereupon...the general (Zhao) led his troops forward, and when he arrived he did not see any trace of the rebels. The captured local people said, 'Several days ago, there was a head lama who had been sent from Batang, and at this place he provoked and assembled the common people. The ramparted fort was well guarded, but upon seeing the great armies coming forward, no one was willing to fight. So the night before they dispersed on their own.'
>
> On the twenty-second day at daybreak, the general's troops advanced forward, and upon arriving at the top of the great Shuo Mountain, we saw there were many rebels and spies, whom we followed closely, sought, and attacked up to the fourth bell of the afternoon. Then we ran away to Chamu, and it happened that the bandits made a furious assault. We were unable to withstand the rebel's strength, so we retreated to Little Bachong.... Consequently we chose from each camp two hundred vigorous soldiers and irregulars, and divided them into two flanks. The first [flank]... searched and then advanced as far as the southeast Duoban Mountain, and they saw the bandits in the process of cacophonously transporting trees and boulders. They were preparing to cut off our approach. It came about that our troops painfully routed and dispersed them. The larger army passed through at the foot of the mountain as far as Reshuitang, and then the bandits ambushed over 1,000 of our soldiers. They came swarming like bees.... Ma Ruxian...established a line of resistance against the rebels, [and]...Li Kechang blew them up with a large cannon. They attacked the bandits with abandon. At that time our two armies in the mountains had already seized the bandits, and their strength became disorganized....

---

[157] Xi 1959:477-79, no.443, as quoted in Des Forges 1973:77.

On the twenty-sixth day of this month we entered Batang. Li Ke-chang entered first to take care of the walled fort, and to take prisoner the indigenous official Luo Jinbao.... The military lieutenant Zhu...captured the assistant indigenous official Guozong Zhabao. That night, there were rumbling sounds of explosions in the four mountains, and by daybreak we knew there were bandits still remaining. They had retreated and hidden in Dinglin Monastery. They resisted and would not communicate.

The said monastery is located several *li* west from the walled fort, and at one time it had packed earthen walls as hard as the outer wall of a city surrounding it. We attacked it, but we could not advance. We used the cannon to bomb it, and its great halls went up in flames. Subsequently, by these means it fell into ruins and was destroyed.

The recently captured ringleader is Lama Bage. The remaining bandits ran off to Qicungou. Immediately we sent soldiers hastily to chase after them.... On the one hand, we have searched the mountains and cleaned them of remaining bandits. On the other hand, we have proclaimed amnesty for the rebels and those who have fled.... In general, the schemers of disorder, the rebellious plotters, and the ringleaders have been recently captured, and therefore we report this up to the Emperor.[158]

This first-hand account of the military suppression of the uprising at Batang confirms many of the ideas addressed in my discussion of the cultural nexus of power in Batang. Most important, a division of power clearly existed between monastic officials and indigenous leaders. It is not insignificant that it was a head lama, presumably representing the monks of Dinglin Monastery, and not one of the indigenous leaders who had at least nominal relations with the Qing government, who attempted to meet Qing troops outside Batang and stop them from advancing. Although not specifically mentioned in the passage above, it is also important to note the following. When the Qing army did arrive, the indigenous officials Luo Jinbao and Guozong Zhabao attempted to mediate between the army and the Dinglin monks, who had taken refuge in the monastery along with many other Batang residents. Despite their good intentions to negotiate a return to stability in the region, both indigenous officials were arrested immediately by the Qing army and eventually executed. The quick arrest of Batang's two indigenous officials, in combination with the strong resistance offered by the monks of Dinglin Monastery to the Qing armies, suggests that the monastery had access to

---

[158] Wu 1984:14-15.

considerably more material, and perhaps military, resources than the indigenous officials. We may therefore conclude that, at least in terms of wealth and military might, Dinglin Monastery overshadowed the indigenous officials in Batang's cultural nexus of power.

This account also challenges the assertion presented by other scholars that the Qing empire successfully broke up large estates and divided power among indigenous leaders in Khams by controlling inheritance rights.[159] In contrast, the above passage offers no indication that Batang's two indigenous officials maintained distinct rights or responsibilities. The fact that they, like Batang's original *sde pa* two centuries earlier, were brothers suggests that early Qing attempts to reduce the influence of indigenous leaders in Khams were largely unsuccessful.

Ma Weiqi and Zhao Erfeng pacified Batang in only four months, but other areas quickly rose up against Qing administration and paralyzed the southern road between Dajianlu and Batang. The Qing court therefore ordered Xi Liang to develop a larger plan to guarantee security in the region. Xi Liang's first action was to command Zhao Erfeng to begin preparations to station a large garrison of soldiers in Batang.

Zhao Erfeng responded with strong military force, using his Mauser guns and foreign cannon to kill more monks, and he effectively cleansed Batang of all resistance. However, resistance to the Qing armies still remained in Khams. Both Zhao and Xi Liang knew that neighboring monks, particularly monks from Sangpi monastery in Xiangcheng, had supported, if not outright fought along with, the monks in Batang throughout their struggle. After bringing Batang under his control, Zhao therefore requested permission to lead his armies south to Xiangcheng on a punitive mission. However, Xi Liang was still hesitant to use excessive military force, and he initially refused. Instead, he attempted to negotiate directly with the Xiangcheng monks in hopes of reaching a compromise. His efforts soon failed. Realizing what was required to bring peace to Khams, Xi Liang wrote, "The policy of managing barbarians by humbling one's self to conquer their hearts only nourishes an abscess and encourages rebellion."[160] With this change of heart, the precarious balancing act

---

[159] Herman (1993:15-109) presents such an argument.
[160] Xi 1959:470-71, no.438, as quoted in Des Forges 1973:78-79.

that the Qing empire had maintained in Khams since the Yongzheng era collapsed, and a policy of sustained direct involvement in the region began. The cultural nexus of power in Khams was forever changed.

After a long-fought battle in Xiangcheng, Zhao Erfeng defeated the monks of Sangpi monastery and restored order to the region. Following this military triumph, the Qing court in 1906 (Guangxu 32), appointed Zhao Erfeng Border Commissioner for Sichuan and Yunnan (*duban Chuan Tian bianwu dachen*), a newly created position charged with managing land reclamation and military training in Khams and northern Yunnan. The creation of this position, and Zhao's appointment to it, is further evidence of the empire's desire to increase its presence in the cultural nexus of power. Zhao quickly became the most important figure in Qing administration of Khams. Departing from Xi Liang's moderate policies, he radicalized Qing policy in Khams and Tibet from his new position. With the right to memorialize directly to the Emperor, he proposed that the Border Commissioner be allowed to establish offices, open mines, direct trade, and establish Chinese schools to teach Chinese language and Confucian morality to Tibetans throughout Khams. He also immediately instituted *gaitu guiliu* in Batang and Litang, promulgated a series of regulations designed to bring Tibetan customs more in line with Chinese Confucian values, and (at least publicly) promoted Han immigration into Khams.[161] The Qing court approved Zhao's programs, including his proposed annual budget of over two million taels, again clearly showing that the court wanted to strengthen its influence in Khams' cultural nexus of power.

Because of Xi Liang's reluctance to pursue an aggressive policy toward Tibet, he was removed from his position as Sichuan Governor-General in 1907 (Guangxu 33). Maintaining his position as Border Commissioner, Zhao Erfeng was appointed interim Governor-General, during which time he allowed foreign missionaries to penetrate further into Khams, engaged Chinese and foreign advisors to develop schools, mines, and agricultural projects, and established more district magistracies in the region. When his younger brother, Zhao Erxun, took office as permanent Governor-General of Sichuan in 1908 (Guangxu 34), Zhao Erfeng was appointed High Commis-

---

[161] Sperling 1976:19-22; Adshead 1983:82.

sioner to Tibet, a position he held concurrently with the position of
Border Commissioner until 1909. Zhao soon departed with his army
to assume his new position in Lhasa, but a succession struggle in
Derge and a series of other events during his journey allowed him to
remove from power all the remaining indigenous leaders in Khams
(including Nyarong). By 1910 (Xuantong 2), Zhao had effectively
brought the entire area under direct Chinese administration.[162] In his
own words:

> Humbly I've found that as for the indigenous tribes beyond the pass,
> historically your Excellency used the indigenous official system to di-
> vide them up and rule them. Now at the beginning of the dynasty, this
> system was still tolerably successful. However, since Zhandui (Nya-
> rong) was incorporated into Tibet (1865), the authority and power of
> the barbarian officials has advanced and pressed their neighboring de-
> pendencies. These officials forcibly oppress others, and they are trou-
> blesome and cruel. The people have difficulty making a living. Be-
> cause the roads are obstructed, Sichuan is far, and there are no people
> to manage things, each and every one of the indigenous officials relies
> on Tibetan barbarians to be his sovereign. We have already lost our
> authority to manage things.
>
> In the last few years, they blatantly incited evil acts. The monks in
> Taining, a small monastery, killed one local official and drove out the
> Han people. In Litang there were private feuds, and they resisted Han
> jurisdiction. In Batang, they actually dared to kill the High Commis-
> sioner. The Tibetan barbarians totally disregard the laws of the dy-
> nasty, and they are certainly making trouble on the frontier. Fortu-
> nately, I've been supported by Heavenly strength, and I have cleaned
> away the chief rebels. In order to make manifest the punishments of
> Heaven, I put them to death. I also took advantage of the situation and
> reincorporated Zhandui, instituted administrative reform (*gaitu guiliu*),
> and established Han officials [in the region] to avoid future calami-
> ties.[163]

After bringing all of Khams under direct Qing control, Zhao continued his march to Lhasa. The Dalai Lama fled to India, and the Qing
empire for the first time in history had direct control over central
Tibet. However, Zhao's interests rested in Khams, not central Tibet.
After restoring order in Lhasa, he returned to Khams and continued
to develop the region aggressively. He began by implementing *gaitu*

---

[162] See Sperling 1976:24-30, for a narrative of Zhao's military activities in Khams
from 1908 to 1911.
[163] Wu 1984:21.

guiliu in the entire region. Then, to legitimize the new magistracies he had established, he proposed new names for each of them and increased the number of soldiers garrisoned there. Moreover, he reformed the salt administration in the region, established a provincial treasury in Batang, drew up contracts with foreign companies to build bridges and explore mining operations in Khams, built a "modern-type" school in Batang, and planned for others to be built in Markham, Nyarong, and Chamdo.[164] The Qing court approved all of Zhao's actions and proposals.

Zhao Erfeng drastically altered the cultural nexus of power in Khams. By successfully implementing *gaitu guiliu*, often accomplished with the use of military force as in the case of Batang, he effectively dismantled the traditional Qing ruling system in Khams. *Sde pa* and *rgyal po*, if they were still living, were no longer tusi, and the resulting loss of this source of legitimacy disempowered them and their descendents in the cultural nexus. In the resulting power vacuum, monasteries, even those damaged by Zhao's military activities, were able to increase substantially their ideological and socio-economic influence in the cultural nexus of power. Qing civil and military officials were stationed in place of the indigenous leaders, but as an obvious unwelcome foreign presence their influence within the cultural nexus was tenuous at best. Nevertheless, we must not overlook the fact that the mere presence of such a large number of newcomers drastically increased demands on the region's limited resources of food, fuel, housing, labor, and transportation, demands which inevitably altered the cultural nexus as well. Also, although Zhao's efforts to promote permanent Han migration to Khams failed, he did lay a foundation that allowed the region to be opened up to further trade. As a result, Han merchants and entrepreneurs willing to conduct business in the region were able to increase their influence and power in the cultural nexus.

The balance of power formerly shared by indigenous leaders, monasteries, representatives of the Qing empire, and merchants in the cultural nexus had disintegrated by the end of the Qing dynasty, and a new system of order had emerged in its place. Indigenous leaders were now non-existent, Qing representatives were no longer welcome, and monasteries and merchants had substantially greater influ-

---

[164] Adshead 1983:86-89.

ence. However, we must not overlook the fact that the Qing empire collapsed in 1911. In the years immediately following the fall of the Qing empire, Khams, like much of western and southwestern China, suffered from lawlessness and banditry. Many of the Qing soldiers stationed in the region either left their posts or joined forces with warlords. Zhao Erfeng himself was murdered in 1911, and many of his achievements were undone. His yet to be implemented proposals were largely abandoned. As a result of the collapse of the Qing empire, the people of Khams witnessed yet another wave of radical fluctuations in the cultural nexus of power. Mapping these fluctuations, however, demands a separate study.

Khams in Chinese Notions of Modernity and Nationalism

The study of the events surrounding the uprising at Batang, as well as Khams history in general, sheds new light on our understandings of Chinese modernity and nationalism. Regarding modernity, historians often portray officials of the late Qing dynasty as conservative actors either opposed to modernization, or unable to modernize successfully. Zhao Erfeng, in contrast, was no such official. Characteristic institutions of modernity appear throughout Zhao's actions in Khams.

Zhao Erfeng's actions in Khams were driven by an ideology of imperialism, and this ideology was fundamentally modern. The fact that Zhao compared his actions in Khams with the imperialist projects of the British in Australia, the French in Madagascar, the Americans in the Philippines, and the Japanese in Hokkaido[165] reveals the modernity of his imperialist ideology. These were the very same nations whose modern ideologies and technologies had allowed them to humiliate, conquer, and colonize not only other lands, but Qing China as well in Zhao's lifetime.

Several other activities reveal Zhao's modern ideology of imperialism. When local Tibetans refused to provide labor for construction of a telegraph line in Litang, Zhao did not co-opt the 'u lag system of corvée labor as was commonly done by Qing civil and military officials. Rather, he entered into a contract with the indigenous official

---

[165] Sperling 1976:23.

in which the Qing government unprecedentedly *paid* for local labor. Zhao writes:

> I...have made a preliminary agreement with one of the indigenous offi-
> cials. The *'u lag* (*wula*) which the common people will provide is to be
> treated as chartered by the government, and between each station the
> wage to be issued is forty cents. All are very pleased to do so. With
> this very method, *'u lag* will not result in trouble in the future.[166]

To promote trade, Zhao also established the Border Tea Limited Liability Company (*Biancha gufen youxian gongsi*) in 1908. In classic imperialist style, this *guandu shangban* (official supervision and merchant company) was designed to "modernize the tea trade and insure China's continued monopoly."[167] As I have mentioned above, Zhao moreover initiated several modern projects to build bridges, increase agricultural production, develop mines, and establish schools in Khams. Many of these projects were abandoned following the collapse of the Qing empire, but Zhao's modern schools remained. While the positive effects of these schools are debatable (their primary purpose was to teach Chinese language to Tibetans), we should not overlook the fact that several important Tibetan intellectuals and political figures, including Phuntsog Wangyal, emerged from Batang and other areas of Khams in the 1930s.[168]

It is also important to note that Zhao frequently used modern technology to implement his programs. Preparing to depart for Batang in 1905, Zhao begins his first telegram to Xi Liang by discussing the progress of telegraph construction in the region. He suggests that completion of a modern telegraph line from Dajianlu to Batang is a fundamental part of his mission, and he completes the line successfully. This telegraph line greatly facilitated Zhao's later plans to build bridges, open mines, construct modern schools, and promote trade in the region. We have also seen that Zhao utilized modern technology, *e.g.*, Mauser guns and cannons, to bring Batang and the rest of Khams under direct imperial administration. Finally, Zhao had had his soldiers trained in modern western field techniques, which no doubt facilitated their military success in the region.

---

[166] Wu 1984:14.

[167] Gardella 1992:111.

[168] For more information on Phuntsog Wangyal, see Barnett 1999:16 and Stoddard 1985:82-84. Special thanks to Robert Barnett for making these references available to me.

While much of Qing China struggled with the forces of modernity in the late nineteenth century, Zhao Erfeng's activities in Khams show that the Qing empire not only accepted various institutions of modernity, but also actively employed them to their own advantage. Although many of his programs either were never implemented or were abandoned with the collapse of the Qing empire, through *gaitu guiliu* Zhao did succeed in developing and laying the foundation for modern imperialist institutions in Khams that were later built upon by the Republican and Communist governments.

The uprising at Batang and the events surrounding it also play a significant role in Chinese nationalism. The British invasion of Tibet in 1904 greatly influenced nascent feelings of nationalism in the early twentieth century Qing empire. Not wanting to face another national humiliation, the Qing court, acting first through Xi Liang and then through Zhao Erfeng, began to adopt a more aggressive Tibet policy. I have shown how this shift in policy directly contributed to the uprising in Batang. This uprising, in turn, ultimately allowed Zhao Erfeng to solidify Qing control in Khams and central Tibet by removing all of Khams' indigenous leaders from power and successfully implementing *gaitu guiliu* throughout the region. Flexing the empire's nationalist muscle, Zhao was able "to convert the British invasion of Tibet into a Chinese nationalist triumph" in less than six years.[169]

The failed Simla Conference in 1914 also reveals the importance of Batang in the development of Chinese nationalism. In tripartite discussions to define more clearly the relationship of Tibet vis-à-vis China, the status of Batang was a major sticking point. Given Batang's relatively strong Chinese (Han) presence since the Yongzheng era and the fact that Batang had undergone *gaitu guiliu*, Chinese representatives steadfastly held that Batang was part of Sichuan province, and not merely part of "Inner Tibet" as the British contended.[170] Effectively used to resist what was perceived to be potential foreign encroachment on Chinese territory, Batang as early as 1914 had become a symbol of an emerging Chinese nation.

Most important in terms of nationalism, the events surrounding the uprising at Batang brought Tibet into contemporary Chinese con-

---

[169] Des Forges 1973:81.
[170] Teichman 1922:45-46.

sciousness. While Tibet was previously absent from Chinese popular discourse, discussions of Zhao's success in Khams became part of a growing movement of public culture in early twentieth century China. Book-length publications such as Fu Songmu's *Xikang jiansheng ji*, Xie Bin's *Xizang wenti*, and Mei Xinru's *Xikang* offered heretofore unavailable information on Tibetan history and culture. The popular bimonthly magazine *Yugong* even dedicated an entire issue to the problems of Tibet and Xikang in 1937. Evincing a growing interest in border areas, study societies were also established during the Republican period to better understand Khams and its culture, now more accessible thanks to Zhao's implementation of *gaitu guiliu*. Moreover, the formal incorporation of Khams into the Qing administrative system by 1910 facilitated the later establishment of Xikang Province in 1939, an event which further bolstered Chinese nationalism in the Republican period.

Interestingly, some Chinese scholars realized the significance of the uprising at Batang in terms of China's emerging national identity in the early twentieth century. Wu Fengpei, who went on to become the most prolific and learned twentieth century Chinese scholar of Tibetan history, wrote prophetically in 1937, "Although the time did not exceed several months before the unrest and trouble at Batang was pacified, Tibetan affairs from this point have been difficult to mend."[171] Zhao Erfeng's efforts in the waning years of the Qing dynasty clearly have had long-lasting effects on both Tibetans and Chinese.

Conclusion

Cassinelli and Ekvall state, "Eastern Tibet had a reputation for political instability and governmental impotence."[172] In this paper I have argued, in contrast, that an identifiable cultural nexus of power existed in late nineteenth and early twentieth century Khams. It is precisely in the interaction between the four primary players in the cultural nexus—indigenous leaders, monasteries and their representatives, representatives of the Qing empire, and merchants, that Khams' unique sense of socio-economic order can be discerned. Al-

---

[171] Wu 1937:43.
[172] Cassinelli and Ekvall 1969:362.

though Khams was rarely at peace from the early seventeenth to the late nineteenth century, it had successfully maintained a delicate balance in its cultural nexus. However, following the uprising at Batang, this balance was lost forever. Indigenous leaders were removed from the nexus as viable participants, and monasteries subsequently increased their power. The stationing of large numbers of Qing soldiers in the region also altered the nexus in terms of both heightened ethnic tension and increased demands on the region's resources. Finally, merchant influence in the cultural nexus of power increased in the wake of Zhao's activities in Khams. The cultural nexus of power is clearly an important component in the process of understanding Khams history.

In this paper I have also discussed the importance of Khams in western and Chinese understandings of modernity and nationalism in early twentieth century China. I have shown: one, that the late Qing empire effectively employed institutions of modernity to its own advantage; and two, that the events surrounding the uprising at Batang greatly strengthened China's feelings of nationalism in the early twentieth century. Critical analysis of the uprising at Batang therefore demands that we rethink our understandings of the Qing empire, China, and Tibet, both then and now.

BIBLIOGRAPHY

Adshead, Samuel A.M. *Province and Politics in Late Imperial China: Viceregal Government in Szechwan, 1989-1911*. London: Curzon Press, 1983.

Barnett, Robert. "The Babas are Dying: Preliminary Notes on Elite Formation in Tibet." Modern China Seminar Paper, Columbia University, January 1999.

Batang xianzhi. Sichuan sheng Batang xianzhi bianzuan weiyuanhui, comp. Chengdu: Sichuan minzu chubanshe, 1993.

Carrasco, Pedro. *Land and Polity in Tibet.* Seattle: University of Washington Press, 1959.

Cassinelli, C.W., and Robert B. Ekvall. *A Tibetan Principality: The Political System of Sa sKya.* Ithaca: Cornell University Press, 1969.

Cooper, T.T. *Travels of a Pioneer of Commerce.* London: John Murray, 1871.

Des Forges, Roger V. *Hsi-Liang and the Chinese National Revolution.* New Haven: Yale University Press, 1973.

Dictionanaire Thibétain-Latin-Français, par les Missionaires Catholiques du Thibet. Hong Kong: Société des Missions Étrangères, 1899.

Duara, Prasenjit. *Culture, Power, and the State: Rural North China, 1900-1942.* Stanford: Stanford University Press, 1988.

Fu Songmu. *Xikang jiansheng ji.* Chengdu: Chengdu gongji yinzhi gongsi, 1912.

Ganzi Zangzu zizhizhou minzu zhi. Kangding minshizhuan bianxiezu, comp. Beijing: Dangdai Zhongguo chubanshe, 1994.

Gardella, Robert P. "Qing Administration of the Tea Trade: Four Facets over Three Centuries." In J.K. Leonard and J.R. Watt, eds. *To Achieve Security and Wealth: The Qing Imperial State and the Economy, 1644-1911.* Ithaca: East Asia Program, Cornell University, 1992.

Guo Qing. "Qingdai Zangqu yichuan zhidu lice." *Xizang yanjiu* 1:71-78, 1996.

Herman, John. *National Integration and Regional Hegemony: The Political and Cultural Dynamics of Qing State Expansion, 1650-1750.* Ph.D. dissertation, University of Washington, 1993.

Hucker, Charles O. *A Dictionary of Official Titles in Imperial China.* Stanford: Stanford University Press, 1985.

Lu Chuanlin. *Chou Zhan shugao.* In Shen Yunlong, ed. *Jindai Zhongguo shiliao congkan*, Vol. 28. Taipei: Wenhai chubanshe, 1974.

Mei Xinru. *Xikang.* Nanjing: Zhengzhong shuju, 1934.

Niu Pinghan. *Qingdai zhengqu yange zongbiao.* Beijing: Zhongguo ditu chubanshe, 1990.

Shakabpa, Tsepon W.D. *Tibet: A Political History.* New York: Potala Publications, 1984.

Sperling, Elliot. "The Chinese Venture in K'am, 1904-1911, and the Role of Chao Erh-feng." *The Tibet Journal* 1(2):10-36, (April/June) 1996.

Stoddard, Heather. *Le Mendiant d' Amdo.* Paris: Societe d'Ethnographie Paris, 1985.

Teichman, Eric. *Travels of a Consular Official in Eastern Tibet: Together with a History of the Relations Between China, Tibet and India.* Cambridge: Cambridge University Press, 1922.

Tsering Thar. "The Dralag Monastery and its Tribes." In Ernst Steinkellner, *et al.*, eds. *Tibetan Studies: Proceedings of the 7th Seminar of the International Association for Tibetan Studies, Graz 1995.* Wien: Verlag Der Osterreichischen Akademie Der Wissenschaften, 1997, pp. 981-85.

Wu Fengpei, ed. "Ji Qing Guangxu sanshiyi nian Batang zhi luan." *Yugong banyue kan* 6(12):43-52, 1937.

Wu Fengpei, ed. *Zhao Erfeng Chuanbian zoudu*. Chengdu: Sichuan minzu chubanshe, 1984.

Xie Bin. *Xizang wenti*. Shanghai: Shangwu yinshuguan, 1926.

Xi Liang. *Xi Liang yigao zougao*. Zhongguo kexueyuan, comp. 2 volumes. Beijing: Zhonghua shuju, 1959.

Zhu Shoupeng, ed. *Guangxu chao donghua lu*. 5 volumes. Beijing: Zhonghua shuju, 1958.

FRONTIER PROCESS, PROVINCIAL POLITICS AND MOVEMENTS FOR KHAMPA AUTONOMY DURING THE REPUBLICAN PERIOD[173]

PENG WENBIN (UNIVERSITY OF WASHINGTON)

In recent years, amidst much scholarly attention to Chinese national-ism, there has also been growing interest in regional and provincial politics in China, offering us an important perspective to understand the process of constructing, as well as deconstructing, China's na-tion-building project. Scholarly analyses have not only dwelt upon rampant regional economic disparities and the emergence of cultural regionalist tendencies in the post-Mao reform era,[174] but have also delved into the Federalist versus Centralist debate of the early Re-publican years.[175] Historical and contemporary studies of regional discourses in twentieth-century China have shed much light on the contingency, complexity and ambiguity of Chinese nation building and modernization projects. Yet most of these studies, illuminating as they are in suggesting competing visions of the Chinese nation and modernity, have been confined to China's coastal regions, focusing largely on provincial and regional politics in Han Chinese areas. They appear to have had little connection to the line of inquiry trav-ersing vast regions of China's frontiers, explicating the interplay of

---

[173] The original version of this paper was presented at the 9th Seminar of the International Association for Tibetan Studies, Leiden, and was entitled "Frontier Politics and Indigenous Movements for Khampa Autonomy During the Republican Period." Analysis of nativist movements in Kham is part of my long-term project on the provincial politicization of Xikang (Sikang) in Republican China. Regrettably, the writing of this paper has largely been based on my research of Chinese resources so far. Relevant data in Tibetan literature are in the process of being collected, and will be included in my later phases of the Xikang Project.

In revising this paper for publication, I would like to thank Larry Epstein for his insightful comments and laborious editing work. I also extend my thanks to Siu-woo Cheung, Uradyn Bulag and Shih-chung Hsieh for their support in a joint project on frontier politics and indigenous movements in Republican China.

[174] See Falkenhausen 1995; Friedman 1994; Goodman 1994, 1997.

[175] See Chen 1999; Duara 1995; Fitzgerald 1996.

ethnicity and nationalism, and the contested relationships between center and periphery.[176]

Building on insights from approaches to the ethnic frontier, as well as to (coastal) provincial politics, this paper explores the hybridity of provincial and ethnic politics in Republican China. As a specific case, this paper analyzes the discursive process regarding the creation of eastern Tibet (Kham) and other minority areas as Xikang (or Sikang) Province in the 1930s.[177] It highlights various historical moments during which Khampa identity politics intersected with the Xikang provincial building project, affirming Kham regional autonomy while engaging Chinese nationalism and international politics. Central to this paper is the issue of how the rhetoric of "Kham for the Khampas" transformed the social experience of Khampa Tibetans into three political movements during the formative years of Xikang Province: the Baan (Batang) Incident in 1932, the Nuola Incident in 1935, and the Ganze Incident in 1939.

In historicizing the trajectory of Xikang, this paper intends to address the complex ethno-provincial politics which unfolded in local space. It involves the struggle of a Khampa intellectual elite to advance its interests by co-opting Nationalist politics, and whose efforts in turn were appropriated by the central Nationalist government to contain Liu Wenhui's provincial warlordism and the dissemination of Tibetan nationalism in Kham. By placing the Khampa autonomy movement within the global-national-local framework, this paper also intends to register a process in which the local had been indispensable to the localizing of global or national politics, and at the same time, the product of this process.

---

[176] See Brown 1996; Gaubatz 1996; Harrell 1995; Lipman 1996, 1997; Litzinger 2000; Millward 1996; Schein 2000.

[177] Xikang Province, established on January 1, 1939, with Kangding (Dar rtse mdo) as its provincial capital, was composed of counties east of the Jinsha River ('Bri chu). It consisted of Khampa Tibetans, various Yi counties in Ningyuan (presently Liangshan Yi Autonomous Prefecture), and several Han Chinese counties in Yaan, southwestern Sichuan.

*Nation-Building and Boundary Making: Crafting Centrality of
Frontiers in Chinese Geopolitical Thinking*

China's metamorphosis from empire to nation-state did not, as Duara argues,[178] suggest a radical and totalizing departure in political self-consciousness, substituting national identity for all other forms of identification (*e.g.,* provincial or native place identity). It was, however, accompanied by a novel imagining of territorial boundaries of China within the world system of nation-states, eroding the Sinocentric cosmos of *tianxia* (All Under Heaven) that had dominated Chinese geopolitical thinking for millennia.

In previous scholarship on Chinese nationalism, there has been an overt emphasis on the emergence of treaty ports along the coast, after the defeat of the Qing by maritime powers, in provoking the Chinese sense of national territoriality and identity[179]. Yet the process of reconceptualizing the vast expanses of land frontiers inhabited predominantly by non-Han ethnic minorities has been no less significant in China's transition to a modern nation-state at the turn of the twentieth century. In the process, areas previously considered barren and peripheral to China proper achieved prominence in the Chinese political thinking.[180] Chinese frontier discourse, now inscribed with new spatial referents, was imagined to be positioned between "internal" and "external" others.[181] It territorialized not only the sovereignty of the Chinese state vis-à-vis foreign powers, but also the "internally primordial and genealogical tie" of the Chinese nation to the multiplicity of ethnic groups in China's fuzzy frontier zones. As such, frontier discourse in twentieth century China was caught up in a web of relationships linked to global, national, and local political economies. The Xikang Provincial project to be discussed below well captured this changing process, and its sociopolitical ramifications reverberated beyond its provincial boundaries,

---

[178] See Duara 1993.

[179] See, *e.g.*, Barlow 1991:210-212.

[180] Mosley 1969.

[181] Terms such as Internal Others, Internal Orientalism or Internal Colonialism have been frequently employed by some analysts in studies of ethnicity in China (see, *e.g.,* Schein 2000). The use of the term 'internal', however, runs the risk of being ahistorical. It suggests that the boundaries of China within which minorities are currently included are permanent or fixed, without a process through which they are historically constituted. I put the term in quotations here to call attention to its complexities.

suggesting the centrality of the "peripheral" or the "ethnic" in the narratives of the nation at a particular historical juncture in modern Chinese history.

Xikang: A Contested Historical Terrain for Global Politics, National Policies and Provincial Warlordism

The making of Xikang as an administrative *place* out of an essentially fluid frontier *space* caught between the centers of China and Tibet proceeded along a tortuous path.[182] Almost thirty years had elapsed since its official proposition to the Qing court in 1911 to its final establishment under the Republican regime in 1939. Yet the province was short lived; sixteen years after its creation, it was abolished by the socialist regime in 1955, after the Communists consolidated the southwestern frontiers.[183] Because of its short duration, many contemporary writers tend to overlook this crucial period in Sino-Tibetan history. Warren Smith, for example, calls the creation of Xikang "illusory," as if it merely fulfilled some Nationalist Chinese expansionist dream, referring to its "almost entirely imaginary nature."[184] This line of thinking, however, does little justice to the complex politics concerning the establishment of Xikang, once a focal point for contestation and appropriation, crucially linked to the nation-building projects both of China and Tibet, as well as to an incipient Khampa self-rule movement.[185]

The idea of Xikang emerged during the turbulent years of the late nineteenth century, at a time when the Qing Empire was severely shaken by the encroachment of foreign states in its frontier regions, and was desperately "using Chinese imperialism to counter foreign imperialism." The attempt to bring peripheral areas under its firm grip had pushed the Qing court to encourage "Chinese colonization of the frontier regions, in many cases suppressing the local autonomy

---

[182] For a subtle distinction between space and place, see Certeau 1984:117ff.

[183] Xikang Province was officially abolished in November, 1955. Its administrative region east of the Jinsha River, the Xikang Tibetan Autonomous Region, was annexed into Sichuan, and was later changed to Ganze Tibetan Autonomous Prefecture in 1956, a name still in use today (Pu 1986:577). For a detailed analysis of the political integration of Southwest China into the PRC, see Solinger 1977.

[184] See Smith 1996: 226, 242.

[185] Cf. Epstein and Peng 1998; Peng 1998.

which the non-Chinese peoples in these regions had previously enjoyed."[186]

The Sino-Tibetan frontier was no exception to this process. The British invasion of Lhasa in 1904 created a deep anxiety among Chinese frontier officials concerned with the safety of China's southwestern border. In their minds, immediate steps were needed to redress the vulnerability of the Sino-Tibet frontier, soon to be materialized in Zhao Erfeng's "civilizing project" in Kham, including reforms of the *tusi* system, extensive colonization, and agricultural, mineral and educational development.[187] In 1911, Fu Songmu, Zhao's successor in Kham, formally proposed to the Qing court to convert Kham into a province so that this part of the frontier could be consolidated and used as a stepping stone to fully assimilate Tibet. Yet the project failed to be implemented upon the eve of the Qing Empire's collapse.[188]

The Xikang project was revived again in 1928 by the Nationalist government along with plans to create four other new provinces: Rehe, Chahaer, Suiyuan, and Qinghai.[189] Upon their victory over the Northern Expedition, the Nationalists perceived this as a crucial step to construct a New China as a sovereign state, a unified nation with a fixed boundary. In the case of Xikang, its establishment could be used to counter the emergent nation-building project of central Tibetans, who were then also attempting to fix their boundaries with China by mounting a series of attacks in Kham to reclaim lost territory.[190]

---

[186] Moseley 1969:301. On the other hand, the Qing doubled the lands under Chinese imperial rule during the eighteenth and nineteenth centuries. It was a period, as Millward (1996:113) accurately puts it, that witnessed the "combination of demographic growth with territorial expansion," with consequences no less dramatic than those of American westward expansion in the same period.

[187] See Sperling 1976:10-36; Lee 1979:63-68. Zhao's brutal suppression of local rebellions earned him the nickname "Butcher Zhao," widespread among local Khampas, who were said to often use his name as a bogeyman to subdue obstinate children.

Apart from a blueprint for establishing Xikang Province, Zhao's notorious reforms, largely Han-chauvinistic, could hardly be called successful, as Louis King (as quoted in Mehra 1979, 1:185), the last British Consul at Dartsendo, observed.

[188] See Dong 1996:21.

[189] See Moseley 1969:309; Wen 1994:340-341.

[190] See Dong 1996. In 1913, the Thirteenth Dalai Lama declared the "independence" of Tibet and sent an army to attack various Kham counties, but he was thwarted by the joint forces of Sichuan and Yunnan. In 1917, military actions in

Liu Wenhui, then Governor of Sichuan, however, was not enthusiastic about the Xikang project,[191] but was busy expanding his power in civil war with other contenders for Sichuan's unification.[192] It was not until 1935 that a Xikang preparatory committee was set up with Liu serving as its chair. By then Liu had already lost his war against other Sichuanese warlords, like Liu Xiang, Deng Xihou, and Tian Songyao, and had retreated to Kham.[193] Liu Wenhui's renewed interest in Xikang was to use it as a stronghold for the survival of his 24th Army, and if possible, to restore his political and military might in southwest China. Liu's enthusiasm about Xikang, at the time, overlapped with Jiang Jieshi's plan to stem the arms and ambitions of Liu Xiang in Sichuan, as well as to stabilize southwestern China as the "rear" or "backyard" pending the massive Japanese invasions. In 1939, at the height of the Anti-Japanese War, the province of Xikang officially came into existence, with more than thirty counties, and a population of 1.5 millions, consisting principally of Khampa Tibetans of the area east of the Jinsha River, and Yi in the southeastern counties.

Kham for the Khampas: Political Incidents, Provincial Narratives, and Identity Politics

The authors of *Sichuan Tongshi* (*General History of Sichuan*) write that the creation of Xikang Province during the War against Japan was "of great significance to strengthen the ties between Tibet and

---

Kham resumed with eleven counties captured by Central Tibetan troops. In 1930, Lhasa again sent soldiers to aid monks at Dargye Monastery in their dispute with the Sichuan army, and captured Ganze and Nyarong, but were driven back to the west bank of the Jinsha River by the coalition forces of Sichuan and Qinghai in 1932.

[191] Liu Wenhui's control over Kham dates back to 1927 when his troops drove Liu Chengxun, another Sichuanese warlord, out of the region. Liu then assumed the post of Chuan-Kang bianfang zongzhihui (Sichuan-Xikang Border Defense Commander-in-Chief).

[192] Wen 1994. At that time, the other four provinces were established. Little is known as to how the Nationalist government reached the decision to set up Xikang as a province. The "unification" of China under Jiang Jieshi in 1928 did not end the chaos in Sichuan, as the province was being fragmented by warlordism. Various provincial militarists, including Liu Wenhui and his rival Liu Xiang, did not have substantive relationships with Nanjing, and pledged loyalty to Jiang rather symbolically. See Kapp 1973.

[193] For a detailed analysis of provincial warlordism in early Republican China, see Kapp 1973.

the motherland, to consolidate the southwest as the rear during war-time years, and to smash the British imperialist conspiracy to invade Kham and Tibet."[194] However, the chapter on Xikang in *Tongshi*, like many other "authoritative" versions of Xikang history in Chinese, makes no specific mention of how Khampa Tibetans responded to the making of Xikang in their homeland. The three autonomy movements that had shaken the Kham political landscape in the 1930s were simply "forgotten" by official historiography.[195] Yet, memories of these episodes were still kept in various *wenshi ziliao* (cultural-historical data) at the local level,[196] unofficial publications consisting of materials not yet sanitized into History, suggesting strongly that Khampas not only reacted, but also reacted militantly according to their own versions of the Xikang provincial project.

---

[194] Wen 1994:345.

[195] The omissions point to some gaps in PRC post-liberation historiography, which, at times, has not been quite capable of holding the themes of Nation and Revolution together. For all their struggles against Han Chinese chauvinism, exploitation and corruption in Kham, these political incidents may well be called "revolutionary uprisings." Yet, such leaders of these movements as the Central Guomindang's stout followers complicated their historical evaluation, diminishing their "progressiveness" by revolutionary history standards. Moreover, these militant movements in the name of "Kham for the Khampas" rub uncomfortably against the nation-building project under the socialist regime, which places heavy emphasis upon the consolidation of ethnic frontiers and the unity of nationalities by attacking various forms of *defang minzu zhuyi* (local nationalism) in China.

Not quite coincidentally, neither have these Khampa autonomy movements in the 1930s been catalogued as epic histories in Tibetan nationalist discourse. These versions of "autonomy" are perhaps too tainted with the agendas of the Central Nationalists in Kham to be compatible with either the cause of Tibetan independence, or the Dalai Lama's recent proposition of "genuine autonomy" for Greater Tibet. Thus they appear to have been deleted from the "foundational saga" of the Tibetan nation.

[196] The writing of *wenshi ziliao* (cultural-historical data) has been sponsored by *zhengxie* (Political Consultative Conference) at various levels, an organization formulated by the Chinese Communist Party for "united-front work," to win support from the non-Communist elite, including those of other parties. *Wenshi ziliao* are generally regarded as collections of raw materials for official histories, covering a wide range of areas about a particular locality in history (*e.g.*, politics, economy, education, religion, folk culture) in forms of memoirs, archives, dairies, or manuscripts. Large portions of *wenshi ziliao* have been devoted to political events in Republican China, written mostly as eye-witness accounts by the participants themselves.

The Baan Incident (1932)[197]

Zhao Erfeng's "reforms" went on mostly in Baan (Batang), a county in southern Kham bordering China and Tibet. Nearly 30 years later, this place was again pushed to front stage in Kham politics, this time by a self-rule movement led by a native Baanese, Gesangzeren (Tib. Skal bzang tshe ring; Chin. Wang Tianjie), in 1932.

Gesangzeren attended both a public school established by Zhao Erfeng and also Huaxi Xiaoxue (West China Primary School), founded by missionaries, in Baan. He completed his high school education in Yunnan before he was admitted into the Xikang Officers Training Institute.[198] In 1924, Gesangzeren joined the Nationalist Party (Guomindang) and became "the Party's first Tibetan member, then a delegate on behalf of Tibet or Xikang in the Party's third to the sixth plenary sessions," as he proudly recalls in his memoirs.[199]

When Gongdentashi, representative of the Panchen Lama was on a mission to Nanjing through Kham in 1926, Gesangzeren served as his interpreter and accompanied him to the capital. While sojourning in Nanjing, Gesangzeren's proficiency in Chinese and Tibetan and his knowledge of Sino-Tibetan issues were highly regarded by top Guomindang officials. Dai Jitao, president of the Examination Yuan (Council) and a devotee of frontier affairs, recommended Gesangzeren to the Meng-Zang Weiyuanhui (Mongolian and Tibetan Affairs Commission), which appointed him as Commissioner and head of the Tibetan Affairs Division in 1927.[200]

In 1931, the Central Nationalist Party Committee dispatched Gesangzeren as Xikang Dangwu Tepaiyuan (Xikang Party Affairs Special Commissioner) to organize a provincial party branch in Kham. This assignment certainly carried the Central Government's intention to weaken Liu Wenhui's power in Kham as Liu was not directly under the control of Nanjing and had not been submissive to the

---

[197] "Baan" or "Batang" have been used alternatively in historical literature. Strictly speaking, it was not until 1951 that "Batang" appeared as the official county name. Virtually throughout the Republican period, 1913-1950, the county was called "Baan." See Pu 1986:488, 578. I thus use "Baan" to avoid an anachronistic error.
[198] The Institute was established by Liu Chengxun, Xikang Military Farming Commissioner, in Kham before Liu Wenhui's takeover.
[199] Gesangzeren 1974:3.
[200] See Feng 1992:116; Qing 1975:45.

Central Authorities.[201] Yet, it also fit into Gesangzeren's own agenda to reform Xikang. [202]

Gesangzeren's return (1932) as a native Khampa of high ranking position caused suspicion and dissatisfaction among Liu Wenhui's civil and military personnel in Baan.[203] They spread rumors, and even assassinated one of Gesangzeren's propaganda workers. Gesangzeren seized the opportunity to disband Liu's army in Baan, and proclaimed his "five-point" reform policies, including local self-rule, equality among the various nationalities, abolition of corvée labor, improvement of agriculture and animal husbandry technology, and development of culture and education in Kham. Meanwhile, he established a preparatory committee of Xikang Province, and declared himself Xikang Provincial Commander of the Nationalist Army.

A dispute between Gesangzeren and Gongga Lama of Yanjing led to a protracted battle between Gesangzeren and Central Tibet, lasting

---

[201] See Jiang and Lai 1982:104. Liu Wenhui had been Jiang Jieshi's political enemy since the late 1920s. In 1929, Liu Wenhui joined Zhongguo Guomindang Geming Da Tongmeng (the Great Revolutionary League of the Chinese Nationalist Party), organized by the party reformists, Wang Jingwei and Chen Gongbo. The League also included Tang Shengzhi, Li Zongren, Zhang Fakui, He Jian, and Shi Yousan, factional leaders attempting to topple Jiang's rule. Twice in 1929, Liu joined Tang Shengzhi in sending telegrams to Jiang Jieshi calling for the latter's resignation. In 1930, Liu Wenhui again sent a telegram to openly support the war against Jiang Jieshi by the coalition forces of Yan Xishan, Feng Yuxiang, and Li Zongren (Liu 1979:4-5; Xie and Feng 1994:117).

[202] Long Yun, a famous Yi warlord who ruled Yunnan at the time, saw potential benefits in Gesangzeren's return to Kham, too. Long met Gesangzeren in Kunming, appointed him Dianbian Xuanhuashi (Yunnan Border Region Pacification Commissioner), and supplied him with rifles and ammunition when Gesangzeren was on route to Baan through Yunnan. The aid, in turn, would help Long consolidate the regions bordering northern Yunnan and southern Kham (Jiang and Lai 1982:105). Since Liu Wenhui had once assisted Long's political enemies in Yunnan's provincial power struggle, Long and Liu were not on good terms. Long's support to Gesangzeren could be interpreted as a form of retaliation by creating a potential enemy for Liu, as one analyst suggests (Qing 1975:45).

[203] On the other hand, Gesangzeren's party activities in Baan also encountered numerous difficulties among local Tibetans. At the sight of "political rituals" (e.g., bowing before Sun Yat-sun's picture, chanting Sun's will, and singing the Party song at the headquarters), they "misunderstood" Gesangzeren's Party affairs as a foreign religion resembling that of missionaries in Baan, but in opposition to Tibetan Buddhism. To accommodate Tibetan Buddhists, Gesangzeren had to put up a picture of the Buddha next to Sun Yat-sun's at the party branch headquarters. This, however, immediately drew fire from an American missionary who refused to bow in front of the Buddha. But, as it was a courtesy visit, he did bow to the national flag and Sun's picture (Gesangzeren 1974:4-5).

over three months, from mid-April to mid-July 1932. Although Gongga Lama had followed Gesangzeren's order to disarm Liu Wenhui's garrison in Yanjing, he refused to turn over the weapons.[204] Gesangzeren sent soldiers to attack him. Lhasa, already alarmed by Gesangzeren's party mission and his reforms in Kham, agreed to help Gongga by sending troops to besiege Baan. Gesangzeren held Baan for months, but was forced to resign his commanding position pending an attack by Liu Wenhui. Accusing Gesangzeren of "rebelling against party orders," Liu ordered a military expedition to Baan, and, simultaneously sent telegrams to Nanjing, requesting that Gesangzeren be recalled. By July 1932, Gesangzeren left for Nanjing, thus ending the Baan Incident, an event which, according to characterizations by the parties involved in it, had caused much controversy.

The Incident's legitimacy was central to its characterization. Liu Wenhui's rhetoric portrayed the incident at Baan, a *coup d'etat* against his own rule in Kham, however as a "plotted rebellion against Zhongyang (the Center) through "mobilizing various gangs of local Tibetan bandits" as well as "contacting" troops from Central Tibet for support. The Incident escalated the "already precarious situation in the border region of Kham,"[205] making it all the more important and urgent to have a "quick and thorough suppression" unless Gesang-zeren "repents of his wrongdoing."[206]

To the Tibetan government in Lhasa, the Baan Incident, appeared to be internal or regional strife in the Nationalist camp, which was, strictly speaking, part of Chinese long-term strategies to assimilate Central Tibet into China. However, it differed from previous at-

---

[204] Before Gongga turned to Lhasa for military assistance, he is said to have sent a telegram to Liu Wenhui, saying he had confiscated the garrison's arms to keep them out of Gesangzeren's hands, and that they would be returned to the garrison when Liu's army arrived in Yanjing (Qing 1975:47).

[205] The severity of frontier situation in Kham in the statement was by no means exaggerated, as both Liu Wenhui and Gesangzeren mentioned it in their telegrams to Nanjing. The war in northern Kham between Tibetan troops and Han Chinese garrisons, triggered by the Dargyas-Beri Incident had been intermittent since 1930, and continued well into 1932 when the Baan Incident broke out in the south. In May 1932, the joint forces of Liu Wenhui and Ma Bufang from Qinghai defeated the Tibetan army and drove it back to the west of the Jinsha River. For a detailed discussion, cf. "The Ganze War of the 1930s," presented by Lawrence Epstein at the 9th Seminar of the International Association for Tibetan Studies, Leiden.

[206] Qing 1975:46.

tempts which had for the most part been carried out by Chinese themselves (*e.g.,* Zhao Erfeng, Yin Changheng, and Liu Wenhui). This time, the effort to undermine Central Tibet's independent status had been orchestrated through the "unprecedented treachery" of a native Khampa, Gesangzeren, who had pledged loyalty to the Chinese Nationalist Party, "propagating dangerous thoughts, instigating a so-called 'revolution', and pushing monks and lay people in Xikang to a crazy war against the Tibetan army...."[207]

In Gesangzeren's own terms, however, the Baan incident was no more than a "conflict" between his party headquarters and the Sichuan garrison at Baan. Though he did not deny that he had exceeded Central Party orders in disarming local Han troops and appointing himself Xikang Provincial Army Commander, his party headquarters, however, "received unanimous support from the people in their unsurpassed revolutionary spirit while fighting against the garrison."[208] For Gesangzeren the legitimacy of the Incident, though hard to apply in his dispute with Liu Wenhui, certainly lay in what had happened during its course. Gesangzeren fully recounted the process, during which he firmly refused to cooperate with Central Tibetans, despite their frequent visits and repeated evocations of *tongzu tongjiao* (a common bond based upon religion and ethnicity).[209] He told how he led troops to fight a hard and courageous battle to defend Baan, inflicting heavy casualties upon the Central Tibetans. Such a contribution, Gesangzeren hinted, could at least parallel, if not actually exceed, that of Liu Wenhui and Ma Bufang's coalition forces in repelling Tibetan soldiers from northern Kham and southern Qinghai.[210]

Commenting on the process and ramifications of the Baan Incident, Qing Feng, a historian in Taiwan, attributes Gesangzeren's failure to his miscalculation of his strength and also his impatience at the Central Government's gradualist approach to political reforms in Kham. Qing, however, gives Gesangzeren high marks for his "outstanding leadership and enthusiasm in local reforms,"[211] in stark contrast to Liu Wenhui's poor performance and corrupt politics in Xi-

---

[207] Gesangzeren 1974:7.
[208] Gesangzeren 1974:5.
[209] Gesangzeren 1974:6.
[210] Gesangzeren 1974:6.
[211] Qing 1975:48.

kang, which were also accountable for the eruption of the Incident. The real traitor, Qing writes, was none other than Liu himself who later allowed the Red Army to slip through his region, and eventually surrendered himself when the Communists returned in 1949.[212]

The Nuola Incident (1935)

During his inaugural speech as governor of Xikang Province on 1 January 1939, Liu Wenhui recalled the difficult path of building up the new province. The year of 1935 had been a turning point for Xikang, as its Preparatory Committee officially came into existence.

> That year, the Central Government sent Nuola to Kham as Pacification Commissioner to assist in building the Province. But Nuola took the opportunity to stir up trouble, murdering civil officials and disarming resident troops. The disastrous state finally ended with his own death in 1936.[213]

Nuola Hutuketu (Tib. Mgar ba bla ma), a Nyingmapa incarnate lama of Riboche Monastery, was certainly a legendary figure in Kham politics and history. He had assisted the Chinese garrison in Riboche, led by General Peng Risheng, in the Sino-Tibetan conflict of 1917, but was captured and sentenced to life imprisonment by orders of the Dalai Lama a year later. Nuola managed to escape, however, and miraculously showed up in Beijing in 1924 after a few months' hard journey through Nepal and India.[214] He petitioned the Beijing Gov-

---

[212] Qing 1975:48.

[213] Feng 1992:225. Nuola obviously had reason not to support Liu's provincial project. Both he and Gesangzeren had their blueprints for the future of Xikang. Gesangzeren would have liked to see the new province modeled on Fu Songmu's proposal with the addition of various counties from Sichuan, Yunnan, and Qinghai, and Baan, his home county, as capital of Xikang. Nuola had an even bigger plan. He proposed abolishing Xikang altogether and creating two provinces, Kangding and Chamdo. He certainly hoped to become governor of Chamdo Province that would include Riboche, his home county (Ren 1933:70-80).

[214] There were two versions of Nuola's escape in 1923 after he had been imprisoned since 1918 in Lho brag Bya yul, southern Tibet. One, as mostly narrated by Nuola himself or his followers, was that during his six years' imprisonment in which he was repeatedly poisoned, Nuola survived with enormous courage and wisdom. After his feigned death one day in 1923, the cave where he was held prisoner was sealed, and Nuola managed to flee by digging a hole out of it. The other was simply that Nuola bribed the wardens and was set free secretly (Hu 1971:112; Jiang, Lai, and Deng 1982:108).

ernment, then headed by Duan Qirui, to recapture Chamdo, but did not succeed.[215]

Nuola's trip to Nanjing around 1927 was a turnabout in his political career. Aided by Gesangzeren, Nuola received an appointment as Commissioner of the Mongolian and Tibetan Affairs Commission, and Dai Jitao was said to have often consulted him on Sino-Tibetan affairs. Leaders in Nanjing had great expectations that Gesangzeren and Nuola would curb warlord forces in Kham, and extend central authority to that part of frontier and ultimately to Central Tibet.[216]

In 1935, Nuola was appointed Xikang Xuanweishi (Xikang Pacification Commissioner) to mobilize resistance against the Red Army's march into Kham.[217] He convened his first pacification meeting in Kangding, attended by *tusi*, local headmen, lamas, and local gentry of Kham. In addition to the open propaganda against the Red Army, Nuola held secret meetings to solicit charges against the brutality and heavy taxation of Liu Wenhui's army, and is said to have sent 300 written complaints to the Central Government. Liu Wenhui, on the other hand, accused Nuola of acting beyond his authority as a Pacification Commissioner in Kham and destablizing the region instead.[218]

Tensions between Nuola and Liu escalated as Nuola embarked on his pacifying missions in northern Kham. After disarming a regiment of Liu Wenhui's troops in September 1935, Nuola proclaimed Khampa self-rule, ordered the removal of several of Liu's magistrates in northern Kham, and an attack on Baan in southern Kham. General Li Baobing, commander of the Central Nationalist 16th Army dispatched to fight the Red Army in Kham, also despised Liu's troops, and intended to have them driven out so that he could replace

---

[215] Jiang, Lai and Deng 1982:108. Nuola is said to have arrived in Chongqing in 1926 upon the invitation of Li Gongdu, a devout Buddhist serving then as representative of Liu Xiang in Beijing. While Nuola was in Chongqing propagating Buddhism, Liu Xiang and many of his top officials became Nuola's converts. Liu Xiang, Liu Wenhui's nephew and also a rival in Sichuan provincial politics, later sent two companies of soldiers as Nuola's security forces while the latter was in Kham in 1935, attempting to create hindrance to Liu Wenhui's monopoly of Xikang (Feng 1992:144; Jiang Lai, and Deng 1982:110).

[216] Feng 1992:143.

[217] Zhou 1985:289-294.

[218] Feng 1992:145.

Liu as future governor of Xikang Province. Thus he lent full support to Nuola's actions against Liu Wenhui.[219]

As news spread that the Red Army was marching toward Ganze in 1936, Nuola was ordered to thwart their movements, but he was beaten twice in the areas of Daofu (Tib. Rta'u) and Luhuo (Tib. Brag 'go), and forced to flee. On his way to Baan through Nyarong, Nuola was captured by Badenduojie (Tib. Dpal ldan rdo rje), and was turned over to a party of Red soldiers on their way to Ganze.[220] In jail, Nuola is said to have repeatedly refuted Red Army leaders' propaganda, attacking the Red Army's policies and practices, and expressing his firm allegiance to Jiang Jieshi's Nationalist government in Nanjing.[221] Seriously ill, Nuola died in Ganze in 1936, and his legendary career ended at the age of 73. So too did his autonomy movement in Kham.[222]

In contrast to the Baan Incident led by Gesangzeren in 1932, which lasted only half a year and was confined to Baan, the Nuola Incident had a wider range in time, space and resources, suggested by Feng Youzhi, author of *Xikang Shi Shi Yi* (*Supplementary Collections of Xikang History*). The Incident "began when Nuola was dispatched to Kham in April 1935, and ended upon Nuola's death in May 1936, lasting over a year, and covered both northern and south-

---

[219] Feng 1992:135-141.

[220] To explore in detail the reasons for Dpal ldan rdo rje's capture of Nuola would take us too far afield here. Suffice it to say that there was yet another set of rival factions vying for control of the Nyarong region. One of these, the Rgya re family, had allied themselves with Nuola's political movement in Kham, and were Dpal ldan rdo rje's enemies. Cf. Epstein and Peng 1998 and note 54, *infra*.

[221] Zhou 1985:294.

[222] But one month after Nuola's death in Ganze, the Red Army had its own version of Tibetan autonomy put into practice there. In June 1936, the Red Army led by Zhang Guotao and Zhu De, set up the "China Soviet Ganze Boba Government." During about one year's stay in Kham, the Fourth Front Army instituted various autonomous Tibetan governments, but "most were simply empty in all but name," (Zhang Guotao, quoted in Sperling 1976:15). However, the one in Ganze seemed to have won some sympathizers. Geda, an incarnate lama in Ganze who was once Vice Chair of the Soviet Boba Government, provided help to the Red Army during the Long March and gave full support to the PLA's march into Tibet in 1950.
Interestingly, Gesangzeren appears also to have been fascinated by the novelty of a self-determined Boba government in Kham. Bya rgod Stobs ldan, a participant in the Soviet government in Ganze, told him the whole story. When Gesangzeren proposed the change of "Zangzu" back to the Tibetan self-appellation "Bod," he cited the Red Army's creation of the "Boba government" as a specific case, suggesting perhaps its appropriateness in name if not its substance (Gesangzeren 1974:13-14).

ern Kham," taking place "when the political situation in Xikang was to the advantage of Nuola."[223] The Baan Incident happened in the hey-day of Liu Wenhui's power—Liu was said to have commanded a for-midable army of about one hundred regiments by then. But by the time the Nuola Incident took place, Liu's forces had already been se-verely crippled by the coalition forces of Liu Xiang, Deng Xihou, and Tian Songyao in 1933.

During the Nuola Incident, in addition to General Li Baobing's support, Nuola had an army of more than five hundred soldiers as his escort team, led by Jiang Anxi, Pangda Tobgye, and Qin Weiqi, re-vealing divergent sources of support for his mission in Kham.[224] In contrast, during the Baan Incident Gesangzeren had no immediate resources to turn to other than a minimal amount of arms and ammu-nition supplied by Long Yun on his way to Baan. Long himself had no desire to meddle directly in Xikang affairs, as he did not foresee the prospect of Gesangzeren's overwhelming success in Xikang.[225]

Additionally, although he was adept in Nanjing politics, Gesang-zeren was not an active and influential figure in the political arena of Xikang, and was thus less successful in soliciting local support dur-ing the Baan Incident. This was not the case in the Nuola Incident. As an incarnate lama, a charismatic religious and political figure in Kham, Nuola was capable of mobilizing a sizable local force, and in-deed he had already done so in 1917 in his fight with Central Tibetan forces. Now he was joined by such powerful figures as Bya rgod Stobs ldan from Derge, and Rdo rje rnam rgyal from Upper Nyarong in his military operations.[226]

---

[223] Feng 1992:141

[224] Jiang Anxi (Blo bzang don grub), a political instructor in the special detach-ment under Jiang Jieshi's Chongqing Office of the Central Military Commission, was sent to accompany Nuola to Kham with eighty solders. Qin Weiqi, an ex-brigadier in Liu Xiang's troops, was assigned by Liu to lead two companies as Nuola's escort troops. Pangda Tobgye with two hundred of his own troops was ap-pointed leader in charge of military affairs during Nuola's pacifying mission. During the Nuola Incident, he was key to the capturing of Baan and disarming the Chinese garrison there (Feng 1992:144-146, 153-156).

[225] Feng 1992.

[226] Bya rgod took part in Nuola's campaigns against the Red Army but was cap-tured in Ganze. He was later appointed Minister of Military Affairs in the China Soviet Ganze Boba Government. Rdo rje rnam rgyal and his daugher, 'Chi med sgrol ma, led Rgya re troops to fight Liu Wenhui's troops and the Red Army. Encouraged by Nuola, Chimedrolma disarmed Liu's garrison in Nyarong and also executed the Chinese magistrate assigned to the county (Feng 1992: 151).

The Ganze Incident (1939)

In spite of their sometime striking spontaneity, the three incidents in the 1930s, did not really belong to a type of "accidental, or isolated events," but were "political ones orchestrated by goals, calculations, and organization."[227] They were basically campaigns against Liu Wenhui, *couched in* the appeal of "Kham for the Khampas,"[228] *supported by* (albeit tacitly at times) the "Center" striving to curtail provincialism and Tibetan nationalist expansion in Kham,[229] and *operating upon* ties of native place, as well as ethnicity. Various figures, who had been active in Kham politics of the 1930s and had played important roles in the three incidents, were native Baanese, such as Gesangzeren (the Baan Incident), Jiang Anxi (the Nuola Incident),[230] and Liu Jiaju (the Ganze Incident).[231]

Liu Jiaju (Tib. Skal bzang chos 'byor) attended the Baan Primary School, and the "West China School." In 1917, Liu was wounded in a battle against troops from Tibet when serving as a secretary in the Sichuan Border Army. Liu went to join Gesangzeren in Nanjing in 1929. His talent soon became recognized, leading to his promotion from an employee in the Mongolian-Tibetan Affairs Commission to its Commissioner, and, upon Dai Jitao's recommendation, he became

---

[227] Feng 1992:140, and 114, where the original Chinese is *you mudi, you yumou, you zuzhi de zhengzhi shijian.*

[228] Feng 1992:140.

[229] The centrality of Kham is captured by Zhao Erfeng's notorious "axiom," "*zhi Zang bi xian an Kang*" (Kham must be pacified before Tibet can be ruled). This surely fit Central Nationalist practices in Kham, but also continued into Maoist times, except in a guise called "Democratic Reforms" which, however, ended in uprisings that soon spread to Central Tibet. But the rationale appears to have been the same: Kham must be transformed and consolidated before social, economic, and political reforms could be carried out in Central Tibet.

[230] Jiang Anxi, Nuola's Tibetan secretary and commander of body guards, played a decisive role in disarming Liu Wenhui's troops in northern Kham, and in participating in the attack on Baan. He is said to have led twenty guards to take one of Liu's battalion by surprise, and disarmed more than 200 solders in a night (Feng 1992:147-148).

[231] The three incidents were "regarded by some as products of these 'three elite members of Baan' ('*Baan sanjie*')" (Feng 1992:140). Together the three founded the "Baan Youth (or Friends) Association" in 1929 (Li 1991:73). When Gesangzeren was staying in Nanjing, he also sponsored a Xikang Training Class at the Central Political Institute, recruiting students from Xikang, whom he later took back for his party provincial project (Jiang and Lai 1982:104). Additionally, he founded the "Xikang Youth Spirit Promotion Association" in Nanjing with the active participation of Liu Jiaju when he joined Gesangzeren in 1929 (Li 1991:74).

Secretary-General of the Panchen Lama's Office in 1932. In 1934, Liu was also appointed a Member of the Xikang Provincial Preparatory Committee officially established later in Yaan in 1935.

In 1939, the Ganze Incident, or the "Panchen Office Incident in Ganze" as it is sometimes called, turned Liu Jiaju and the Panchen Office into the political spotlight in Xikang. After the Sixth (Ninth) Panchen Lama's death in late 1937,[232] the Central Government allowed the Panchen Lama's Office to be retained, and later, to move from Qinghai to Ganze in northern Kham in 1938.[233] In August 1938, Dai Jitao led a delegation to Ganze to mourn the late Panchen Lama. Liu Jiaju proposed the establishment of a special administrative region consisting of eight northern Kham counties as a base for the Panchen Office. Meanwhile, he and other senior members of the Office encouraged Yixiduoji (Tib. Ye shes rdo rje), an officer of the Panchen Lama's entourage, to marry Deqinwangmu (Tib. Bde chen dbang mo), chieftain of Ganze Khangsar, one of the most powerful families in northern Kham.

Liu Wenhui, of course, was deeply aware of the political implications of this marital relationship, and of the Panchen Office's ambitions to take over northern Kham, which would pose a serious threat to his provincial agendas. Previously, he had made an arrangement to ally himself with the Khangsar family to stabilize his control over politics in northern Kham. He first adopted Deqinwangmu as his "nominal daughter" (Chi. *gan nuer*), and then took upon himself a "father's role," arranging for her to marry one of his Han officers in

---

[232] The Panchen Lama died in Yushu, Qinghai (Skye rgu mdo) on 1 Dec. 1937, on his return trip to Tibet, which was, however, repeatedly delayed by the disagreement between Lhasa and Nanjing as to the Chinese escort's entry into Tibet. The Panchen Lama's death was certainly a heavy blow to the Central Nationalist Government, keen on having him back to stem the Dalai Lama's power (Lai and Deng 1982:123-125).

[233] In making the decision to move from Muslim-centered Qinghai to Kham, an area where inhabitants were predominately Tibetan Buddhists, the Panchen Office also took into consideration Liu Jiaju's native ties to Kham, and his official position as Member of the Xikang Provincial Preparatory Committee. In addition, Liu Wenhui also welcomed the move, based upon a calculation that the arrival of the Panchen Lama's remains could turn Kangding into a pilgrimage center, thus potentially benefiting his rule. Afterwards, the Panchen Office decided to stay away from Kangding, and stationed itself in Ganze to avoid being controlled by Liu (Feng 1992:331).

Ganze.[234] But, to his disappointment and anger, neither Deqin-wangmu nor his own officer accepted the "arranged marriage," each citing the obstacle of "ethnic and religious differences."[235]

When a report reached Liu that Deqinwangmu was planning to wed Yixiduoji, the Panchen's officer, Liu decided to interfere. He ordered Zhang Zhenzhong, Ganze garrison commander, and Zhang Jialin, magistrate of Ganze, to imprison her and block her marriage. Deqinwangmu was told that she would be set free after she repented of her "disobedience" (unfilial action?) and terminated her marriage with Yixiduoji. The Khangsar family petitioned Liu to have her re-leased, but failed.

Outraged, the Khangsar headmen decided to attack. The Panchen Office and the Khangsar family convened a joint meeting, chaired by Liu Jiaju, to discuss the military action. At the meeting, the slogan "Kham for the Khampas" was proposed in opposition to rule by the warlord, Liu Wenhui. Liu Jiaju was appointed commander to lead the assault. Their military operation began on 25 October 1939, and lasted 4 days. The joint forces of the Panchen Office and Khangsar captured Ganze, released Deqinwangmu, took the Ganze garrison commander and magistrate prisoner, appointed magistrates to various Northern Kham counties, and proclaimed Khampa self-rule.[236]

In December 1939, Liu Wenhui's army launched a counterattack and recaptured Ganze. The Panchen Office and the Khangsar family fled to Qinghai in early 1940. Ironically, in this victory, Liu Wenhui failed in his original calculation that he could have the Panchen Of-fice invited to Kham to "borrow" some of the late Panchen's relig-ious influence to shore up his own rule in Xikang.[237] This miscalcula-tion cost him dearly, resulting, for a while, in the presence of two "centers" competing for power over local politics in Kham.

---

[234] Obviously regional politics, or the politics of Center, is dependent upon local politics, and vice versa. During Dai Jitao's visit to Ganze, he too accepted Bde chen dbang mo as his "nominal daughter," so that intimate ties between the Central Gov-ernment and local politics could be established to ultimately remove Liu Wenhui's provincial warlordism. It was said that Dai secretly told Dechen that if Ganze wanted to be self-ruled, she could contact him directly to obtain the Central Gov-ernment's intervention (Luo *et al.* 1996:19).

[235] Feng 1992:337.

[236] Feng 1992:339-350; Lai and Deng 1982:128-132.

[237] Feng 1992:331.

Visions of Authority: Provincial Legitimacy Betwixt and Between National Unification and Local Autonomy

Having been frustrated by a chain of political incidents against him in Xikang, Liu Wenhui, once "confided" to Hu Gongxian, chair of Xikang Canyihui (Xikang Provincial Assembly): "I'm really tired of Xikang administrative affairs, and want to train some native Xikangese to take over so that I can develop elsewhere." As one analyst commented, "what he said might not have been straight from the heart, but it sure reflected his dilemma in Xikang at that time."[238]

Liu had repeatedly claimed that he was indispensable both to the creation and administration of Xikang Province. But he was now confronted with the dilemma that his birth place was in Dayi, a county in Sichuan outside the jurisdiction of Xikang Province, which made it impossible for him to claim a "native" identity in Xikang. Liu's lack of "ancestral ties" to the newly invented province often led some "Xikangese" to challenge his legitimacy as their governor. Also joining in the attack were some Han Chinese in Yaan who had vehemently opposed the annexation of their home region into Xikang when the province was being conceived, but who now realized their membership in Xikang gave them a "natural" advantage in the provincial power struggle.[239] While the Khampa self-rule movements in Xikang targeted Liu's brutal chauvinistic rule in their homeland as a Han Chinese colonizer, local Han Chinese appeals for autonomy in Xikang were intended to topple Liu's rule in their "native" province as a Sichuanese outsider.

Related to the above, and more vexing to Liu Wenhui, was the Central Government's de facto denial, or at least lack of support, of his legitimacy in Xikang, patterns of which were discernable in the string of incidents directed against him in the 1930s. Liu characterized all these incidents as being launched by

1. organs authorized by the Central Government,
2. using the name of the Central Government to instigate the Khampa people,

---

[238] Feng 1992:325.
[239] Huang and Feng 1996:10-14.

3. proclaiming to fight against local government and garrisons only while pledging loyalty to the Center. Hence, neither the Center nor the populace treated the incidents as rebellions.[240]

What Liu complained about most was the syndrome of "provincial dislocation" he had experienced in handling these incidents. Most often he found that his provincial authority was circumvented by the circuit of power between the Center and Khampa local politics, and, at the same time, he was the target of both, be it in public or in private. Thus, during the Ganze Incident, he said he had to defend his officially sanctioned position by clearing up clouds of "rumor" in Kham, which said that the Panchen Office's self-rule movement had been authorized by the Central Government in Nanjing. Meanwhile, Deqinwangmu of the Khangsar family also needed to be "reminded" of who her immediate authority in Xikang was by being reprimanded with "disciplinary" measures taken by Liu's soldiers in Ganze.[241]

The Central Government in Nanjing surely had a vested interest in the explosive forces unleashed by various Khampa incidents, if not a genuine desire for Khampa autonomy. The scenario of a bit of "supervised" chaos in various Kham regions did not concern the Center so much as it did Liu Wenhui. Ethnic revolt in Kham could erode Liu's provincial power, something Liu desperately wanted to avoid, but that the Center certainly desired. To the Central government, Liu as a warlord commanding an army and a province posed a much greater threat to the overall stability of the nation than the Khampa incidents could have done. After all, Liu's continuing rule in Xikang haunted Jiang Jieshi's unification imaginary, reminding him of his unfinished campaigns against those "lesser" warlords on Chinese frontiers since the Northern Expeditions.

An analysis of the Khampa autonomy movement in the Republican era enhances our understanding of what Barlow calls the "localization of the sign." This signifies a process whereby the appropriation of pieces of knowledge ("signs") out of a "stronger" language into a "weaker" language works within "specific, autonomous, local political contexts," and where the same sign might take on "a different discursive force, powers unknown to its previous context."[242]

---

[240] Liu, quoted in He 1988:30.
[241] Sichuan Sheng Danganguan 1990:461-469.
[242] Barlow 1991:211, 212.

The historical milieu in which the Khampa self-rule movements were embedded had been very dynamic, characterized by a burgeoning trend of indigenous movements in southwest China in the 1930s and 40s. Siu-woo Cheung has done seminal research in this regard, writing on nativist development in Guizhou in Republican China. In contrast to the Khampa movements that evolved militantly toward the goal of autonomy, various Miao intellectuals battled for Miao official representation through discourses of ethnography and historiographical revisions of Miao categories to empower their legal petitions.[243] What is perhaps more significant is that indigenous movements in southwest China rose to prominence in the 1930s, at a time when *defang zizhi yundong* (local self-rule movement), a political and intellectual current which characterized much of Chinese politics in the 1920s, had already receded in Han Chinese provinces.[244]

Like various Miao elite in Cheung's case, leaders of the Khampa incidents, from Gesangzeren, to Nuola, and to Liu Jiaju, had considerable exposure to the global and national political currents of their times, either through schooling in missionary or Chinese educational institutions, or, more, by participating in Chinese frontier politics. Yet, their appropriations of local self-rule in ideology and practice differed remarkably from the Han Chinese model in the 1920s. While the Chinese provincial movement played on regional variations as part of its political ideology, the provincial project pushed forward by the Khampa incidents had been injected with an ethnic dimension, made public by the slogan of "Kham for the Khampas" vis-à-vis Han Chinese overlords in Kham. This process of "provincial ethnicization" was to be operated upon a reworking of the Khampa identity by re-equipping their "ancient sense of centrality"[245] on the Sino-Tibetan

---

[243] Cheung 1996:70-113

[244] Fitzgerald 1994:39-42. The ideology of local self-rule championed by the Federalists began to wane in the Chinese political arena the late 1920s. Federalism, in the Centralist assault, was equated with warlord separatism, then feudalism, one of the greatest enemies of the nation and the revolution, in conjunction with imperialism. Centralist ideas gradually prevailed after the battle against Chen Jionming's "rebellion" against Sun Yat-sen in 1922, followed by the Northern Expedition, and a series of campaigns against provincial militarists in the late 1920s.

[245] Aris, in Rock 1922:13. In talking about frontier as a historical process, Aris reminds us of the existence of "strong forms of local rule" on frontiers, *e.g.*, those of "local princes, clan chieftains, monastic prelates" within their own worlds since ancient times. Much attention, Aris argues, needs to be given to the "local perspective of those actually living on the periphery," which runs counter to our stereotypical perceptions.

frontier with the novel and "derivative" concepts of "self-determination" and "self-rule," which resonated globally during the first half of
the twentieth century.[246] Participating in the Chinese national and
frontier politics was a tactic to achieve the possibility of Khampa
autonomy, or to reclaim a Khampa "subjectivity," however partial
and paradoxical it might have been as leaders of the Khampa incidents sometimes recognized.[247]

To reach the goal of a Khampa ethnic-provincial agenda, a form
of "strategic partnership" was forged between the local and the Center to wipe out provincial warlordism in Kham. Viewing themselves
as spokespersons for both sides, leaders of the Khampa incidents also
saw their provincial project as embodying the interests of both the
Central government and the local Khampa Tibetans. In their minds,

---

There, rather than "a sense of marginality or alienation, so often one meets instead with
a confident and ancient sense of centrality." Such has certainly been the case of
Khampa Tibetans, whose "independent nature," Sperling suggests, led them to fight
against "both Peking and Lhasa" in the twentieth century, though their differences with
Lhasa "are nowhere near as basic as those with China" (1976: 10).

[246] Chatterjee 1986. Chatterjee's use of "derivative discourse" to characterize the
relationship of postcolonial nationalist projects to European nationalism is conducive
to our thinking of the Khampa autonomy movements in the 1930s. The term "derivative" suggests a point of origin rather than a process of wholesale importation of
nationalist ideology from the "West." This importing process, Chatterjee asserts,
"could lead to a change in the sorts of theoretical ideas which nationalist thought had
borrowed from Western rationalism, giving up older theories and adopting, even
devising, new ones" (p.42). In analyzing the Khampa self-rule movements in Republican China, we should neither reduce them to some mechanical reproduction of
global political currents, nor to the "outbursts" of their age-long "independent nature." Rather, these movements are part of a communicating process between Khampas' historical identity and ideas flowing from various "metropoleis" around the
globe. Seen this way, the notion of frontier could be regarded not only as a zone
characterized by movements of people (indigenes, immigrants, merchants, soldiers,
pilgrims, etc.), but as a zone dynamic in the contact of ideas jostling for meanings of
place, history, and identity.

[247] Gesangzeren 1974. Autonomy, however poorly defined in these various incidents, and however ambiguous even to leaders of the Khampa autonomy movements, was believed to be the "middle of the road" in solving frontier problems.
Among various leaders, Gesangzeren wrote the most on the political issue. In es-
pousing autonomy for Kham, Gesangzeren tried to grapple with the tension between
"independence" and "autonomy." "Frankly," he explained, "I am opposed to both
the independence of frontier nationalities and Han chauvinism" (p.2). Autonomy, in
his various propositions to the Central Nationalist Government, seemed to be mostly
concerned with the establishment of autonomous regions and shifts of administrative
power to indigenes. Autonomy of Tibetans or Mongols in their respective regions
occupied most of his concerns. Other agendas (economic, cultural and social) did not
quite follow in his blueprints.

as the goal of their provincial movement overlapped to a large extent with that of the Center, the boundaries between the two were not necessarily distinct. This would not be the case in the local self-rule movement in Han Chinese regions. There the Center became a focal point of contestation for power, a target for both ideological and military attacks from the provinces.

Conclusion

Agency and locality have been the two major concerns underlying this *historicized* anthropological approach to the building of Xikang. Agency involves strategizing, defined by Certeau as the "calculation (or manipulation) of power relationships,"[248] which locates different players in a process of negotiation, contestation, or accommodation with each other. The historical milieu that situated the making of Xikang was extremely fluid and complex, involving different parties motivated by different political agendas at different times. In this paper, I have analyzed some in greater detail while merely touching upon others. These agendas may all be summed up as:

1. The Chinese imperial expansionist project under the perceived threat of the British colonial power;

2. The nation-building projects of both Chinese and Tibetans;

3. Liu Wenhui's strategy of provincial warlordism;

4. Native Khampa ambitions for autonomy, manipulating, and being manipulated by, the Central Nationalist government[249];

5. The Red Army's version of Tibetan autonomous movements for the imaginary of the "Soviet Federalist State," a project whose legacy remains controversial and awaits further probing in a separate paper.[250]

---

[248] Certeau 1984:35.

[249] This does not, however, suggest that all the political incidents taking place in Kham in the 1930s were somehow moving in one direction, more or less in favor of the Central Nationalist Government. The "Dargyas-Beri Incident" between 1930 and 1932 displayed a more complex scenario of frontier politics. The two contending local forces built alliances with either Central Tibet or the Han Chinese garrison, with monks of the Dargyas Monastery standing firmly on the side of Central Tibet. The Center's mediating role was not quite heeded by Liu Wenhui's troops and the Central Tibetan Army during the Incident.

[250] Projects of Tibetan autonomous governments, like the "Ganze Boba Republic" created by the Red Army during the Long March, were short lived, and looked mostly empty even to their designers and practitioners (Sperling 1976:15).

An inquiry into the process in which Xikang was discursively constructed and contested in the Republican era certainly leads to our
rethinking about politics of the "local," a topic that has increasingly
come under critical scrutiny in anthropological field. As this paper
intends to show, the local is neither autonomous nor timeless, but is
shaped by a concatenation of historical forces, exemplified by the
interplay of global, national and regional factors in the Xikang-mak-
ing process of Xikang. Local politics in Kham had essentially been
built into the historical forces negotiating the transformation of the
frontier space of Kham to the provincial place of Xikang. A closer
look at Khampa autonomous movements in the 1930s further reveals
the dynamics of the local, the complexity of which can be neither reduced to a complete passive form, nor romanticized as a site of pure
resistance. Rather, the local constitutes a site both of empowerment
and predicament,[251] and this dialectic will facilitate a better understanding of the essential fluidity and ambiguity of identity politics on
the Sino-Tibetan frontier.

Yet, to historians of the Chinese Communist revolution, they were important and
practical steps in instituting the spirit of a Party Politburo meeting held in Shawo,
Songpan in August 1935. During this meeting "nationalities issues, for the first time,
were realized to an extent that they could determine success or failure of the Chinese
revolutionary cause" (Zhonggong Sichuan 1986:349). It was considered important to
win over minority nationalities by acknowledging their rights of self-determination
and by helping them build their own governments.

    Of course, as Dreyer (1976: 67-69) argues, lessons could also be learnt from the
Red Army's encounters with minorities, and from experiments of minority policies,
including the building of minorities' autonomous governments, which, subsequently,
led to a rethinking of minorities' rights of self-determination and rights of secession
from China. Substituting these early versions of ethnic policies has been the limited
autonomy in minority regions in post-Liberation China.

[251] Cf. Dirlik 1996.

BIBLIOGRAPHY

Barlow, Tani. "*Zhishifenzi* (Chinese Intellectuals) and Power." *Dialectical Anthropology* 16:209-232, 1991.

Brown, Melissa J., ed. *Negotiating Ethnicities in China and Taiwan.* Berkeley: University of California Center for East Asian Studies, 1996.

Certeau, Michel de. *The Practice of Everyday Life.* Translated by Stevan Rendall. Berkeley, Los Angeles, and London: University of California Press, 1984.

Chatterjee, Partha. *Nationalist Thought and the Colonial World: A Derivative Discourse.* Minneapolis: University of Minnesota Press, 1986.

Chen, Leslie H. Dingyan. *Chen Jiongming and the Federalist Movement: Regional Leadership and Nation Building in Early Republican China.* Ann Arbor: University of Michigan Center for Chinese Studies, 1999.

Cheung, Siu-woo. *Subject and Representation: Identity Politics in Southeast Guizhou.* Ph.D. Dissertation. Seattle: University of Washington, 1996.

Dirlik, Arif. "The Global in the Local." In Rob Wilson and Wimal Dissanayake, eds. *Global Local: Cultural Production and the Transnational Imaginary.* Durham and London: Duke University Press, 1996, pp.21-45.

Dong Enqiang: "Xikang Jiansheng Shi Mo Ji (A Record on the Establishment of Xikang Province)." *Minguo Chunqiu* (*Spring and Autumn of the Republican Era*), 2:21-23, 1996.

Dreyer, June. *China's Forty Millions.* Cambridge, Massachusetts and London, England: Harvard University Press, 1976.

Duara, Prasenjit. "De-Constructing the Chinese Nation." *The Australian Journal of Chinese Affairs* 30:1-26, 1993.

———"Provincial Narratives of the Nation: Federalism and Centralism in Modern China." In *Rescuing History from the Nation: Questioning Narratives of Modern China.* Chicago: University of Chicago Press. 1995, pp.177-204.

Epstein, Lawrence and Peng Wenbin. "The Making of Xikang." Paper presented at the Annual AAS Meeting, Washington, D.C., 1998.

Falkenhausen, Lothar von. "The Regionalist Paradigm in Chinese Archaeology." In Philip L. Kohl and Clare Fawcett, eds. *Nationalism, Politics, and the Practice of Archaeology.* Cambridge: Cambridge University Press, 1995, pp.198-219.

Feng Youzhi. *Xikang Shi Shi Yi* (*Supplementary Collections of Xikang History*). Kangding: Zhongguo Renmin Zhengzhi Xieshang Huiyi Ganze Zangzu Zizhi Zhou Weiyuan Hui Wenshi Ziliao Weiyuan Hui Bianyin (Printed by the Cultural-Historical Data Committee, the Chinese People's Political Consultative Conference of Ganze Tibetan Autonomous Prefecture), 1992.

Fitzgerald, John. "'Reports of My death have been greatly exaggerated': The history of the death of China." In David S.G. Goodman and Gerald Segal, eds. *China Deconstructs; Politics, Trade and Regionalism.* London and New York: Routledge, 1994.

———*Awakening China: Politics, Culture, and Class in the Nationalist Revolution.* Stanford, California: Stanford University Press, 1996.

Friedman, Edward. "Reconstructing China's National Identity: A Southern Alternative to Mao-Era Anti-Imperialist Nationalism." *The Journal of Asian Studies* 53.1:67-91, 1994.

Gaubatz, Piper R. *Beyond the Great Wall: Urban Form and Transformation on the Chinese Frontiers.* Stanford, California: Stanford University Press, 1996.

Gesangzeren. *Bian Ren Chu Yan* (*Humble Speeches of A Frontier Person*). In Shen Yunlong, ed. *Jindai Zhonguo Shiliao Congkan Xubian* (*Supplements to the Series of Historical Data of Modern China*), no.11 (reprint). Taibei: Wenhai Chubanshe (The Culture Sea Publishing House), 1974.

Goodman, David. "The Politics of Regionalism: Economic Development, Conflict and Negotiation." In David Goodman and Gerald Segal, eds. *China Deconstructs: Politics, Trade and Regionalism*. London and New York: Routledge, 1994, pp.1-20.

——ed. *China's Provinces in Reform: Class, Community and Political Culture*. London and New York: Routledge, 1997.

Harrell, Stevan. "Civilizing Projects and the Reaction to Them." In Stevan Harrell, ed. *Cultural Encounters on China's Ethnic Frontiers*. Seattle: University of Washington Press, 1995, pp.3-36.

He Juefei. *Xikang Jishishi Ben Shi Zhu* (*A Chronicle of Important Events in Xikang Presented in Poems*). Xizang Xue Hanwen Wenxian Congshu Di Er Ji (Series of Han Chinese Literature in Tibetan Studies, Vol. 2). Lhasa: Xizang Renmin Chubanshe (Tibetan People's Publishing House), 1988.

Hu Jilu. *Xikang Jiangyu Su Gu Lu* (*A Historical Study of Xikang Territories*). Taibei: Taiwan Shangwu Yinshuguan (Taiwan Commercial Press), 1971.

Huang Qiguang and Feng Youzhi. "Xikang Sheng Canyihui Shi Mo Ji (A Note on the Beginning and End of Xikang Provincial Assembly)." In *Sichuan Wenshi Ziliao Jicui: Minzu Zongjiao Huaqiao Pian* (*Selected Publications of Sichuan Cultural and Historical Data: Chapter on Minorities, Religions and Overseas Chinese*) 5:3-18. Chengdu: Sichuan Renmin Chubanshe (Sichuan People's Publishing House), 1996.

Jiang Anxi and Lai Zuozhong. "Yi Jiu San Er Nian Baan Shibian Jiankuang (A Brief Introduction to the Baan Incident in 1932)." *Sichuan Sheng Ganze Zangzu Zizhi Zhou Wenshi Ziliao Xuanji Ti Yi Ji* (*Selections of Cultural-Historical Data, Ganze Tibetan Autonomous Prefecture, Sichuan Province*), Vol. 1:104-107, 1982.

Jiang Anxi, Lai Zuozhong, and Deng Junkang. "Nuola Shibian Gaishu (A Brief Introduction to the Nuola Incident)." *Sichuan Sheng Ganze Zangzu Zizhi Zhou Wenshi Ziliao Xuanji Ti Yi Ji* (*Selections of Cultural-Historical Data, Ganze Tibetan Autonomous Prefecture, Sichuan Province*), Vol. 1:108-122, 1982.

Kapp, Robert. *Szechwan and the Chinese Republic: Provincial Militarism and Central Power, 1911-1938*. New Haven and London: Yale University Press, 1973.

Lai Zuozhong and Deng Junkang. "Ganze Shibian de Qianqian Houhou ("The Process of the Ganze Incident)." *Sichuan Sheng Ganze Zangzu Zizhi Zhou Wenshi Ziliao Xuanji Ti Yi Ji* (*Selections of Cultural-Historical Data, Ganze Tibetan Autonomous Prefecture, Sichuan Province*), Vol. 1:123-134, 1982.

Li Mingzhong. "Liu Jiaju Zhuan (Biography of Liu Jiaju)," *Sichuan Sheng Ganze Zangzu Zizhi Zhou Wenshi Ziliao Xuanji Ti Shi Yi Ji* (*Selections of Cultural-Historical Data, Ganze Tibetan Autonomous Prefecture, Sichuan Province*), Vol. 11:73-79, 1991.

Lipman, Jonathan. "Hyphenated Chinese: Sino-Muslim Identity in Modern China." In Gail Hershatter, Emily Honig, Jonathan Lipman, and Randall Stross, eds. *Remapping China: Fissures in Historical Terrain*. Stanford, California: Stanford University Press, 1996, pp.97-112.

——*Familiar Strangers: A History of Muslims in Northwest China*. Seattle and London: University of Washington Press, 1997.

Litzinger, Ralph. *Other Chinas: The Yao and the Politics of National Belonging.* Durham and London: Duke University Press, 2000.

Liu Wenhui. *Zou dao Renmin Zhenying di Lishi Daolu (A Historical Path by Which I Joined the People's Camp).* Beijing: Shenghuo, Dushu, Xinzhi Sanlian Shudian (The United Press of Life, Reading, and New Knowledge), 1979.

Luo Jiangze, Luo Nima, and Luo Xini. "Huiyi Ganze Shibian Jingguo (The Ganze Incident in Retrospect)." In *Sichuan Wenshi Ziliao Jicui: Minzu Zongjiao Huaqiao Pian (Selected Publications of Sichuan Cultural and Historical Data: Chapter on Minority Religions and Overseas Chinese)*, 5:19-36. Chengdu: Sichuan Renmin Chubanshe (Sichuan People's Publishing House), 1996.

Mehra, Parshotam. *The Northeastern Frontier: A Documentary Study of the Internecine Rivalry between India, Tibet and China*, Vol. 1. Delhi: Oxford University Press, 1979.

Millward, James. "New Perspectives on the Qing Frontier." In Gail Hershatter, Emily Honig, Jonathan Lipman, and Randall Stross, eds. *Remapping China: Fissures in Historical Terrain.* Stanford, California: Stanford University Press. 1996, pp.113-129.

Peng Wenbin. "Remapping Southwest China: Politics of Nation-Building and the Discourses of Regional Culture Construction, 1930-1940." Presented at the Annual Meeting of Asian Studies on the Pacific Coast, Whitman College, 1998.

Pu Xiaorong. *Sichuan Zhengqu Yange yu Zhidi Jinshi (Historical and Contemporary Analyses of Regions Administered by Sichuan).* Chengdu: Sichuan Renmin Chubanshe (Sichuan People's Publishing House), 1998.

Qing Feng. "Xikang Gesangzeren Shijian Jingguo (The Process of the Gesangzeren Incident in Xikang." *Sichuan Wenxian (Sichuan Historical Literature)*, 157:44-48. Taipei, 1975.

Ren Naiqiang. *Xikang Tujing: Jingyupian (Xikang Geography-Territory).* Nanjing: Xin Yaxiya Xuehui (New Asia Association), 1933.

Rock, Joseph F.C. *Lamas, Princes and Brigands: Rock's Photographs of the Tibetan Borderlands of China.* Michael Aris *et al.*, eds. New York: China House Gallery China Institute of America, 1992.

Schein, Louisa. *Minority Rules: The Miao and the Feminine in China's Cultural Politics.* Durham and London: Duke University Press, 2000.

Sichuan Sheng Danganguan (Sichuan Provincial Archive Bureau) and Sichuan Minzu Yanjiusuo (Sichuan Nationalities Research Institute), eds. *Jindai Kangqu Dangan Ziliao Xuanbian (Selected Publications of Archival Data of Modern Kang Region).* Chengdu: Sichuan Daxue Chubanshe (Sichuan University Press), 1990.

Smith, Warren W. *Tibetan Nation: A History of Tibetan Nationalism and Sino-Tibetan Relations.* Boulder, Colo.: Westview Press, 1996.

Solinger, Dorothy. *Regional Government and Political Integration in Southwest China, 1949-1954: A Case Study.* Berkeley, Los Angeles, London: University of California Press, 1977.

Sperling, Elliot. "The Chinese Venture in K'am, 1904-1911, and the Role of Chao Erh-feng." *The Tibet Journal* 1(2):10-36, 1976a.

——"Red Army's First Encounters with Tibet—Experiences on the Long March." *Tibetan Review* 10:11-18, 1976b.

Wen Xianmei, ed. *Sichuan Tongshi (General History of Sichuan)*, Vol. 7:336-353. Chengdu: Sichuan Daxue Chubanshe (Sichuan University Press), 1994.

Xie Benshu and Feng Zuyi, eds. *Xinan Junfa Shi* (*History of Warlords in Southwest China*), Vol. 3. Guiyang: Guizhou Renmin Chubanshe (Guizhou People's Publishing House), 1994.

Zhonggong Sichuan Shengwei Dangshi Gongzuo Weiyuanhui (Party History Work Committee, Sichuan Provincial Committee of the Chinese Communist Party), ed. *Hongjun Changzheng zai Sichuan* (*Red Army's Long March in Sichuan*). Chengdu: Sichuan Sheng Shehui Kexue Yuan Chubanshe (Sichuan Provincial Academy of Social Sciences Press), 1986.

Zhou Xiyin. "Nuola Hutuketu." In Ren Yimin, ed. *Sichuan Jinxiandai Renwuzhuan* (*Biographies of Contemporary Sichuanese Dignitaries*) 1:289-294. Chengdu: Sichuan Academy of Social Sciences Press, 1985.

——*Zhongguo Shaoshu Minzu de Lishi Zuoyong* (*The Historical Role of China's Minority Nationalities*). Chengdu: Sichuan Nationalities Press, 1989.

THE SIXTH PANCHEN LAMA'S CHINESE TITLES

FABIENNE JAGOU (ÉCOLE FRANÇAISE D'EXTRÊME-ORIENT)

We know a considerable amount about the investiture of titles and seals given to Tibetan masters by the Thirteenth Dalai Lama (1876-1933) and the Chinese Republican Government (1912-1949) as well. The modern historical period was subject to many disruptions and reforms. Tibetan and Chinese leaders had to determine how to proceed from imperial rules to independent and republican ones. The Thirteenth Dalai Lama's decision to modernize Tibet met with resistance from the clergy, while Chinese Republican leaders tried to establish a new regime in their relations with Tibet without accepting its new status.[252]

The Sixth Panchen Lama (1883-1937), confronted with these ambiguous worlds where the systems were in transition and poorly defined, finally decided to go on working as before. First, he rejected the demands of his government, and then left Tibet to resist them.[253] Finally, he was coöpted by Chinese Government leaders who granted him titles.

First, I present a descriptive explanation of the titles themselves, and then focus on the last two titles the Chinese Government gave the Sixth Panchen Lama in order to understand what the aim of the Chinese Republican Government was and what the Sixth Panchen Lama attained.

The Historical Background

In 1912, the Thirteenth Dalai Lama, temporal and spiritual ruler of Tibet, declared his country's independence and Sino-Tibetan relations were severed. He decided to begin reforms and, first of all, to create an army. Toward this end, he ordered funds be raised from

---

[252] Goldstein 1989.

[253] Indian Office Records (IOR) L/P&S/12/4174 (PZ 1769/24), letter written by the Sixth Panchen Lama before leaving Tibet in December, 1923, translated by D. Macdonald, British trade agent in Rgyal rtse and sent to F.M. Bailey, Political Officer in Sikkim in March 1924.

aristocratic and religious estates. The estates of the Sixth Panchen Lama Blo bzang chos kyi nyi ma, one of the highest spiritual authorities of the Dge lugs pa school, were so vast that Bkra shis lhun po Monastery was faced with a huge demand. The Sixth Panchen Lama refused to submit to the new taxes, arguing that the previous Dalai Lamas had made generous endowments to him and had given him the guarantee that no levy would be raised from his estates due to their master-disciple relationship.[254] Eleven years later, negotiations were deadlocked.

On 23 December 1923, the Sixth Panchen Lama secretly left his monastery located near Gzhis ka rtse in the province of Gtsang and headed for Northern Tibet. He wanted to go to the new Republic of Mongolia, but Russian influence there represented a possible danger for him. So he changed his mind, and for several months he roamed about in Gansu.[255]

As soon as this news came to Cao Kun, then President of the Beijing Government in China, he ordered the Chinese warlords of Gansu to locate the Sixth Panchen Lama and invite him to Beijing. One of the warlords, Lu Hongtao, tracked him down in April 1924. From then until early 1925, the Sixth Panchen Lama was placed under the protection of the Chinese warlords, who took turns in providing for his security and material requirements, and he was directed to Beijing.[256] This was the first contact between the Sixth Panchen Lama and the Chinese warlords. From that moment on, the Sixth Panchen Lama became involved in Chinese policy towards Tibet and Inner Mongolia.

In 1928, the Nanjing Central Government in China was founded, and Chinese policy towards Tibet and Inner Mongolia became clearer. In December, the Mongolian and Tibetan Affairs Commission was created. Its aims were to examine the local situations in Tibet and Inner Mongolia, to modify the status of those countries as autonomous regions, and to avert the foundation of an independent Inner Mongolia. The Sixth Panchen Lama had been well received by

---

[254] Original copy of the decree's thirteen articles issued by the Tibetan Cabinet (*dpyad mtshams bka' rtsa 'dra bcu gsum pa'i zhal bshas he pag med pa*), 1923.

[255] Chen 1943:1; Liu 1943:36; Wang 1969:58-66; Don khang 1984:8-10; Srung 1984:117.

[256] Chinese Ministry of Foreign Affairs to military strategist Ma, telegram, 25/3/24; Chinese Ministry of Foreign Affairs to Lu Hongtao, telegram, 24/4/24.

the Inner Mongolian princes from 1925 on, and he was also honored
in Amdo and Kham. The Chinese Government therefore felt that he
might well serve its interests in realizing its own aims. Although he
had been granted his first Chinese title in 1913, this is the principal
reason the Chinese Nationalist Government granted the Sixth Panchen Lama more titles between 1923, when he left Tibet to go to
China, and 1937, when he passed away.

Description of the Titles

These titles appear in many primary Chinese sources, such as archive
documents issued by the Chinese Government and official letters
signed by the Sixth Panchen Lama when he was in China.[257] They are
also mentioned in two Chinese hagiographies written by the Panchen
Lama's disciples.[258] However, the meaning and usage of the Tibetan
version of these titles is less obvious. For example, in the Thirteenth
Dalai Lama's biography these titles are never used to refer to the
Sixth Panchen Lama. However, it must be specified here that the
Thirteenth Dalai Lama's biographer makes no mention of the Sixth
Panchen Lama at all in his writings after he left Tibet in 1923.[259] Pha
bong kha Rinpoche, who met the Sixth Panchen Lama in 1937, or
rather Blo bzang rdo rje, his biographer, calls him "All-seeing Omniscient Panchen" (*kun gzigs pan chen thams cad mkhyen pa*). His
Chinese titles were not mentioned at all.[260] Actually, the article by
Srung Kri hru'u, which gives the Tibetan version of the Sixth Panchen Lama's Chinese titles, cites the Tibetan sources used in this article. The other source is a contemporary work by Ya Hanzhang.[261] In
fact, the Tibetan sources are quite silent about the Sixth Panchen
Lama's activities in China, so it is not surprising that we find no information about his Chinese titles in Tibetan sources.

The Chinese titles received by the Sixth Panchen Lama are as
follows.

The first title, "Faithful Orator Devoted to the Propagation of Values" (*zhizhong chanhua*; the Tibetan version of the title was *gzhung*

---

[257] I have seen these documents in the Nanjing Number Two Archive in 1993.

[258] Chen 1943; Liu 1943.

[259] Phur lcog 1981.

[260] Blo bzang rdo rje 1981:608a-609a.

[261] Srung 1984; Ya'a 1992.

bstan spel, "Propagator of the Main Doctrine"), was conferred on him under the troubled circumstances of 1913.[262] He received it in Beijing in 1924 from Cao Kun, then President of the Northern Government.[263] So far, we know nothing further about this title.

The second title, "World Savior who Propagates Orthodoxy" (*xuancheng jishi, blo dkar spel nas 'jig rten phan pa*),[264] was given, with a golden or jade seal, to the Sixth Panchen Lama by Duan Qirui, President of the Chinese Northern Government in 1925.[265] The conferment of this title appears to be a unique political action on the part of the Chinese Northern Government towards the Sixth Panchen Lama.

The third title, "Great and Glorious Master Panchen who Protects the Country and Propagates its Values" (*huguo xuanhua guanghui dashi*), was granted by the Nanjing Government in 1931. The literal translation of the Chinese term *xuanhua* (an abbreviation of *xuanchuan wenhua*) is "transmit government orders" or "educate the people."[266] As we shall see later, the first translation seems more appropriate to describe the role that the Nanjing Government envisioned for the Sixth Panchen Lama. However, the second meaning could also be appropriate.

The question here concerns the term *hua*. Etymologically speaking, the Chinese character *hua* connotes one who can be transformed by education. First, *hua* means "education" with the implicit extension of "civilized" through Confucian (that is to say Han) values as opposed to others. Regarding the assimilation policy of the succeeding Republican Government, when the Chinese nation was unified and its territorial borders defined in 1912, the Han, Muslim Turks, Mongols, Tibetans and Manchus were included in the Chinese nation, as they were during the Qing empire. According to Sun Yatsen's thoughts, which he clarified in 1924, these five nationalities would abide in a climate of "harmonious coexistence" (*wu zu gonghe*) and have equal rights (*yi lü pingdeng*). At that time, he dis-

---

[262] Tang 1997:45.

[263] Chen 1943:1-2; Liu 1943:11, 38; Srung 1984:118.

[264] Srung 1984:119.

[265] Nanjing Archives, letter n°156 from the Mongolian and Tibetan Affairs Commission to the Sixth Panchen Lama, August 1925; Chen 1943:7; Liu 1943:39; Srung 1984:119.

[266] Luo 1994, 3:1404.

tinguished between a race-nation (*minzu*, which derives from natural forces, historical evolution and is founded on race) and a nation-state (*guojia*, which is created as a result of military actions). According to him, the race-nation could be established by people who shared the same blood (*xuetong*), a way of life (*shenghuo*), a language (*yuyan*), a religion (*zongjiao*) and habits (*fengsu*). Additionally, he said that the blood criterion is innate, while the other four criteria are acquired. Thus, he thought it would be easy to change the last four elements, since the first one is innate for the people living within Chinese territory. Consequently, he considered that the Muslim Turks, Mongols, Tibetans and Manchus would adopt Chinese habits without much difficulty.[267] This was his own way of making them equal to the Han people. For Sun Yat-sen, it was a matter of numbers: these four nationalities had to unite with the Han simply because the Han were the largest community, and they had to learn Chinese culture in order to be equal to the Han. This viewpoint was self-evident to Sun Yat-sen, and he was ready to credit the four nationalities with self-determination and free association with China.

When the Sixth Panchen Lama received his title, Chiang Kai-shek was president of the Republic of China. Although Chiang Kai-shek adopted Sun Yat-sen's thoughts as a legacy, his policy was more assimilationist than Sun Yat-sen's. Two years before, during the third congress of the Guomindang in 1929, the concept of state-nationality (*guozu*) was created. The five nationalities became part of the Chinese nation rather than parts of the Chinese territory,[268] and the ideas of self-determination and free association were abandoned. At that time, such terms as *ronghe* "fusion" and *tonghua* "assimilation" appeared more and more in official speeches concerning China's border areas (*bianjiang*).

The bottom line was that Sun Yat-sen and Chiang Kai-shek were convinced of Han superiority over the four other nationalities due to their larger number and their higher level of cultural development. Indeed, if we compare the Chinese title with its Tibetan translation carved on the Sixth Panchen Lama's seal,[269] it is clear that the

---

[267] Sun Yat-sen. *Minzu zhuyi, di yi jiang, di san jiang.*

[268] Qin 1978:96.

[269] *Rgyal skyob bstan spel kun mkhyen slob dpon chen po,* "Great Master Teacher who Protects the Country and Propagates Buddhism," or the one mentioned in contemporary sources, *rgyal khab skyong ba'i dge rgan chen po rgyal btsan yongs kyi*

Chinese term *hua* was used here with the meaning of "Buddhist teaching." In this case, the "education" sense included in *hua* would relate to Tibetan teachings transmitted by the Sixth Panchen Lama. The Tibetan word *'dul* would have been more appropriate to translate *hua*, because its meanings are exactly the same as *xuanhua* ("transmit government orders" or "educate the people").[270] Obviously, the Tibetan title was better fitted to a Buddhist master than the Chinese title, which is more suitable in a political sense. In any case, we might well wonder if this Tibetan translation was merely fortuitous, or whether it was adopted in order to facilitate the Sixth Panchen Lama's task in the field by adhering more closely to the Tibetan.

The title "Great master" (*da shi*) is a deferential appellation, in principle reserved for the Lord Buddha who represents the perfect model to be followed. This title had been given by the Emperors to Buddhist monks since the sixth century. Its attribution implies a very close relation with the Chinese Government.[271]

The fourth title, "Emissary for the Propagation of Values on the Western Frontier" (*xichui xuanhua shi*), was granted by the Nanjing Government in 1932, but the Sixth Panchen Lama received it in 1934. This Chinese title was translated in two different Tibetan versions. The first was *nub mtha'i bstan spel pho nya chen mo*, "Great Emissary who Propagates Buddhism on the Western Border." The second was *nub phyogs skyong ba'i dge rgan chen mo*, meaning "Great Teacher who Protects the Western Region."[272]

The fifth title was "Great Glorious Enlightened Master who Protects the Country and Propagates its Values" (*huguo xuanhua guanghui yuanjue dashi*; *rgyal skyob bstan spel kun mkhyen byang chub slob dpon chen po*). This was conferred on the Sixth Panchen Lama after his death on 20 January 1938.[273]

---

bdag po thams cad mkhyen pa, "Great Teacher who Protects the Country, Omniscient Master of All Buddhist Teachings." See Srung 1984:119; Ya'a 1992:563.

[270] *Bod rgya tshig mdzod chen mo*, 2:1405.

[271] Forte 1994:1019-1934.

[272] Srung 1984:120; Ya Hanzhang 1987:567.

[273] Don khang 1984:126.

The Rituals of Investiture

We know little about Republican China's ceremonies of investiture. What seems very strange in the case of the Sixth Panchen Lama is that these ceremonies sound like imperial ones. This would have been credible under the regime of Yuan Shikai who tried to create a monarchic system in 1914, but not under a Republican government. In any case, we have all the ingredients of an imperial investiture in the ceremonies: titles given by the President of the Republic to the Sixth Panchen Lama in person (Cao Kun in 1924, Duan Qirui in 1925, Jiang Jieshi in 1931 and Lin Sen in 1932), the prostrations; the place where the ceremonies took place—the room of rituals (*litang*).

One ceremony has been described in a few words in the Chinese press and in the Sixth Panchen Lama's hagiographies:[274]

> On 25 December 1932, as planned by the Mongolian and Tibetan Affairs Commission, the Sixth Panchen Lama, dressed in a yellow robe and a yellow morning coat with yellow and red platform boots, was invited to enter the government room of rituals. There, Zhang Ji, who represented the acting President Lin Sen,[275] asked him to take an oath and gave him the seal of the "Emissary for the Propagation of Values in the Western Regions." At the end of the ceremony, Dai Jitao, the Minister of Education, gave him two *thang kas*, because he respected the Sixth Panchen Lama as his spiritual master.

The Use of these Titles

The third and fourth titles initiated the involvement of the Sixth Panchen Lama in Chinese politics. They bring to the fore the role that the Chinese Government intended for the Sixth Panchen Lama, and the way he used those titles (and their functions) as well.

---

[274] *Zhongyang ribao* (*China Central Daily*) 25: 29/12/32; Chen 1943:22; Liu 1943:48.

[275] Lin Sen had been acting President (*daili zhuxi*) since 15 December 1932, the day Jiang Jieshi gave up power (*xiaye*). On Lin Sen (1868-1943), cf. Boorman 1967, 2:379-382. The Sixth Panchen Lama would use this seal for the first time 5/5/32; cf. Nanjing Archives, report from the Sixth Panchen Lama to the Chinese government signed with his new seal, 5/5/1932.

Great and Glorious Master Panchen who Protects the Country and Propagates its Values

At first, from 1924 to 1929, the Sixth Panchen Lama traveled among the Chinese warlords, then among the Inner Mongolia princes, acting as a religious master and as a political figure as well. From 1928 onwards, he attracted the attention of the Chinese authorities when he gathered thousands of people around him for Buddhist teachings, and where he requested the respect of equality between nationalities and the enforcement of Sun Yat-sen's political instructions.[276] His conduct gave the Chinese Government an opportunity to coöpt him. As a result, he was invited to other national meetings, and, on 5 May 1931, he attended the anniversary ceremony for the creation of the Nanjing Government alongside Jiang Jieshi, the President of the Republic of China.[277]

From June 1931 onwards, Dai Jitao, Minister of Education and a disciple of the Sixth Panchen Lama, asked the Chinese Government to give the Sixth Panchen Lama the title of "Great and Glorious Master Panchen who Protects the Country and Propagates its Values." This was carried out on 1 July 1931. This date is important, because from then on the Sixth Panchen Lama became a member of the Chinese Government.

The new mission of the prelate was now to propagate (*xuanchuan*) Sun Yat-sen's "Three Principles of the People," the directives of the Chinese Government, and to comfort the monks and lay Buddhists living in these areas. Should questions connected with the implementation of government policy arise, the Sixth Panchen Lama was obliged to ask the Central Government or provincial authority for advice (*bu de zhijie ganshe*), but he was also allowed to intervene directly in local affairs. Moreover, the Mongolian and Tibetan Affairs Commission indicated the means given the Sixth Panchen Lama to accomplish his new mission. For example, he had at his disposal an amount of money dedicated to the creation of branch offices (*xingshu*) in Amdo and Kham provinces. Each office was composed of a Secretariat (*mishu*), a Propaganda Section (*xuanchuan*) and a

---

[276] Nanjing Archives, letter from the Sixth Panchen Lama to Jiang Jieshi forwarded to the Civil Affairs Office by the Mongolian and Tibetan Affairs Commission, 8/11/1930.

[277] *Minguo ribao* (*Republican Daily*), 5/5/1931; *Dagong bao*, 5/5/1931; Chen 1943:12; Liu 1943:44; Srung 1984:119.

Religious Affairs Department (*jiaowu*). The Sixth Panchen Lama was assisted in his task by two advisers (*canzan*) appointed by the Nanjing Government. He sent employees in charge of propaganda to a targeted province. He created a security team (*jingweidui*) whose chief and members he chose. However, its military instructor (*jiaolianguan*) was designated by the central authorities. The Republican Government provided weapons, ammunition and cars to this guard, plus 30000 yüan per month. Half of this amount was dedicated to the operating funds of the offices, the other half for the security guard. It also granted an annual salary of 200000 yüan to the Sixth Panchen Lama and his retinue.[278] On 24 June 1931, the Republican Government decreed that the Sixth Panchen Lama should be granted the title "Great and Glorious Master Panchen who Protects the Country and Propagates its Values."[279] This was carried out on 1 July 1931.

From then on, the Sixth Panchen Lama commenced a cycle of activities which fell within the Republic of China's political structure. He was given official recognition and funding by the Republican Government, and, in view of his activities in the field, the Republican authorities sponsored and protected him. On his side, the Sixth Panchen Lama accepted a dual political role. First, he became a sort of ambassador in charge of propagating government policy and values in Tibet and Inner Mongolia. Second, he was responsible for informing the Republican Government about the situation in the field. This mission was not new for him. Indeed, he had already been doing so in the past, when he wanted to persuade the Republican Government to provide funds to help the poorest populations of Tibet and Inner Mongolia.

In this way, the Republican Government amiably coöpted this unexpected, yet zealous, ambassador for Sun Yat-sen's principles. From then on, it contrived better to control the Sixth Panchen Lama's field activities in order to promote Chinese Government policy. The trick was to oblige him by giving him allowances, thus forcing him to accept orders. In this spirit, the Republican Government let him go

---

[278] Nanjing Archives, letter from the Mongolian and Tibetan Affairs Commission to the State Council, 21/6/1931.

[279] Nanjing Archives, letter from the rites section of the Military Advisors Department to the Office of Civil Affairs, 30/6/1931; order from the Chinese government, 1/7/1931. Chen 1943:15-16 indicates that this title was given to the Sixth Panchen Lama on 24 February 1932.

back to Inner Mongolia. There the Sixth Panchen Lama faced two situations: the migration of Chinese into Mongolian territory, and the advance of the Japanese army. He chose to use the Nationalist policy statements which had been drafted to safeguard the borders in order to influence the Chinese Government.

In March 1932, the Chinese State Council received a telegram from the Sixth Panchen Lama dated on the fourth. In this telegram, the worried prelate urged the Republican Government to resist the Japanese, using the pretext of safeguarding the national borders.[280] The reaction of the Mongolian and Tibetan Affairs Commission was ambiguous. Should it encourage the Sixth Panchen Lama to act on its behalf, or should it try to remind him that he was a government member, and in consequence moderate his requirements? At this juncture, it was difficult to answer this question. In response, the Mongolian and Tibetan Affairs Commission decided to send Blo bzang rgyal mtshan (who had been appointed director of its Tibetan Affairs Office, the majordomo and the director of the Sixth Panchen Lama Nanjing Office)[281] to Inner Mongolia to bring the Sixth Panchen Lama his seal engraved in Chinese and Tibetan, attached to the title of "Great and Glorious Master Panchen who Protects the Country and Propagates its Values."[282] Apparently, government policy makers opted for the second course of action, since a few days later the Republican Government accepted the proposition formerly made on 21 June 1931 by the Mongolian and Tibetan Affairs Commission after its submission by Dai Jitao. It granted the Sixth Panchen Lama the new title "Emissary for the Propagation of Values in the Western Regions." The official order was published on 14

---

[280] Liu 1943:44.

[281] The Sixth Panchen Lama Nanjing Office *(banchan zhu jing banshichu)* was officially opened by the Nanjing Government on 28 February 1929. This first Sixth Panchen Lama Office became his headquarters in China and was attached to the Mongolian and Tibetan Affairs Commission (Nanjing Archives, order n°414 from the Nationalist government 24/2/1929; Chen 1943:10; Liu 1943:42; Srung 1984:121.

[282] Chen 1943:17.

April 1932.[283] It also attached to this new function headquarters located in Xiangride (or Xiang'erde) in Amdo.[284]

At the same time, the Mongolian and Tibetan Affairs Commission considered the Sixth Panchen Lama's mission to Inner Mongolia to be over, since it appointed the Lcang skya Khutukhtu "Emissary for the Propagation of Values in the Mongolian Leagues" (*meng qi xuan-hua shi*).[285]

Why did the Republican Government decide to grant the Sixth Panchen Lama his new title of "Emissary for the Propagation of Values in the Western Regions" at this moment, and, at the same time, effectively remove him from Inner Mongolia? It appears that the prelate was overzealous in promoting the unity of the five nationalities and the defense of borders, to the point where he was hampering Chinese Government policy. Jiang Jieshi, too preoccupied by his Communist enemies' schemes, decided to abandon Inner Mongolia to the Japanese and bend the policy of the unity of the five nationalities. It is likely that the Republican Government judged as embarrassing, maybe risky, all the Sixth Panchen Lama's activities in favor of Inner Mongolia and decided to recall him. In the meantime, the Republican Government tried, as far as possible, not to offend the Sixth Panchen Lama's sensibilities, because the prelate could be used again in some other cause, such as the Chinese interest in Tibet.

Despite this, the Sixth Panchen Lama stayed on in Inner Mongolia, where he carried on with his political and religious activities. Over the years, he had created chaplain-donor relations with many Mongolian princes. He had given many Buddhist teachings in Inner Mongolia, and the Mongolian princes had offered him hospitality and gifts such as monasteries.[286] But, it is difficult to say whether the

---

[283] Chen 1943:17 proposes the date 19 April 1932, but in that case, the directive n°1042 from the State Council to the Mongolian and Tibetan Affairs Commission, forwarding order n°354, was concerned. Cf. Nanjing Archives, order n°354 from the government to the State Council, 14/4/1932.

[284] Nanjing Archives, directive n°1207 from the State Council to the Mongolian and Tibetan Affairs Commission, 30/4/1932.

[285] *Zhongyang ribao*, 23/11/1932 ; Jiang 1957:33.

[286] The "Panchen Lama Monastery" (*panchin boγdo yin süme*) was built in the Silingol League, West Sunit Banner, in Prince De's domain in 1931-1932. Later, Prince De gave the Panchen Lama the Bayanqota Monastery (Dga' ldan chos gling phun tshogs dgon) in August 1933. Chen 1943:32; Kasuga 1936:49-65; Hyer and Jagchid 1983:134.

Sixth Panchen Lama acted in his own interests or those of the Republican Government. From this time on, the Republican Government conspired to make him return to Nanjing. They invited him to
attend the third session of the plenary meeting, a ceremony organized
in his honor to give him his seal of "Emissary for the Propagation of
Values in the Western Regions," and to attend the fifth anniversary
of the Mongolian and Tibetan Affairs Commission's founding. Finally, the Sixth Panchen Lama changed his mind and went to Nanjing, mainly because he was invited by lay Buddhist Associations
which wanted him to come to Nanjing to teach.

However, we read in a contemporary newspaper that the Sixth
Panchen Lama suddenly left Nanjing on 7 February 1933, to return
to Inner Mongolia, instead of going to the Western regions as he had
announced. Hence, we wonder what the relevance of these titles was
as far as he was concerned.[287] Despite the trick the Sixth Panchen
Lama played on it, the Republican Government was busy framing the
office of "Emissary for the Propagation of Values in the Western
Regions," which was supposed to help the prelate in his new functions. Indeed, the only way for the Chinese authorities to remove the
Sixth Panchen Lama from Inner Mongolia was to give him a good
reason to go to the Western regions. The opening of this office based
in Amdo could have been one.

However that may be, by 23 April 1933, the Amdo office had not
yet opened. The State Council began to hasten its organization, because the Sixth Panchen Lama was still very active in Inner Mongolia.[288] For example, on 16 March 1933, the Sixth Panchen Lama had
sent a telegram to the Government of the Republic attempting to
have his voice heard. He wrote that he was very worried about the
advance of the Japanese troops in Jehol, and he asked "those who are
far away from the battle field or who control the Chinese armies to
strengthen the defenses and safeguard the borders." He then ex-
pressed his indignation about the tragic events that he was facing in
the field.

His testimony (and its large number of addressees) embarrassed
the Chinese authorities; he indirectly accused them of making no
serious attempt to save Inner Mongolia. On the one hand, the Repub-

---

[287] *Zhongyang ribao* 7-9/2/1933.

[288] Nanjing Archives, telegram from the office of the Shahukou train station to
the Mongolian and Tibetan Affairs Commission, 23/4/1933.

lican Government appreciated the Sixth Panchen Lama's work of "propagating values" in Inner Mongolia. On the other hand, the seriousness of the problems described by the prelate, and the expensive solutions he proposed (such as sending more troops), hampered the Chinese Government. Therefore, the State Council urgently tried to regain control of the Sixth Panchen Lama, and send him to the Western regions where his activities would not interfere with urgent Chinese national interests.

Emissary for the Propagation of Values in the Western Regions

On 27 May 1933, with this objective in mind, the State Council sent a directive to the Mongolian and Tibetan Affairs Commission, saying in essence that the office of the "Emissary for the Propagation of Values in the Western Regions" would now come directly under the State Council. Its mission would be to manage all the affairs concerning the propagation of values in the Western regions. The office was to be divided into two departments (*chu*). The first, general administration of affairs, would distribute, copy and keep all documents received and sent, and do the accounting. The second would be responsible for propaganda and manage all activities concerning the propagation of values. The "Emissary for the Propagation of Values in the Western Regions" would be the director of the office. Four secretaries (*mishu*) would assist him, and among them, two would be designated by the Chinese president and two chosen by the Sixth Panchen Lama. The prelate would be assisted by skilled advisers (*mingyu guwen*). Two directors, directly appointed by the Chinese President, would manage each department. Four to six section chiefs (*kezhang*) would be chosen by the Sixth Panchen Lama and eight to ten section employees (*keyuan*) would be appointed by their respective directors (*weiren*).

The Mongolian and Tibetan Affairs Commission forwarded this directive to the Sixth Panchen Lama, who sent it on to each of his offices, which awaited the advice of the Republican Government before taking action.[289] From now on, every time the Sixth Panchen Lama communicated with the Chinese Nationalist Government, he

---

[289] Nanjing Archives, letter n°11 from the Office of the Great and Glorious Master Panchen who Protects the Country and Propagates its Values to the Mongolian and Tibetan Affairs Commission, 29/6/1933.

had to proceed as follows: he first wrote and signed a document, then sent it to his Nanjing office. The latter forwarded it to the Mongolian and Tibetan Affairs Commission, which sent it on to the State Council.

From then on, the Sixth Panchen Lama's offices in Beijing, Chengdu, Xining, Shenyang, Nanjing and Kangding (Dar rtse mdo), founded between 1925 and 1930, became the offices for the "Emissary for the Propagation of Values in the Western Regions." And by this means the Republican Government brought into line the independent propagator of values.

The Chinese authorities hoped thus to regain control over the Sixth Panchen Lama. Finally, Republican Government efforts succeeded, when in mid-June 1935, the Sixth Panchen Lama went to Ningxia Province, and on 8 February opened his first Office of "Emissary for the Propagation of Values in the Western Regions" in Xiangride (although he was back in Inner Mongolia by 11 August 1934).

Besides his roles as ambassador of values and informant on the situation in Tibet and Mongolia, the Chinese authorities gave the Sixth Panchen Lama a third mission attached to the title of "Emissary for the Propagation of Values in the Western Regions." This was to create local offices and to publish a special newsletter intended to spread and increase Republican Government messages in the field. This newsletter was published in both Tibetan and Chinese. It contained articles on the main Chinese and international news, Republican Government policies, the social situation in the West, and political and religious activities related to Tibet and Mongolia. It also provided information about the Sixth Panchen Lama's travels and teachings. It was dispatched to all the Sixth Panchen Lama's offices and to all the military camps on the borders.[290] On the front page a signed photograph of the Sixth Panchen Lama was always displayed. The first thirty pages (written in Tibetan) were on the subjects mentioned above, plus reprints of the Sixth Panchen Lama's political discourses and Buddhist teachings, while the second part summarized them in Chinese. As well as the monthly newsletters, which

---

[290] Nanjing Archives, letter n°271 from the Mongolian and Tibetan Affairs Commission to the Office of the Emissary for the Propagation of Values in the Western Regions, 26/1/1935.

were published irregularly between 1935 and 1937, the Xiangride office also published magazines, slogans and small dictionaries.

Conclusion

We can say that the Republican Government supported the Sixth Panchen Lama when the prelate propagated values in Tibet and in Inner Mongolia, when he informed local leaders about Chinese policies and encouraged them to rally to the unity of the five nationalities. In this case, the Republican Government seemed to appreciate his unexpected ambassadorship. On the other hand, the Republican Government systematically abandoned the Sixth Panchen Lama as soon as he started taking political initiatives in the field, behavior which might have been considered legitimate because of the titles he had been given by the Chinese Government. The Republican Government's reactions when the Sixth Panchen Lama asked for financial or practical help (*e.g.*, to protect the Mongolian princes attacked by the Japanese, or to provide assistance to the people of Amdo and Kham) could have discouraged him. These reactions indicate that the Chinese authorities had backed him in the hope that he might have been able to produce a political miracle among the inhabitants of the border areas. Nevertheless, the Sixth Panchen Lama remained faithful to Sun Yat-sen's ideas and to the Nanjing Government. In fact, could he have done anything else, given that the Republican Government was, after all, his most powerful donor?

Practically, and beyond well-meaning discourses, what did the Sixth Panchen Lama expect from the Republican Government? He probably hoped that the Chinese authorities would clearly show their intentions towards the Tibetan and Mongolian peoples in order to gain their confidence and facilitate their acceptance of the unity of the five nationalities. He also expected that the Chinese Government would set up a meaningful development project. It was for this reason he first testified to the Chinese authorities on the situation he found in Tibet and in Inner Mongolia. It was with this aim that he wrote to Yan Xishan, president of the Mongolian and Tibetan Affairs Commission in 1929, and to Jiang Jieshi in 1930. Then, because he got no real answer, he himself set up a development project which he later submitted to the Chinese authorities in the hope they would adopt it.[291]

A few points remain unanswered. We still do not know how the Lhasa authorities reacted to the titles granted by the Republican Government to the Sixth Panchen Lama. And the standpoint of the Mongolian authorities is difficult to assess; they played a strange game with the Sixth Panchen Lama, who was for them the embodiment of strong political and spiritual powers. Finally, every actor of this period seems to have manipulated the inherent ambiguity of the chaplain-donor relationship in a Republican environment.

---

[291] Discourse by the Sixth Panchen Lama before Ma Hongkui, then Provincial President of Ningxia, and all the members of his government, 24/1/1935. When his departure to Tibet looked imminent, the Sixth Panchen Lama proposed to Huang Musong, the new director of the Mongolian and Tibetan Affairs Commission, a project to propagate values in Tibet, 19/3/1935. Discourse by the Sixth Panchen Lama in Xining, Qinghai Province, where he explained his reasons for choosing to return to Tibet through Qinghai, 12/5/1935.

BIBLIOGRAPHY

Blo bzang rdo rje. *Rigs dang dkyil 'khor rgya mtsho'i khyab bdag he ru ka dpal ngur smrig gar rol skyabs gcig pha bong kha pa bde chen snying po dpal bzang po'i rnam par thar pa don ldan tshangs pa'i dbyangs snyan* (*Biography of Pha bong kha pa Bde chen snying po dpal bzang po*). 2 Vols. New Delhi, 1981.

Boorman H.L. *Biographical Dictionary of Republican China*. 5 Vols. New York: Columbia University Press, 1967.

Chen Jinzhong. "Zhongyang zhengfu banshou lishi dalai, banchan zhi jin ce jin yin" ("The Gold Seals and their Certificates Given by the Chinese Central Government to the Dalai and Panchen Lamas"). *Zhongguo Zangxue* (*China Tibetology*) 1:38-48, 1996.

Chen Wenjian. *Banchan da shi dong lai shiwu nian dashiji* (*Record of Events for Fifteen Years after the Great Master Panchen Came to the East*). Chongqing, 1943.

Danqu. "Labuleng si zang yin kaoshu" ("Research Report on the Collection of Seals at Bla brang Monastery"). *Zhongguo Zangxue* 3:72-78, 1996.

Don khang Skal bzang bde skyid. "Pan chen sku phreng dgu pa mes rgyal nas nang khul du gsang phebs kyi snga rjes" ("Discussion of the Dispute Between the Ninth Panchen Lama and the Tibetan Government"). *Bod kyi rig gnas lo rgyus dpyad gzhi'i rgyu cha bdams bsgrigs* (*Selection of Materials on Tibetan History and Culture*) 4:1-32. Lhasa: People's Publishing House, 1984.

Forte A. "Daishi." *Hôbôgirin* 7:1019-1034, 1994.

Goldstein M.C. *A History of Modern Tibet, 1913-1951. The Demise of the Lamaist State*. Berkeley: University of California Press, 1989.

Hyer P. and S. Jagchid. *A Mongolian Living Buddha. Biography of the Kanjurwa Khutughtu*. Albany: State University of New York, 1983.

Ishihama Yumiko. "A Study of the Seals and Titles Conferred by the Dalai Lamas." In Ihara Shoren and Yamaguchi Zuiho, eds. *Tibetan Studies. Proceedings of the 5th Seminar of the International Association for Tibetan Studies* 2:501-514. Narita: Naritasan Shinshoji, 1992.

Jiang Yangni. "Banchan lama yi wei daxi lama zhi yanjiu" ("Research on the Translation of the Title 'Panchen Lama' into 'Tashi Lama'"). *Meng zang yuebao* (*Mongol-Tibetan Monthly*) 4(4):24-34, 1936.

Jiang Zhongzheng. *Hu guo jing jue fujiao da shi zhangjia hutuketu shi* (*Biography of the Lcang skya Khutukhtu*). Taibei, 1957.

Kasuga R. "Môko ramabyô chôsa hôkoku" ("Report on the Mongol Lamaseries"). *Tôhô Shukyô* 35:49-65, (16 July) 1936.

Liu Jiaju. *Banchan da shi quanji* (*Complete Works of the Great Master Panchen*). Chongqing, 1943.

Luo Zhufeng, comp. *Hanyu da cidian* (*Large dictionary of Chinese Language*). 12 Vols. Shanghai: Hanyu da cidian, 1994.

Ou Chaogui. "Zhonghua minguo cigei xizang difang de fengyin" ("Titles Given to Local Tibet by the Republic of China"). *Xizang yanjiu* (*Tibetan Studies*) 4:28-32, 1996.

Phur lcog yongs 'dzin Thub bstan byams pa tshul khrim bstan 'dzin. *Lhar bcas srid zhi'i gtsug rgyan gong sa rgyal ba bka' 'drin mtshungs med sku phreng bcu gsum pa chen po'i rnam thar rgya mtsho lta bu las mdo tsam brjod pa ngo mtshar rin po che'i phreng ba* (*Biography of the Thirteenth Dalai Lama*), Vols. 5-7. Śata-

Piṭaka series, Vols. 287-288. New Delhi: International Academy of Indian Culture, 1981.

Qin Xiaoyi *et al.*, comp. *Geming wenxian, di qishijiu ji, zhongguo guomindang lijie lici zhongquanhui zhongyao jueyi an huibian* (*Revolutionary Documents, No. 79. Assorted Volumes on Important Decisions of All the Plenary Sessions of the Chinese Central Guomindang*). Taibei: Zhongguo guomindang zhongyang weiyuan hui dangshi weiyuanhui, 1979.

Srung Kri hru'u. "Pan chen sku 'phreng dgu pa dbus gtsang dang zhal bral ba dang dbus gtsang du phyir phebs pa'i skor bshad pa" ("The Relations of the Ninth Panchen Lama with Central Tibet and his Return to Central Tibet"). *Mtsho sngon gyi rig gnas dang lo rgyus dpyad gzhi'i yig rigs 'dem sgrig* (*Selection of Articles on Amdo Tibetan Province History and Culture*) 1:115-127. Xining: Qinghai Publishing House, 1984.

Tang Jingfu. "Minguo shiqi lijie zhongyang zhengfu weihu xizang zhuquan de cuoshe" ("Measures Taken by Successive Governments to Safeguard Tibetan Sovereignty during the Republic of China"). *Zhongguo Zangxue* 1:42-58, 1997.

Wang Chengsheng. "Xizang banchan jiu shi yisheng shenji" ("The Miraculous Life of the Ninth Panchen Lama"). *Zhongwai zazhi* (*China Foreign Magazine*) 1:5, 1969.

Xu Wenshan, comp. *Guofu yijiao sanmin zhuyi zongji* (*Collection of the Three Principles of the people: Teaching inherited from Sun Yat-sen*). Taibei: Zhonghua yeshu, 1960.

Ya Hanzhang. *Banchan e'erdeni zhuan* (*Biographies of the Panchen Lamas' Lineage*). Beijing: People's Press, 1987.

Ya'a han krang. *Pan chen sku phreng rim byon gyi mdzad rnam* (*Biographies of the Panchen Lamas' Lineage*). Lhasa: People's Press, 1992.

Zhongguo di er lishi dang'anguan, comp. *Jiu shi banchan yuanji zhiji he shi shi banchan chuanshi zuochuang dang'an xuanbia* (*Compilation of Documents Preserved in the Nanjing Archives on the Death of the Ninth Panchen Lama and the Enthronement of the Tenth Panchen Lama*). Nanjing: Zhongguo Zangxue, 1991.

——*Jiu shi banchan neidi huodong ji fan zang shouzu dang'an* (*Compilation of the Nanjing Archives Documents on the Ninth Panchen Lama's Activities in Inner China and the Obstacles in the Way of his Return to Tibet*). Nanjing: Zhongguo zang xue, 1992.

Zhou Ziyin. "Cong minguo shiqi dalai banchen de chuanshi tan zhongyang zhuquan de xingshi" ("Discussion on the Sovereignty Exercised by the Chinese Central Government on the Dalai and Panchen Lamas' Reincarnations since the Republic of China"). *Xizang yanjiu* 2:40-48, 1995.

SA SPANG MDA' GNAM SPANG MDA': MURDER, HISTORY, AND SOCIAL POLITICS IN 1920S LHASA[292]

CAROLE MCGRANAHAN (UNIVERSITY OF COLORADO)

Sa spang mda' gnam spang mda'
The earth is Pangda's, the sky is Pangda's.

On a dark and stormy night, people had gathered in Lhasa's Twentieth Park, (*nyi shu'i gling ga*), to celebrate *'dzam gling spyi bsangs,* the Universal Smoke Offering Day. Throughout the day, people picnicked and gambled in tents set up throughout the park. With the exception of the weather, the atmosphere was festive—people eating, drinking, and otherwise enjoying themselves. Beer maids roamed from tent to tent refilling *chang* bowls,[293] singing, and flirting. Much of Lhasa's high society was there. The flaps of their tents were down, perhaps as much as to prevent prying eyes as to provide shelter from the weather. Inside one particular tent, dimly lit by oil lamps and candles, a group of men played mahjong and drank chang. As they played, a thunder and lightning storm developed. Outside the tent, two men huddled, nervously preparing for their own festival activities. Then, as one or another of the men inside the tent contemplated his next play, there was a ferocious roar of thunder, followed by a flash of lightning. The lightning illuminated the tent, and through chang-glazed eyes, they saw that one of the men had fallen over. Outside the tent, the two men were already gone, swiftly making their escape through the alleys of Lhasa. The man who had fallen was dead, murdered with just one shot fired precisely at the time of the thunder, so as not to be heard and thus giving the assassins just

[292] The original title of this paper, as delivered at the Ninth Seminar of the International Association for Tibetan Studies, June 24-30, 2000, in Leiden, The Netherlands, was "Sa spom mda' gnam spom mda': Earth, Sky, and the Pangdatsang Family." The Social Science Research Council (U.S.A.) and the American Institute of Indian Studies provided funding for research. Many people provided gracious assistance and advice in the research for and writing of this paper; thank you to Tashi Tsering, Lobsang Shastri, Chophel, Champa Lhunpo, Tenzin Bhagen, Larry Epstein, Ann Stoler, and Leslie Pincus. A very special thank you to members of the Pangdatsang family in the United States, Switzerland, and India.

[293] *Chang* is Tibetan barley beer.

enough time to make their get away. This was 1921 and the murdered man was Pangda Nyigyal, the head of the Pangdatsang family,
a Khampa trader settled in Lhasa and a favorite of the Thirteenth
Dalai Lama.

The dramatic story of the murder of Pangda Nyigyal is still told
today by Tibetans. Eyes wide, voices lowered, narrators seven decades distant from the event drape their narration in suspense and conspiracy enabled first, by the fact that the murder was never solved,
and second, by the controversial place of the Pangdatsang family in
modern Tibetan society and history. This article follows both
branches of suspense, and is two stories in one. It is first a study of
the murder of Pangda Nyigyal and the histories his murder has gen-
erated, and it is also the beginnings of a history of the Pangdatsang
family and of the relations between region, class, and politics in Tibetan society.

In the first half of the last century, simultaneous with Tibet's un-
easy exploration of outside ideas about modernity and the nation-
state, the Tibetan merchant class was attempting to carve out a new
bourgeois social space in Lhasa's aristocrat-dominated society. The
attempts of this group, many of who were trading families from the
eastern Tibet region of Kham, were a challenge to rigid hierarchies of
regional status and social class in a national imaginary that privileged
the Central Tibetan aristocracy. Genealogy and heritage trumped
earned wealth and power in early twentieth century Lhasa, but financial success was beginning to infringe on the bastions of social pres-
tige. Thus, although ascribed status still prevailed over achieved
status, Tibet's new bourgeoisie did have its share of success stories.
Among Khampas, the two most successful trading firms were those
of the Sadhutsang family from Kanze and the Pangdatsang family
from Markham. Along with the Reting Labrang,[294] they were referred
to as *re spom sa gsum,* "Reting-Pangda-Sadhu, the Three."[295] In Kalimpong today, forty-odd years after the trade route between India

---

[294] A labrang is the property and wealth of an incarnate lama accumulated over a
series of incarnations. Reting Rimpoche, the incarnate lama associated with Sera
Monastery's Je College, had a substantial labrang that was, among other things,
successfully engaged in trade.

[295] In 1952, American intelligence officers observed that "Pangdatsang,
Sadutsang, and Reting Labrang...have formed a syndicate operating at
Kalimpong...to promote the wool trade." U.S. Intelligence report, June 27, 1952,
NARA document.

and Tibet was closed, they are remembered as "the sun, star, and jewels of Tibet."[296]

Sa spang mda' gnam spang mda'. "The earth is Pangda's, the sky is Pangda's." I first heard this phrase from one of Pangda's former mule herders. Since then numerous Tibetans have quoted it to me, often telling me stories of how Pangda's servants would invoke it when committing an offense, saying, "I am connected to Pangda, what are you going to do to me?"[297] This insolence was possible only through the power of the Pangdatsang family, one that rose seemingly from nowhere to great power, and which in the span of two generations became one of the wealthiest—if not *the* wealthiest—families in all of Tibet. From Kham, the family was wildly successful in Lhasa. The story of its members ranges back and forth between India, China, Kham, and Lhasa, covering ground ranging from the Tibetan economy and trade to politics both lay and monastic, from relations with Nationalist China and British India to intrigues of all sorts of shapes and sizes. In this article I draw on an eclectic array of oral and written sources to present less well-known aspects of the family. Thus, instead of bringing new material to bear on the 1934 Pangda rebellion in Kham or Rapga's Tibet Improvement Party in 1940s Kalimpong, I focus on Nyigyal, the family patriarch, and his shepherding of the family in their rise to national prominence.

Lightning Strikes: The Making of the Pangdatsang Family

Our story begins in Chamdo. The rise of the Pangdatsang family from local power to regional power, and then to national power took place in a relatively short span of time and under two different names—Pangdatsang and Pomdatsang. In the mid-nineteenth century, the Pomdatsang (Spom mda' tshang) family,[298] based in a Sakya

---

[296] Interview, Dawa Dhondup, March 24, 1998, Kalimpong.

[297] An off-color version of this story also circulates. One of Pangda's mule herders was caught relieving his bowels on the side of the road in Kalimpong, and upon being scolded, responded, "The earth is Pangda's, the sky is Pangda's. If I don't shit here, where am I supposed to shit?" *(sa spang mda' gnam spang mda' skyag pa 'di ru ma btang na ga par gtong dgos red).* Most versions of the story that I was told included only the first phrase, whether the second phrase was edited out for me or added to the original by others for comic effect, I do not know.

[298] Khampa family names often affix *tshang,* romanized as "tsang," to them. *Tshang* literally means "nest," but "Pangdatsang" may be translated as "House of

area of Chamdo called Rdza ba Spom mda',[299] were traders and sponsors of the Sakya family and sect.[300] At this time, Tenzin Zangmo, one of the sisters of the head of the Sakya family, was married into the Pomda family. The family was given a Sakya post in Markham, an important district south of Chamdo, and relocated there. One offspring of the Pomda-Sakya union was Nyima Gyaltsen, or Nyigyal, under whom the family's power would be consolidated through a combination of business acumen and religious patronage. Connections to the Sakya family were an important part of the ascent of the Pangdatsangs.

The Sakya family was one of the most powerful in all of Tibet. From the town and monastery of Sakya in central Tibet, they had risen to power in the thirteenth century.[301] Sakya rule over Tibet lasted for only about a century, but the importance of the family and religious tradition did not wane. Unique in Tibet, Sakya is the name of a family, their estate, a monastery, and one of the four main schools of Tibetan Buddhism. In addition to the Sakya monasteries found throughout Tibet, the Sakyas maintained a degree of political autonomy in eleven different areas of Tibet through the 1950s, including two territories in eastern Tibet—Damthog and Markham.[302]

The Sakya post in Markham was one of the eighteen *dpon* or chieftain positions in Markham and was called the Gyakeg Pon (Rgya skeg dpon).[303] This is the position given to the Pomda family.

Pangda." In Lhasa, the word *gzim shag,* an honorific for house, was used instead of *tshang.*

[299] Known as Rdza ba sgang or Rdza ba Dpa' shod Rdzong. Oral information from Tashi Tsering, Phupa Tsetop, and Baba Lekshay. Pangda family members that I have interviewed were unaware that the family was originally from Chamdo.

[300] The story of the family's rise to local power requires further investigation. Pangdatsang family members contend that the family was locally powerful for generations. Wangmo Yuthok Pangdatsang recalls that in the first half of the twentieth century, the Pangdatsang brothers could recite family history going back four or five generations. Their ancestral stories were of powerful and respected local chieftains who had good relations with the people they governed. Interview, Wangmo Yuthok Pangdatsang, Seattle, June 2, 2000.

[301] On the Sakya family and religious tradition, see Samuel 1993, Cassinelli and Ekvall 1969, and Chogay 1983. For personal narratives, see Sakya and Emery 1990, and Norbu 1987.

[302] Cassinelli and Ekvall 1969:32.

[303] Phupa 1998:7. Phupa gives the spelling as *rgya dkar;* Cassinelli and Ekvall as *rgya khag.* I choose to follow instead Sakya Trichen Takshu Tinley Rinchen who spells the name *rgya skeg.*

The domain included the nomad area of Jindok and the mixed farming-nomadic area of Gushod, as well as the Gyakeg monastery and community.[304] The position was usually given to a lama from Sakya who would stay for three to five years as both head of the monastery and the lay community.[305] In contrast to this system, the Pomda family was awarded the post as a hereditary one in perpetuity. This meant that the family was now ruler of a unique area, one which paid taxes to Sakya, but from which the Lhasa government could levy work, or collect an "outer tax."[306] The granting of this Sakya post provided material benefits to the family, spiritual benefits in the form of strong protector deities Dorje Dakden (Rdo rje grags ldan) and Thog goe (Thog rgod), attendants of the powerful deity Tsi mar (Tsi'u dmar ra), as well as one of the Sakya *'bag mo,* or witches,[307] and an identity change in the form of a new name. The area of Markham that they moved to was called Spang mda', and the family took on this name, referring to themselves as Spang mda' tshang, or Pangdatsang, rather than the earlier Spom mda' tshang. This relatively recent change of name means that both names—Spom mda' and Spang mda'—are still used to refer to the family. The family themselves prefer the Spang mda' name, transliterating it as "Pangda," and I follow their preference here.[308]

The new position in Markham did not curtail the Pangda trading business, but rather provided the financial means for expansion. Pangda Nyigyal moved to Lhasa and began coordinating long-distance trade from there. It is at this point that the family gains recognition preserved in broader historical memory within the Tibetan community. Over the course of several dozen interviews with Khampa and Lhasa Tibetans about the Pangdatsang family, of those

---

[304] Phupa 1998:7

[305] Phupa 1998:7. Cassinelli and Ekvall 1969:30 downplay the importance of the eastern Sakya areas. In addition, they erroneously claim that "no people from these eastern regions were of any importance in the governmental and religious affairs of Sa sKya proper."

[306] Cassinelli and Ekvall 1969:361.

[307] On Tibetan deities, see Nebesky-Wojkowitz 1956. On the Sa skya *'bag mo,* see Wangdu 1995.

[308] Wangmo Yuthok Pangda recalls that papers her father, Pangda Yamphel, submitted to the Dalai Lama would come back with the name Spang mda' crossed out and Spom mda' written in instead (Interview, June 2, 2000). Several individuals have suggested that the reason for preferring Spom mda' could be because Spang mda' is a close homonym for the term *sprang po* which means "beggar."

who were able to explain the origins of the family's rise to power, all told me similar stories. Collectively, they were as follows:

> When the Thirteenth Dalai Lama fled Lhasa to the Tibetan border with India following the fall of the Qing Dynasty in 1911, Pangda Nyigyal provided free transport of all his goods to and from Lhasa, as well as a bodyguard of some 2-300 Khampa troops.[309] Once His Holiness was safely returned to Lhasa, he called Pangda Nyigyal to see him, asking him what he wanted in return for services provided. Nyigyal replied that he was a businessman and didn't know about politics, but could His Holiness give him the business powers of the Central Government? His Holiness said very well and sent the orders to the Kashag, the Tibetan cabinet. The Kashag asked Nyigyal, "If we give you one million gormo, then what will you give us next year?" He wisely replied, "Two million." The deal was struck, and Pangda's star began to rise. As the Central Tibetan Government business agent, Pangda bought wool at half the regular price from the sellers and others were not allowed to buy until he had bought his fill. He also paid only half the transportation costs, and others had to wait to move their goods until all of his had been transported. Other traders, wool sellers, and transporters did not like this and became jealous.

This oral history of Pangda's fortuitous encounter with, and service to, the Thirteenth Dalai Lama sets the date of the family's rise in 1912. But while Nyigal did aid the Dalai Lama, and was later favored for this service, the Pangda family was on the rise prior to 1912. British colonial records housed in London help us extend this study further back by several years. Although Tibet was never colonized by Britain, the British Empire and its agents amassed and created massive amounts of documentation regarding Tibet. The importance of knowledge in the imperial project of rule extended to places and peoples outside the boundaries of rule. In Tibet we see this through British attempts to ensure that Tibet developed in ways compatible with the interests of Great Britain and British India.[310] British policy in Tibet in the early twentieth century had three objectives: first, to cultivate a pro-British sentiment among the Tibetan elite; second, to influence Tibetan diplomatic affairs; and third, to develop trade as a key component of British-Tibetan relations. With this third concern in mind, they noted with alarm every time the Tibetan Government

---

[309] Tsepon W.D. Shakabpa also writes about "Nyima Gyalpo Pandatshang of Markham" aiding the Dalai Lama in 1912; see his 1967:243, and 1976:208.

[310] On European colonialism as a project of knowledge as well as rule, see Cohn 1996; on British policy towards Tibet, see McKay 1997, and McGranahan in press.

made trade decisions that went against British notions of a fair and open market that underlay the various trade treaties between the governments of India and Tibet.

Protest over trade arrangements, often directed at the Tibetan Government's favoring of the Pangda family, was a frequent form of British communication with Lhasa. The first British protest against Pangdatsang favoritism was in 1909, three years before Nyigyal provided aid and escort to the Dalai Lama. On May 26, 1909, the Tibetan Government granted the sole right to purchase wool and yak tails to three traders: "the Kumsang family of Lhasa, Jimpa of Chema (or Garusha from Lhasa, if Jimpa declined), and Pu-nye-chang from the Pom-do-tsang family."[311] The British were joined in their protests over these grants by the eighteen major traders of the Chumbi valley, on the Indian-Tibetan border and through which ran the Kalimpong-Lhasa road. Yu Lien, the Chinese representative in Lhasa, was also against the trade grants and gave orders for the grant to be cancelled. His orders were promptly ignored, as were the other protests, and the grant recipients began to reap their benefits. The trading powers of the Pangda firm in particular began to grow, and monopolies over the wool trade—the chief domestic product of Tibet—continued to be granted to Pangda Nyigyal by the government. Pangda was also a major importer of tea and silks from China, and had representatives throughout China, including Beijing and Shanghai. By 1920, Pangda Nyigyal was recognized as the leading Tibetan trader, a fact not lost on the British. Sir Charles Bell, Political Officer in Sikkim (with responsibilities for Tibet) off and on from 1904 through 1921, provides a rare written description of Pangda Nyigyal.

> During my time in Tibet, the chief Tibetan merchant was a man named Pom-da-tsang. I met him in Lhasa.[312] He had branches in Calcutta, Shanghai, and Peking, and formerly had maintained a branch in Japan also. His business with India was chiefly in wool, but he exported also yak-tails and other commodities. To Peking he sent woolen cloth, as well as the skins of fox, stone marten, lynx, marmot, etc. He imported great quantities of Chinese silk.... Pom-da-tsang emphasized the necessity of knowing the different patterns on the silk, for some districts

---

[311] IOR L/P+S/10/138 Tibet. Trade Monopolies, 1909-1918. In addition, the grant for hides went to the Getutsang family from Kham for Rs. 20,000/- per year.

[312] Bell's meeting with Pangda Nyigyal took place at some point between November 1920 and October 1921, the only time that Bell was in Lhasa. For information on the Bell Mission to Lhasa, see McKay 1997.

in Tibet favor one pattern, others another. The silk which came from
Russia, he asserted, was of good quality only; there was nothing second rate. It was more costly than the most expensive Chinese silk.[313]

Pangda was also one of the few Khampa traders who paid for goods
in Dartsendo or Chengdu with drafts payable in Shanghai.[314]

At some time in the 1910s, as the family became more successful
in Lhasa, they made the decision to join forces with the Jangling
(Byang gling) family, a family of traders from Lhasa.[315] The two
daughters of the Jangling family, Sonam and Tsedon, married with
the two Pangda sons Yamphel and Tobgyal, but this was not all; to
more closely tie the families together, the husbands also married each
other's wives. This was done with an official ceremony, after which
the two families lived together as one. From the unions of the par-
ents, only one child was born, a daughter, Pema Choekyi. She was
given the Pangda name, and the original son of the Jangling family
took the name Spang mda' zur pa, or Pangsur (Spang zur),[316] when he
went into government service.[317] This union of families combined not
only two trading families, but also created deeper ties for the
Khampa Pangda family with communities in Lhasa.

Social divisions in Lhasa were not only along class lines, but regional ones, with Tibetans from the provinces added into Central
Tibetan social hierarchies. Two arenas in which there was considerable latitude for crossing divisions and bringing together different
communities were trade and religion. Both trade and religion cut
across social and regional divides in general, while recreating such
divisions internally, e.g., through regional trade associations and monastic colleges or houses organized around regional affiliation.
Khampa traders passing through Lhasa could easily find Khampa

---

[313] Bell 1992:130.

[314] IOR L/P+S/11/90, File P921. Tibet, Trade in Tachienlu and the Marches. O.R.
Coales letter, Tachienlu, November 22, 1916.

[315] Interviews, Wangmo Yuthok Pangda, June 2, 2000; Surkhang Lhacham, Oak-
land, May 1, 2000.

[316] Zur ("corner") is a suffix given to family names when the occasion arises that
a secondary branch of the family needs a name for official use.

[317] He eventually went as a mag pa to the Tethong family which meant that the
Pangsur name was not continued. Mag pa is the term for a man who at the time of
marriage leaves his family's home to live with his wife's family. He becomes a
member, often the head, of the new family and takes their family name as his own.
This is commonly done in families where there are no sons, and thus no one to carry
on the family name.

worlds in the capital—places to stay and drink, lamas to seek bless-ings from. These were familiar worlds, and most traders were per-haps content to operate within these frameworks.[318] Pangda Nyigyal, however, had aspirations beyond Khampa expatriate life in Lhasa; his merger with the Jangling family, his efforts at business expan-sion, and his relationship with the Dalai Lama are ample evidence. One question remains unanswered by historical memory in exile and British colonial archives: why was Pangda Nyigyal awarded the 1909 trade concession? What exactly had brought him to the attention of the Tibetan Government?

The key to unlocking the story of the Pangdatsang family's suc-cesses in Lhasa was entrusted to Nyigyal's grandson, Manang Sonam Tobgyal. Son of Pema Choekyi, Manang Sonam Tobgyal spent much of his childhood and teen years in the household of his uncle Yam-phel. Pangda Yamphel, along with his brothers Rapga and Tobgyal, would regale the younger generation with stories of the past, includ-ing Nyigyal's early years in Lhasa. As family lore goes, Nyigyal came to Lhasa as an ordinary Khampa trader. He did not have much money, but was a clever man, and he had a plan. Shortly after his arrival in Lhasa, Nyigyal borrowed money from friends and then made large contributions to the "three monasteries"—Sera, Drepung, and Ganden.[319] He gave all of his capital to them, leaving nothing for himself. In Tibet, at this time, there were no banks, so people were responsible for keeping their own money. Across all levels of soci-ety, from poorest to wealthiest, giving alms was a popular means of accumulating merit, and as a result, the monasteries were very cash-rich. After Nyigyal made large donations to each of these monaster-ies, people began to talk. Word spread about Nyigyal's generosity, and the monastic officials thought that Pangda Nyigyal must be a very rich Khampa trader who had just arrived in Lhasa. The monas-teries were not fond of keeping large amounts of money on their grounds, and with no banks available, would store money at the

---

[318] An additional and unofficial realm in which divisions of class and region were crossed was in the world of sexual relations. Although it is beyond the scope of this paper, liberal Tibetan sexual mores allowed for transgressions of social boundaries through male-female sexual relations, especially between traders and women in towns along trading routes.

[319] Sera, Drepung, and Ganden were the three main monasteries associated with the Tibetan Government. Each was Gelugpa, supported thousands of monks from all regions of Tibet, and supplied high-level monastic officials to the government.

homes of their trusted sponsors. Pangda Nyigyal, having shown himself to be a valuable sponsor, was asked to store their money; he agreed, and used this money as the capital with which to build his successful business. Reflecting back on Nyigyal's plan, his grandson says, "That's how it all started. With the protection of these three monasteries, you are safe in Tibet."[320]

Nyigyal was indeed safe. He garnered not only the support of both lay and monastic officials in the Tibetan government, but became a favorite *(spyan gsal)* of the Thirteenth Dalai Lama. The Thirteenth Dalai Lama had several favorites over the course of his tenure; being a favorite of the Dalai Lama meant rare access to His Holiness, and privileges in political, social, and economic realms as well. Manang Sonam Tobgyal suggests that perhaps Nyigyal, a bright and capable Khampa and a devoted religious sponsor, caught the attention of the Thirteenth Dalai Lama, who was an especially open-minded man, interested in building stronger relations with Kham. Pangda Nyigyal's personal acumen and monastic connections aside, his association with the Thirteenth Dalai Lama—and the later close association of his sons with the Dalai Lama and his chief favorite Kumbela—provided the Pangda family with the means to unparalleled wealth as well as social and political influence. If those responsible for killing Nyigyal thought that his death would bring down the family, they were very wrong.

Unsolved Crimes: Storytelling and the Politics of History

> The past is like the scene of a crime: if the deed itself is
> irrecoverable, its traces may still remain.[321]

History is only such when there are two versions of the same story. Pangdatsang family history provides no exception to this rule, and is ripe with gossip, innuendo, secrets, and speculations aired behind mostly closed doors. The story of Nyigyal's assassination—a crime that remains unsolved today—raises important questions about historical knowledge. Who killed Pangda Nyigyal and why? The inability to solve the crime, or perhaps the *unwillingness* to solve the

---

[320] Interview, Manang Sonam Tobgyal, July 1, 2000, Luzern, Switzerland; also phone interview, May 30, 2000.

[321] Kuhn 1995:4.

crime, results in a seemingly unfinished history, in which social politics are hinted at, names are whispered, and truths are sidelined. While the "deed" and its doer may be "irrecoverable" in the present, other aspects of this history are as important as its missing facts. I turn now to explore how this history has been told, and by whom, asking how it has been edited to fit the "central interpretive devices" of Tibetan society at the various times of its telling.[322] Alongside a tracking of the murderer, therefore, we shall also track the possibilities for history as configured by shifts in Tibetan social and political worlds in the 1920s and ensuing decades.

History in this instance is *lo rgyus,* a category with no pre-set subject, told in narrative rather than its earlier format as annals. The histories that I draw on in this discussion of Pangda Nyigyal's murder are both ones written and told shortly after the murder, as well as ones narrated for me in the last several years. In combining sources I look not just for information about the murder, but for the ways that stories about the murder have and have not been told. Historian Alessandro Portelli contends that oral histories tell us as much, if not more, about meaning than about events.[323] To follow, Luise White suggests that historical facts emerge from social truths and vice versa.[324] The case of Pangda Nyigyal's murder offers such a dual commentary on the murder itself as well as on social politics in Lhasa and beyond. Viewing history as a combination of fact and meaning opens our investigation to the conditions that led to Pangda Nyigyal's murder and also to the various possibilities of interpretation and transmission for stories of his murder. This approach recognizes that events are not real solely because they happened, but because their reality is secured by remembering and telling them in culturally meaningful ways.[325]

Nyigyal was a wealthy and important man at the time of his death, but still a Khampa newcomer to Lhasa society, and the possibilities for narrating his murder reflect that status. His death also took place at a time of sparse literacy in Tibet. There were no newspapers in Lhasa in 1921, and any prison or governmental records that might have been kept are not currently accessible. Thus, although crime is

---

[322] Steedman 1986:5.
[323] Portelli 1981.
[324] White 2000:33-4.
[325] White 1987:20; Scarry 1996.

considered by historians to be an event generative of a surplus of sources,[326] in the case of Nyigyal's murder, this expectation does not hold true. To my knowledge, only two individuals wrote about the assassination;[327] the rest of our sources are oral. All accounts of the assassination are second-hand; we have no available eyewitness accounts. Nevertheless, traces remain.

The clearest statement on the murder is short and to the point: "On the evening of the 16th, in Lhasa, the devoted sponsor Pangda Nyigyal was shot by a bad person while he was in a tent during Zamling Kyisang." [328] This diary entry was written in 1922 by Takshu Tinley Rinchen, the Sakya Trichen, head of the Sakya family and religious sect. The Sakya Trichen had kept a diary since the age of eight, and was a fastidious recorder of the world around him.[329] His collected diaries, including many accounts of his interactions with the Pangdatsang family, were edited and published as his autobiography in 1974 by his chief disciple, the Venerable Jampal Sangpo, Abbot of Sakya Monastery.[330] Takshu Tinley Rinchen records his first association with the Pangdatsang family in 1882 at age eleven when he gave a long life initiation teaching to Sonam Palgyal, "the storekeeper of Gyakeg Pomdatsang."[331] In 1915, he assumed the position of Sakya Trichen from his father, Kunga Nyingpo, and in 1920, he made a ceremonial visit to Lhasa.[332] His activities there included at least seven different recorded ceremonies and teachings done on behalf of Pangda Nyigyal.

The year before Nyigyal's murder, 1920, the Year of the Iron Monkey, was a busy one for the Sakya Trichen. He was in Lhasa tending to his own religious activities and monastic responsibilities, as well as giving a large number of teachings to his individual sponsors. Over the course of the year, Sakya Trichen gave Nyigyal his

---

[326] See the collected essays in Muir and Ruggiero 1994, especially their "Afterword: Crime and the Writing of History," pp.226-236.

[327] I thank Tashi Tsering of the Amnye Machen Institute in Dharamsala for directing me to these texts.

[328] Khri chen 1974, 1:840.

[329] Khri chen 1974:4 ("Preface").

[330] Khri chen 1974.

[331] Khri chen 1974, 1:81-2.

[332] Khri chen 1974:3 ("Preface"). In Lhasa, Sakya Trichen had his second visit with the Thirteenth Dalai Lama and made visits to many monasteries and pilgrimage sites. He also did ceremonies for the Tibetan Government, "at which a number of miracles are said to have occurred."

family, associates, and servants numerous long life initiation teachings, rituals for deities (*e.g.*, *rta phyag khyung gsum*), rituals for
prosperity (*g.yang sgrub nor bu'i chog rgya*), and teachings that he
himself had composed.[333] Nyigyal in turn made many generous offerings to the Sakya Trichen, his mother, wife, and three children, including religious objects (such as Mandral Tensum which represents
the body, speech, and mind of the Buddha), high quality brocades,
tea, and barley, as well as cash.[334] During the seven day prosperity
ceremony, Pangda Nyigyal confided to Sakya Trichen that he had
paid back all of his debt to the government and to relatives, and had
now accumulated a large sum of money. He had decided to divide
this money in thirds, with one-third to go to His Holiness the Dalai
Lama, one-third to Gyakeg Monastery in Markham for expansion
and to support 500 monks, and the remaining one-third to Sakya
Monastery. Sakya Trichen records that he praised this plan, telling
Nyigyal, "To give such an amount of money to the great monastery
makes your human life useful and plants a seed of goodness for your
future lives."[335] Shortly after, Pangda Nyigyal was murdered.

Sakya Trichen's account of the year leading up to Pangda Nyigyal's murder offers no direct commentary on why Nyigyal was
killed, much less who the "bad person" behind the deed could be.
Indirectly, however, the character sketch he provides of Nyigyal is
one of a devoted religious sponsor, moreover, one who had just paid
off all of his outstanding debts, and was perhaps poised to take his
trading firm to new heights of success. While Sakya Trichen refrains
from commenting on trade jealousies or speculating on who might
have killed Nyigyal, other narrators do not hold back such comments. In the oral histories of Pangda Nyigyal's assassination that I
have collected, all narrators knew that he had been shot while pic-
nicking, all knew that this had been during a thunder and lightning
storm, and all knew who was suspected of ordering the assassination.
Of those interviewed who chose to share the suspect's name with me,
the same person, a Tibetan aristocrat, was named again and again
without fail, but always with qualification; *e.g.*, "Who killed [Pangda
Nyigyal] remained a mystery. Nobody knew exactly who killed him
or for what reason. Of course, people had their suspicions about who

---

[333] Khri chen 1974:608-649.
[334] Khri chen 1974:645, 648.
[335] Khri chen 1974:626.

the killer was."[336] The only narrator to confidently name the
murderer, and to write about it, was Alo Chonzed.[337]

Alo Chonzed, a Khampa born and raised in Lhasa, a leader of Mi-
mang Tsongdu, the popular anti-Chinese Tibetan People's Organization in the 1950s, was in later decades a vocal critic of the Tibetan
Government-in-Exile. His handwritten and self-published 617-page
history of Tibet was banned by the Tibetan Government-in-Exile,
and circulates in only limited numbers. It is in this book, *Bod kyi
gnas lugs bden 'dzin sgo phye ba'i lde mig zhes bya ba a lo chos
mdzad kyi gdams, spyi lo 1920 nas 1982 bar,* or *The Key That Opens
the Door of Truth to the Tibetan Situation: Materials on Modern Tibetan History,* that the most detailed account of Pangda Nyigyal's
murder is available.[338] Alo Chonzed's interest in the case was personal; his uncle Aten was arrested for the crime, imprisoned and tortured before his innocence was proven and he was released from jail.

The murder of Pangda Nyigyal was not an ordinary crime. His social rank was high enough that the case appears to have been a political rather than legal affair, adjudicated by prison and government
officials rather than through the court system.[339] As Alo Chonzed
tells the story, Nyigyal's assassination was acted upon swiftly. Sakya
Trichen confirms this, writing that he received a letter from Pangda
Nyima stating that "about ten men" confessed to being involved in
Nyigyal's murder, and except for two who were still at large, the cul-
prits had all been put in jail.[340] Nyima concluded the letter by saying
that they were not sure who else was involved in the murder, and
requested religious objects from Sakya Trichen to protect the remaining family members against harm from weapons. In response,
Sakya Trichen sent him shirts that his father and uncle had worn, and
a *kha btags*, a white silk scarf, with eleven knots tied in it. While the
Pangdatsang family was now well protected, Khampa Aten's trou-
bles were just beginning. In the following paragraphs, I present a
paraphrase of Alo Chondzed's narration of the story.

---

[336] Interview, Anonymous, November 3, 1997, Kathmandu.
[337] The Tibetan spelling is *A lo chos mdzad.* I transliterate this name as Alo Chonzed, following his own preference—Alo Chhonzed—but with a single rather than
double 'h.'
[338] Chonzed 1983.
[339] See French 1995 on political and legal status of murder cases and those involving important persons, especially pp.115-6.
[340] Khri chen 1974, 2:51-3.

Khampa Aten was arrested for the murder of Pangda Nyigyal be-cause of his association with the Dzangtsatsang family. This family, Khampa traders from Lithang, was suspected of competition with the Pangdatsang family. Based on his association with the Dzang-tsa-tsangs, Khampa Aten was placed in the Shol Pangting Prison below the Potala, the Dalai Lama's palace and monastery. He protested his innocence to no avail. He was whipped with the "Interrogation Whip" *(tsha 'dri rta lcag mang po gzhus)* and received the stone hat *(rdo zhwa)* treatment of popping out one's eyeballs *(mig hril phyir 'don ba'i khrims gcod byas)*. He was made to kneel on tiny stones in front of Pangda Yamphel, but he still did not confess to the murder. Finally, without any resolution on his innocence or guilt, he was dismissed from prison. Upset that his innocence had not yet been proved, Khampa Aten demanded to know who had accused him of the crime. There was "nothing Aten could do—he had been wrong-fully accused, severely tortured, and he thought to himself, "I need to temporarily accept this suffering and retaliate against my enemy in the future."" He went home, continued to press for details about his accuser, and as time passed, became more and more agitated with the lack of movement on the case. He decided to take action, specifically to kill two people—one prison official and one member of the Pang-datsang family—the two groups that he thought "were the only ones against me." He began to make arrangements to get his family safely out of town to distant Golok in Amdo and to draft up his own assas-sination plans.

In the midst of his planning, Khampa Aten received two important visitors. Two officials of Sera monastery, from the Mey Pomra Col-lege, the Venerable Adzadipijak and the administrator Lori came to visit. They advised Aten keep his Khampa bravado in check and to seek redress through legal channels. Their counsel to him was as follows:

> Concerning your problem, by immediately retaliating without knowing who caused the problem, that is, if you go past the point of no return by showing the Sign of Kham (*i.e.*, by retaliating),[341] then it will be difficult for those [family members] who have left and those who have stayed. Beyond that, it is important for you to wait for a legal decision on your innocence or guilt. We think that we should all go together to see the current powerful renowned aristocrat of the Tibetan Govern-

---

[341] In Tibetan, *khams rtags bstan,* meaning to retaliate, to kill, to be brave.

ment, Ara Karpo, the Chamberlain of the Potala (*mgron gnyer chen mo*).[342] We will ask him to tell His Holiness the Dalai Lama that you were wrongfully accused of killing Pomda Nyijang[343] and were tortured by means of the stone hat, etc., and finally, no decision was ever made on your innocence or guilt. By telling this, a decision on your innocence or guilt will be made in a short time and we will have no regrets.

These two lamas were the family's spiritual advisors and Aten accepted their advice, shelving his assassination plan. Twice the three men appeared before Ara Karpo, the Chamberlain. Aten was told that the case would be resolved gradually, and that he was to remain calm until the resolution. Ara Karpo gave him religious offerings (*phyag tsha* and *dam rdzas*), and told him to accept that "through the grace of the Three Jewels *(dkon mchog gsum)*,[344] the power of truth, and the uncheating nature of karma, the wrongfully accused may be cleared. The recent torture of the wrongfully accused will cleanse the bad karma from the murder of Takya's son, etc."[345] This advice calmed Khampa Aten, such that "the fire went out and the smoke disappeared." The crime remained unsolved for many years. Finally, the situation became clear—the murder was due to jealousy, but the jealous party was not the Dzangtsatsang family.

Earlier, His Holiness the Thirteenth Dalai Lama had appointed two of his favorites, the Honorable Tsarong Dasang Damdrul and Pangda Nyigyal, to high government posts. Tsarong and Pangda were equally wealthy and there were jealousies between them. During the Universal Smoke Offering Festival, Tsarong hired General Tsogo to shoot Pangda in Lhasa's Twentieth Park. General Tsogo, however, was not just the "red-handed murderer," but wealthy and powerful in his own right. Neither he nor Tsarong were ever accused of or punished for the crime. Eventually Tsarong confessed that Gen-

---

[342] "Ara Karpo" means "white beard," a nickname for the Potala Chamberlain, Tempa Dargye.

[343] Alo Chonzed uses not just the Spom mda' spelling of the family name, but gives Nyigyal's name as Nyi jang. This appears to be a variation on the Khampa contraction of Nyi rgyam for Nyigyal.

[344] The "Three Jewels" are the Buddha, the dharma, and the sangha.

[345] Although Alo Chonzed writes that Aten believed his connection to the Dzangtsatsang family was the cause for his arrest, it appears that his connection to another murder, *i.e.*, of "Takya's son," was also a cause for suspicion. Later in the text, Alo Chonzed states that "Killer" Uncle Aten's reputation for great bravery also cast suspicion on him.

eral Tsogo was the culprit, and as a result, Uncle Aten was released from jail.[346] Following this, Chamberlain Ara Karpo, who had clearly known the persons involved, pardoned Khampa Aten.

His name cleared, Khampa Aten benefited from acts of contrition by the Tsarong and Pangdatsang families. Both families gave Aten generous assistance as a result of his suffering from being wrongfully accused. He received "money, goods, start-up funds for business *(tshong rtsa)*, and so on." The families were also generous to Alo Chonzed, sharing their secrets with him *(nga rang la snying gtam bshad pa)* and providing him with business assistance *(tshong mkhos)*. The new bonds between Aten's family and the Tsarong and Pangda families seemingly erased his suffering in prison. Alo Chonzed closes his discussion of Pangda Nyigyal's assassination with this confirmation of the new good relations between families—"From that, we remained as friends with sincere minds clear as a cloudless sky and dustless ground." Thus ends Alo Chonzed's version of the Pangda Nyigyal's murder.

For Aten and Alo Chonzed, the story had a happy ending. Things were well in Lhasa. However, was the murder solved? Were Tsarong and Tsogo really responsible for the murder? In exile, most people claim "they have heard" that the person behind the killing of Pangda Nyigyal was Tsarong. However, there have always been other stories in circulation, and recently one of these was revived. In addition to the suspicions cast on Tsarong, people would say that a Khampa family was behind the assassination. While some were possibly referring to the Dzangtsatsang family, others meant a different family, from a different part of Kham altogether. A recent arrival to New York, a man from Derge, claims that a Derge Khampa was responsible for Nyigyal's murder. His story was told to me by a third party, a Khampa man who had always believed that Tsarong was behind the assassination. This story goes as follows:

> Pangda Nyigyal had two Khampa business managers, brothers who had worked for him for many years and who were from Derge. They decided to desert his firm without telling him and set off for Jyekundo. Pangda got word of their scheme and got the Central Tibetan Government to arrest them upon their arrival in Jyekundo. There was a scuffle during their arrest and the eldest brother was killed. The younger

---

[346] A biography of Tsarong, written by his son, was recently published. The Pangdatsang family is not mentioned in it. See Tsarong 2000.

brother made his way back to Derge where he stayed for several years, plotting his return to Lhasa and his revenge on Pangda. When he did go back to Tibet, he and a servant carried out the plan, enlisting the services of a Khampa beer maid to find Pangda Nyigyal in the closed tents. The Khampa man—whose name I don't know—escaped back to Derge, but his servant was eventually arrested, sent to jail, tortured and died there. The story was kept as a community secret by the villagers who feared the repercussions from the Pangda family. It is only now, they say, in the times of the Chinese, when Pangda is no longer power-ful, that the story can be told.[347]

Histories untold are not necessarily forgotten. Khampas from this area of Derge, for example, preserved this story about Pangda Nyi-gyal's murder, restricting its circulation until the repercussions for telling the story diminished. The lack of a need for closure for this history of a murder is partially a product of Tibetan forms of truth. In her study of the Tibetan legal system, Rebecca French identifies two forms of truth: as "an ideal and separate standard" and "as consen-sus." Truth as consensus was factual consonance: "the facts given by both sides had to agree, not with reality, but with each other."[348] The story of Pangda Nyigyal's assassination contains elements of both kinds of truths without assigning ranked value to them. Truth as ideal and separate standard told the story of what happened, while truth as factual consonance revealed (partially) who did it. In the 1920s, both Pangda and Tsarong were families that were on the rise, and as the next three decades passed, each family only grew more powerful. The possibilities for history, and for types of historical truth, were limited by the social politics of the day.

Feuds between powerful families in the insular world of the Ti-betan aristocracy could be socially and economically destructive, something that these ambitious families could not afford. It was not in the best interest of either to carry on a public and violent feud with the other family. Nor was it in the interest of curious spectators to solve crimes of murder and history that those in power chose to leave publicly unsolved. Tibetan society in 1920s Lhasa was full of rigid social divisions that have spilled over into the exile community. To-day's narrators in exile include the same cautious qualifications in their story of who was responsible for the murder that their mothers and grandfathers included in the versions they told them: "People

---

[347] Interview, Kalsang Gyatotsang, April 6, 2000, New York.
[348] French 1995:137.

suspect it was Tsarong," "Tsarong was always said to be the killer," and the like. To level such a charge at a powerful aristocrat—for Tsarong represented not just himself, but his family, as did Pangda Nyigyal—would be to invite trouble upon oneself, and it might also be lying.

The passage of time brings with it changes in sociopolitical arrangements, some drastic, such as the creation of a refugee community and exile government, and some more subtle, such as the persistence of ascribed status amidst a new recognition of achieved status in exile. These changes shift the boundaries for history and for truth. Alo Chonzed, socially and politically estranged from the Tibetan status quo, and "sharing secrets" with the Tsarong and Pangda families, wrote that Tsarong and Tsogo were the killers, and that this was the ideal and separate truth. Derge villagers, recognizing the Pangdatsang family's loss of retributive power, challenged the consensus truth that Tsarong was responsible for the murder, installing instead their own candidate for the role of singularly true murderer. These shifting parameters of truth do not change the possibility for the joint existence of both forms, nor do they diminish the importance of truth for Tibetans. While Tibetans in general place a high premium on the reliability of one's word, Khampas in particular take pride (to a fault in the opinion of other Tibetans) in being straightforward and honest. They also, however, as was shown with the two monks' scolding of Khampa Aten, are renowned for their bravery and obstinacy. "To show the Sign of Kham," *khams rtags bstan,* meant to retaliate, to kill, to be brave. As the saying goes, the best horses are from Amdo, the best religion from U-Tsang, and the best *men* from Kham.

Pangda Nyigyal's sons were Khampas from head to toe, inside and out, according to their descendants. In this instance, however, they forsook Khampa traditions of honor for aristocratic notions of propriety, choosing not to push for a definitive solution to, or public airing of, the crime. Although they suspected Tsarong, they chose to focus on sponsoring ceremonies for their deceased father rather than seeking revenge for his murder.[349] Years later, when his daughter

---

[349] Sakya Trichen reports conducting numerous ceremonies on behalf of Pangda Nyigyal following his murder; the last recorded one was in 1932, the same year that Nyigyal's mother Tenzin Zangmo died, and four years before Sakya Trichen himself passed away. Khri chen 1974, 2:605.

asked him about the murder, Pangda Yamphel told her not to think or speak about it. "So many people were punished by the government that it is best not to talk about it, just to leave it as it is," he would say.[350] He kept his word, for his daughter learned only later from friends that Tsarong was suspected of the crime; in the Pangdatsang household, at least between generations, the murder was not discussed. Families have their secrets, their censored stories, and they keep these concealed from the rest of the world as well as from each other.[351] Nyigyal's death, however, transcended the realm of family history into that of public story. The public and dramatic murder of Pangda Nyigyal, a small-scale trader from Kham self-made into a man of power in Lhasa—a Tibetan variation on the American dream—was and is a story that people tell conspiratorially, heads shaking in disbelief. We may never know whether Tsarong was indeed behind the murder, or if he merely patronized Khampa Aten and his family to cover for another's deeds. Likewise were the brothers from Derge indeed the killers and not just fabricating their own "Sign of Kham" story once they had returned back home from the big city? We may never know, and yet this history is by no means unfinished.

Conclusion

While Pangda Nyigyal's untimely death left few documentary traces, it left a visible imprint on the social imagination of numerous Tibetans. Implicit in many of the stories I was told about him, and explicit in some, was the linking of his death to his growing economic and social power. Khampa traders were not unique in Lhasa; however, ones who amassed stupendous wealth and who made inroads into insular Lhasa society were unique, and in some regards, unwelcome. Histories of Pangda Nyigyal's murder contain the same sort of social hesitancy that accompanied relations between wealthy Khampa traders and established Lhasa aristocrats. These histories go only so far, following the push and pull between the currents of change and those of social protocol. Nyigyal, from a Sakya family, was not just indebted to the Thirteenth Dalai Lama, but devoted to him, and taught the same devotion to his children. With the death of the Dalai Lama

---

[350] Interview, Wangmo Yuthok Pangdatsang, June 2, 2000.
[351] See the rich discussion of the poetics and politics of family pasts in Kuhn 1995.

in 1933, Pangda Nyigyal's sons were among those who maintained visions of a modern Tibet. Their stories, which I tell elsewhere, are held accountable to the same mix of social hierarchies and political commitments, albeit hierarchies and commitments adjusted in response to a different, and more urgent, series of changes.

In closing, I return to the story of Nyigyal's assassination, to a prophecy of the almost simultaneous rise and fall of a family. For Nyigyal had been warned not to go to the picnic. It was a bad month, *'tshub chen po red,* one full of obstacles, according to Sakya Trichen Takshu Tinley Rinchen. Nyigyal's wife came to the same conclusion. She had the ability to go into trance, which the Sakya Trichen himself had witnessed. He wrote that she "was said to be entered by Dorje Drakden and to prophesy worldly activities which appeared to be surprisingly real." He inspected her while she was in trance, and wrote, "It looked to be true."[352] While in trance, she told Nyigyal not to go to the party. He promised her that he would not spend the night, that there would be lots of servants on watch, and that she should not worry as nothing would happen. As it turned out, it was raining, it was a dark and stormy night, the servants were seeking their own shelter elsewhere, and the rest, as they say, is history.

---

[352] Khri chen 1974, 1:421. He writes, "Yangchen, the wife of Nyigyal Gyakeg Pomdatsang was said to get entranced...."

BIBLIOGRAPHY

Bell, Sir Charles. *The People of Tibet.* Delhi: Motilal Banarsidass Publishers, 1992 [1928].

Cassinelli, C.W. and Robert B. Ekvall. *A Tibetan Principality: The Political System of Sa sKya.* Ithaca: Cornell University Press, 1969.

Chogay Trichen Rinpoche [Thubten Legshay Gyatsho]. *The History of the Sakya Tradition: A Feast for the Minds of the Fortunate.* Bristol: Ganesha Press, 1983.

Chonzed, Alo. *Bod kyi gnas lugs bden 'dzin sgo phye ba'i lde mig zhes bya ba a lo chos mdzad kyi gdams, spyi lo 1920 nas 1982 bar (The Key That Opens the Door of Truth to the Tibetan Situation: Materials on Modern Tibetan History).* Australia, 1983.

Cohn, Bernard S. *Colonialism and Its Forms of Knowledge: The British In India.* Princeton: Princeton University Press, 1996.

French, Rebecca Redwood. *The Golden Yoke: The Legal Cosmology of Buddhist Tibet.* Ithaca: Cornell University Press, 1995.

Khri chen Drag shul Phrin las rin chen. *Rdo rje 'chang drag shul phrin las rin chen gyi rtogs brjod (The Autobiographical Reminiscences of Khri-chen Drag-shul-phrin-las-rin-chen of Sa-skya).* 2 Volumes. Dehra Dun: Sakya Centre, 1974.

Kuhn, Annette. *Family Secrets: Acts of Memory and Imagination.* London: Verso, 1995.

McGranahan, Carole Mei. "On Swallowing a Living Person: Boundary Disputes in Kham between Tibet, China, and Great Britain, 1913-1934." In Alex McKay, ed. *The History of Tibet, Volume 3: The Tibetan Encounter with Modernity,* Richmond, Surrey: Curzon Press, in press.

McKay, Alex. *Tibet and the British Raj: The Frontier Cadre, 1904-1947.* Richmond, Surrey: Curzon Press, 1997.

Muir, Edward, and Guido Ruggiero, eds. *History from Crime: Selections from Quaderni Storici.* Baltimore: Johns Hopkins University, 1994.

Nebesky-Wojkowitz, Rene de. *Oracles and Demons of Tibet: The Cult and Iconography of the Tibetan Protector Deities.* The Hague: Mouton, 1956.

Norbu, Dawa. *Red Star Over Tibet.* New Delhi: Sterling Publishers, 1987.

Phu pa, Tshe ring stobs rgyas. *Gangs can bstan srung blangs dmag: Smar khams sgang gi rgyal srung dmag 'thab lo rgyus (The Volunteer Army to Defend Buddhism and Tibet: The History of Markham's Battle to Defend Tibet).* Dharamsala: Narthang Press, 1998.

Portelli, Alessandro. "The Peculiarities of Oral History." In *History Workshop Journal* 12:96-107, 1981.

Sakya, Jamyang and Julie Emery. *Princess in the Land of Snows: The Life of Jamyang Sakya in Tibet.* Boston: Shambhala, 1990.

Samuel, Geoffrey. *Civilized Shamans: Buddhism in Tibetan Societies.* Washington, DC: Smithsonian Institution Press, 1993.

Scarry, Elaine. "The Made-Up and the Made-Real." In Marjorie Garber *et al.*, eds. *Fieldwork: Sites in Literary and Cultural Studies,* New York: Routledge Press, 1996, pp.214-224.

Shakabpa, Tsepon W.D. *Tibet: A Political History.* New Haven: Yale University Press, 1967.

——*Bod kyi srid don rgyal rabs (Political History of Tibet).* 2 Volumes. Kalimpong: Shakabpa House, 1976.

Steedman, Carolyn. *Landscape for a Good Woman: A Story of Two Lives.* New Brunswick, NJ: Rutgers University Press, 1986.

Tsarong, Dundul Namgyal. *In the Service of His Country: The Biography of Dasang Damdul Tsarong, Commander General of Tibet.* Ani Trinlay Chondron, ed. Ithaca: Snow Lion Publications, 2000.

Wangdu, Pema. "Sa skya'i 'bag mo zhes pa byung tshul lo rgyus ngag rgyun du chags pa 'ga' zhig" ("Some Oral Histories of the Sakya Bagmo"). *Yum tsho* 3(3):46-50, 1995.

White, Hayden. *The Content of the Form: Narrative Discourse and Historical Representations.* Baltimore: Johns Hopkins University Press, 1987.

White, Luise. *Speaking with Vampires: Rumor and History in Colonial Africa.* Berkeley: University of California Press, 2000.

ন্যৃপ নথনব

HISTORY AS ORAL TRADITION: THE CONSTRUCTION OF COLLECTIVE IDENTITY IN BRAG G.YAB (KHAMS)

PETER SCHWIEGER (UNIVERSITY OF BONN)

Introduction

Twenty years ago I collected Tibetan oral literature among refugees from the Eastern Tibetan area of Brag g.yab. The material focussing on fairy tales and merry tales has long been published.[353] But some issues remain which I would like to address here, in particular the longer of two so-called *lo rgyus* that I recorded.

The term *lo rgyus,* which used by the native speakers themselves, is generally translated as "history." In the context of oral tradition it must be understood as a kind of "public local history," *i.e.*, general knowledge about local history circulating in public, often with the additional connotations of "legend" and "description of customs and traditions," but lacking the connotation of "life story" or "personally remembered or witnessed history." Nevertheless it may customarily or traditionally include personal memories. Therefore it seems to lie between what is generally understood by "History as Oral Tradition" and "Oral History."[354] By calling it *lo rgyus*, speakers designate a

---

[353] Phukhang and Schwieger 1982; Schwieger 1989.

[354] I originally chose the more concise term "Oral History" as equivalent to the Tibetan term *lo rgyus*, intending to refer primarily to the external form of how communications about the past is transmitted. Although there is no generally acknowledged definition of the term "Oral History," it is mostly restricted to the history of everyday life and contemporary history (as well as to the specific scientific techniques used in research into those subjects). Nevertheless, the term may, according to Vorländer (1990:11), also refer to oral transmission of historical knowledge through many generations, especially in regard to cultures without writing (*ibid.*:7-12). Apparently the text at hand lays greater stress on the distant past than on contemporary events and situations. To avoid any misunderstanding I therefore call the text in the heading "History as Oral Tradition," following the clear distinction made by Vansina (1985:12ff.): "The sources of oral historians are reminiscences, hearsay, or eyewitness accounts about contemporary events and situations, that is, which occurred during the lifetime of the informants. This differs from oral traditions in that oral traditions are no longer contemporary. They have passed from mouth to

specific kind of text. This not only implies that it has a distinct beginning and end, but also allows us to expect some coherence among the
different parts of the text.

I had not asked the narrators to tell me a *lo rgyus*. Rather it was
they who offered to tell me one, and I just recorded them in passing.
The longer one was narrated by a man called Tshering, then about
sixty, who had already lived in exile in Kathmandu for more than
twenty years.[355]

At first I had naively expected the *lo rgyus* would contain some
"valuable" information on so-called facts of regional history. In this
regard the result was quite thin.[356] So I put the records aside until recently when I wrote an article on how Tibetans construct their past in
their histories.[357]

In comparing historiography with what ordinary Tibetans own to
be history in their oral traditions, I became aware that the gaps,
missing links and corruptions are closer to the contingencies of real
life experience than the synthetically constructed plot structures of
historiographic literature. What I now present is not a regional history, but rather a direct view into how people see themselves, particularly in opposition to others. Thus we are able to gain insight into
how collective identity is created and shaped. Such narratives about
the distant past always refer to the history of a complete community.
Narrators tell us what is important to the way the community sees
itself, and are therefore representatives of collective memory.[358] I
concentrate on the longer version I recorded, because its contents are
more complex and more remote from what I would call the common

---

mouth, for a period beyond the lifetime of the informants." He adds: "As messages
are transmitted beyond the generation that gave rise to them they become oral traditions."

[355] While telling the *lo rgyus* there was no real audience other than me and a
young Tibetan named Sherab Lhawang, who had arranged the meeting. With
Sherab's assistance I did a phonetic transcription and a first translation of the
recording while still in Kathmandu, so that I could go back to the narrator to ask him
questions concerning difficult passages. I thank Tshering and Sherab for their help
and cooperation.

[356] The difficulties regarding the use of Tibetan oral literature as a source for historical studies has been discussed in some detail by Schuh 1994:11, 40ff. He also
presents the edition and translation of two such "narratives" (*ibid.*:12-34).

[357] Schwieger 2001.

[358] Cf. Ungern-Sternberg and Reinau 1988:4ff.

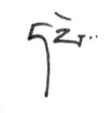

knowledge of monks.[359] I approach the text employing different levels:

1. I begin with what confronts us directly, to wit the language (linguistic-syntactical analysis).

2. I continue on the semantic level.

3. I then determine what kind of text such a *lo rgyus* actually is in the context of oral literature (analysis of the text type).

4. Finally I explore the sociocultural level, asking how such a text constitutes collective identity (function and horizon of the text)

Linguistic-Syntactical Analysis

The whole story contains 232 "parole sentences" and a total of about 4000 lexical formatives, excluding varieties. The vocabulary is simple and limited, and the narrator makes no effort to avoid repetition, for example, by using synonyms. Most of his words are part of simple everyday colloquial language, and lacks honorific language, except the occasional polite form for inviting (*gdan 'dren zhu*) a highly respected lama.

Stylistic analysis shows nothing comparable with what one finds in elaborated written literature. This is typical of oral literature in general, insofar as it is not influenced by literacy. We know from Walter J. Ong's studies[360] that literacy makes it possible not only to write and read a language, but also to speak a written language.

Most of the verbs are simple, common and pale words like "to say," "to do," "to make," "to go," and "to come." Noticeable is the small number of adjectives, the majority of which are restricted to color details (fourteen times) and size, like "small," "large" or "big" (seven times). There are also few single adjectives describing general qualities, like "good," "poor," "rich" and "old." As a superlative the narrator uses the adjectives *dpe*, and *dpe ma srid pa*. There are nearly no colorful adjectives able to evoke sequences of vivid images in the listener's mind.

---

[359] This of course does not in principle exclude the possibility of interactions between the oral and the written. Some of the data or structures, for instance the succession line of the lamas of Brag g.yab, may have originated primarily in written texts.

[360] Ong 1982.

The cohesion[361] of the text is mainly effected by simple temporal adverbs like "then" (*de, de nas*), "now" (*da*), "once" (*gcig*), demonstrative pronouns (*'di, de*) and repetition. Often just one and the same linguistic element is repeated. This element might be just one word or even half a sentence (see, for example: lines 43 and 44 of the translation below.) But, of course, different pronouns, especially deictic ones, also serve the same function (see, *e.g.*, line 26). Most sentences are short and simple. Sometimes several of them are loosely strung together in an additive way through linking particles. Where there are subordinate clauses they use the particle *nas,* which I normally translate in a temporal or modal sense. There are only three causal conjunctions in the whole text. This already hints at the fact that there are no real plot structures, making the *lo rgyus* in the oral context something entirely different from the historiographic literature. Several times the cohesion of the text is interrupted by breaks, incomplete sentences, confusing grammatical constructions or rhetorical questions that indicate uncertainty, gaps in memory, time to think, or in general the openness of what could be said next.

Semantic Analysis

The coherence[362] of the entire text seems to be merely associative. Sometimes we have the impression that we are able to observe how one idea results in another. After a while a string of associations is used up, and a totally new one has to be started, subdividing the text into different chapters. These subdivisions and determining their respective messages allows a further approach. Altogether we may distinguish nine chapters with quite different topics.

I. The text lacks an introductory formula as, for instance, in fairy tales. It starts immediately with the setting (four phrases), an incomplete and undated list of the names of the successive hierarchs of Brag g.yab. This list serves as a pattern for the temporal dimension of what is called Brag g.yab.[363] Before the institution of the so-called

---

[361] *I.e.,* the way the elements of the text are interwoven through linguistic means (Vater 1994:32; Adamzik 2001:284).

[362] *I.e.,* meaning continuity. Coherence is essential for shaping what may be called a text (Vater 1994:43, 65).

[363] "Each culture has its own notions of time, and calendars do not exist in oral society…. Chronology need not be based on an absolute calendar, it can be a relative

Brag g.yab Skyabs mgon Rin po che, there was no area or province called Brag g.yab. As a province it came into existence only through the establishment of the Brag g.yab bla ma. No data are given describing the spatial dimension.

II. After this brief setting, we gain the first impression that the real story has started, and a sequence of different episodes in chronological order unfolds (seventeen sentences). We hear a kind of origin story of how Brag g.yab, and at the same time the institution of its main lama, came into being. As is typical of folk tales, marvelous elements increase throughout the story. The chapter is loosely connected to the following one.

III. The first Skyabs mgon is credited with founding the most important religious ceremony for the common people, the Ma ṇi bum bsgrub (forty-four sentences). But then the narrator abandons the chronological and historical perspective, and continues to describe important public religious ceremonies and feasts in Brag g.yab, especially the 'cham dance.

IV. The next chapter breaks substantively from the previous ones, because we find here no actors or actions at all (twenty-three sentences). This chapter is a short explanation of what and how many monasteries are to be found in the Brag g.yab Ma dgon and Bu dgon monastic complexes.

V. This is a chapter of fairy tale-like stories, fantastic phenomena to be found in Brag g.yab: gold tax-paying ants, grass tax-paying wind, a tax-collecting mule, and a self-created Maitreya statue, later destroyed by the Chinese, but whose torso no one was able to remove from its original place (twenty-nine sentences).

VI. Next is a popular metaphor which relates the different parts of Brag g.yab and their monasteries to the figure of the snow lion (seven sentences).

VII. There follows a very brief description of the people, described as semi-nomads. This topic is not highly elaborated (ten sentences).

VIII. The narrator then returns to a more narrative style, telling us little historical episodes about the Brag g.yab bla ma, the official representative of Brag g.yab, and his relations with the central gov-

---

sequence of events and situations only" (Vansina 1985:73). Vansina (*ibid.*:179) says that "oral lists are kept when they have a social meaning, though they are never very long. If they were, one would suspect backfeeding from writing."

ernment in Lhasa (ninety-two sentences). This is by far the longest chapter. This fact already marks the topic which the narrator emphasizes when he speaks about what Brag g.yab is, concentrating on the relationship between the periphery and the cultural, political and religious center.

IX. The conclusion is a kind of bracket, interpreting the whole *lo rgyus* as a legend (*sgrung*), making it appear less important and reliable than more prestigious written historiography (six sentences).

Analysis of the Text Type (Literary Criticism)

Deducing the actual intent of such a text—why is it composed and what kind of function it fulfills—may let us determine what kind of *lo rgyus* this text is. The narrator himself qualifies it as a *sgrung* (line 227), a word generally signifying "story," "folk tale," "legend," indeed any kind of "fiction." In this way the narrator tries to be modest, saying that what he tells lacks literary or bookish authority. He further describes at the end the way the origin (*'byung khungs*) of Brag g.yab used to be told.

But when we ask where and what the organization of a sequence of events belonging together is—the beginning, center and end of what could be called a well-formed story, we do not find any. Instead we have loosely connected, rather heterogeneous chapters. In some a descriptive character prevails, in others a narrative one. What the individual chapters all have in common is the aim of explaining, from different points of view, the constitution of the phenomenon called Brag g.yab. Brag g.yab is not explained categorically, but in terms of practical situations and situational thinking.[364] The different points of view are connected to each other in an additive, rather than a causal, way. Only in some parts do we recognize narrative features, and only in some parts does the text deal with changes of situation, present events which are combined in sequences, and introduce real actors whose actions are related to changes. Mostly the events and actions are not combined in a real plot structure. Rather than saying, for example, "First the queen died and then the king died of grief," the text would say "First the queen died, then the king." The simple syntax seems to refer to a social world without complex structures.

---

[364] Ong 1982:51.

Only in Chapter VIII do we have real pairs of actors who communicate with each other or who act as opponents. Here we therefore observe more often the use of direct speech that vitalizes the narration, the early stages of distinctive narrative structures like interesting plot construction, resolution of complications and evaluation by the narrator.[365]

I am tempted to assign the single elements of the text to different well-known text types. The element of the fantastic and wonderful I would assign to fairy tales,[366] of cunning, shrewdness and cleverness to picaresque stories,[367] what is told about the monasteries, feasts and people to the descriptive type,[368] the listing of the successive lamas to the genealogical type,[369] and so forth. However, no type is really developed in detail, and the text presents itself as a loosely integrated and fleeting whole. It might appear only once in this specific form. The next time it is told, its parts could just as well be combined in a different way, adding new ones or skipping others.[370]

Function and Horizon of the Text

As originally the case with folk and fairy tales, this *lo rgyus* has its place in an oral environment, lacking the strict forms and formal

---

[365] Regarding the criteria which constitute a well-formed story, see the brief description in Gergen 1998:171-181.

[366] Lüthi 1979:5; Wilpert 1969:463.

[367] Wilpert 1969:683.

[368] *I.e.*, the characteristic feature of this text type is the function of information (Brinker 1997:106).

[369] Strictly speaking, the structure of the genealogies of the Middle Ages was already more complex than a mere list. Hence it often was presented in the form of a genealogical tree (Goetz 1993:98ff.; see also Vansina 1985:182). But the ties of reincarnation constitute more than the loose connection within a list of offices. In this regard, they are similar to the family-based ties of a genealogy.

[370] One is forced to the conclusion that the text at hand is not a memorized speech. It looks more like an account, but it lacks a stabilized form (Vansina 1985:14, 17.) Although the text incorporates features of different text types, it does not just mix any popular type drawn from Tibetan oral literature. Following the narrative style, *i.e.*, everyday language, it entirely lacks verses and formulaic speech patterns which characterize the oral epic poem presented by special bards (cf. *ibid.*:13; for a definition of the "formulaic system," see Parry 1971:272, 275.). Several typical text types in Tibetan oral literature, focussing on oral literature collected in Mustang (Nepal), are briefly described in Kretschmer 1986:421-429.

language of written literature. Like folk tales, this *lo rgyus* is not produced and consumed *in vacuo*, but was told in small communities among families, friends, neighbors, traveling companions, and so on. The narrator includes the audience by slipping in specific explanations of single facts (lines 8-10, 98-99, 101), by using gestures (lines 109-12), by asking spontaneous rhetorical questions, etc. In this way a kind of unity is created among those present, who share this common knowledge, recognizing it as their own. This is possible only when the subjects spoken of have relevance for people and their lives; they would otherwise drop into oblivion. The knowledge shared by this kind of story telling is also kept alive only by the story telling process, since, in an oral economy, there is no place to store it other than in people's minds.

My impression is that the example I recorded twenty years ago in an exile situation already reflects the stage of fading away. The different parts which contribute to the image of Brag g.yab are still there, but have become pale and rudimentary, with many details forgotten. The context in which such a text was originally told is lost, due not only to refugee life, but also to economic, social and cultural changes in general, including the influence of new media. Guaranteed by the individuals who formed the specific community, the atmosphere in which this kind of literature can survive is gone.[371] Moreover, in an oral culture, collective identity is itself to a large degree constituted through story telling.[372]

---

[371] A variety of performance contexts may have originally existed (Vansina 1985:34). When I recorded Tibetan fairy tales among refugees in India, I became aware of the importance of the community for the survival of oral traditions, and first tried to create a suitable story-telling atmosphere (Schwieger 1989:7ff.). However, recording tales in a more traditional milieu makes a huge difference, *e.g.*, the readiness to tell tales (Kretschmar 1986:417-419), or the formal occasions that traditional societies provide for performance (*ibid.*:417; Vansina 1985:19).

[372] There is no other way to constitute identity through time. Monuments, pictures, landmarks, etc. can only act in such a capacity in combination with stories which "explain" how the presence of a community has a common history and origin. Monuments, etc. function as proof for the correctness and authenticity of the story (Röhrich 1988:95; Vansina 1985:44-46). As long as there are no other media, such as written texts, these stories must be retold to keep them alive and shared as common property. Members of a community who especially regard these as stories of their own history, feel the need to tell them to each other. While it is often the case that a community adopts a story from outside, the story is reformulated and adapted to local specifics and circumstances (for examples, see Röhrich 1988:93ff., 97).

In telling these kinds of stories there may always have been a tendency to forget details; parts of the story broke away, but certainly to a minor degree. In a traditional context the audience, familiar with the specific story, was able to confirm, correct or supplement what was told. Like fairy tales, these stories did not function to tell of something new or provide hitherto unknown information. Telling and listening helped to keep specific knowledge alive, and this ongoing process prevented the story from becoming too fragmented.[373]

Heterogeneous texts such as these were told and handed down to give one's own social group a collective identity, functioning like a mirror capable of reflecting features of self and other in temporal and spatial dimension.[374] Identity is a matter of awareness, reflexivity upon an unconscious self-image. Such self-awareness of a specific tribe, people or nation—insofar as it understands, imagines and describes itself in such terms[375]—forms an identity that allows a social group to maintain a social order and to give social life a lasting orientation.[376]

The self-image of Brag g.yab presented in our text contains only a few pale hints about indigenous social relationships. As a homogeneous entity Brag g.yab is confronted with the outer world, and the constitution of its own identity is marked by the opposition of periphery versus center. The only other outsiders are the Chinese, mentioned five times, but only in passing and only to add some relevant explanations. Neither does the narrator differentiate among Chinese, who play no part in constituting local identity. Lhasa alone is substantial as the cultural and religious center.

The relationship to Lhasa is not described in abstract categories or even comprehensive descriptions, but rather in short narrative episodes, containing the elements of actors and of actions. The central actor is the first Brag g.yab bla ma Grags pa rgya mtsho (1572-1638/39). But this figure lacks much in common with the real historical figure, or even with the picture drawn of him in the histo-

---

[373] Assmann (1999:97) maintains that in the world of oral tradition the innovation and information potential of texts is low. Only oral texts which bring up subjects already extensively known are preserved by cultural memory. Quite the opposite is true in regard to the written tradition.

[374] Rüsen 1998:22.

[375] Assmann 1999:130, 132ff.; Gergen 1998:199ff.

[376] Wagner 1998:50ff.

riographic literature.[377] In the context of the oral *lo rgyus,* he is the kind of symbolic figure and "flat" character into which the past is typically condensed in cultural memory. He functions as a hero, who, when confronted with a more powerful opponent, gets what he wants by means of cleverness.

The episodes combined in chapter VIII all present the center as the undoubtedly more powerful and hegemonically superior part. But they also present a model of how to get along with a superior partner and how to get what one wants within such a relationship. In this way such stories help provincial peoples feel less powerless. Their means and methods—cunning and shrewdness—are the typical weapons of the weak, but nevertheless clever, junior partner.

The goal of these actions was to achieve recognition of the Brag g.yab bla ma's high status not only in Khams, but also in the center, Lhasa. Without actually saying so, this recognition includes special esteem for Brag g.yab as a whole, and the narrator explains that the Brag g.yab bla ma, together with the 'Phags pa lha from Chamdo, were revered as the highest lamas in Khams. In his homeland the Brag g.yab bla ma is always addressed as Skyabs mgon Rin po che, a title generally accorded the Dalai Lama. According to the *lo rgyus,* this special respect and veneration was originally restricted to his homeland. It was due only to his cleverness that he also gained the right to use specific symbols of high status in Lhasa as well, such as a sedan-chair, ceremonial umbrellas and a representative building in Lhasa. He did not frankly request permission to use these symbols. For instance, when he wanted to build a house in Lhasa, he modestly requested permission to build a house on a piece of land the size of an animal skin. When this was granted, he cut the skin into a small strip the way one peels an apple. The resulting spiral was laid down so that it covered a much larger piece of land.

These episodes demonstrate vividly the practical aspects of such a text type. They present a kind of moral, telling peripheral peoples the most promising way to deal with a superior center. They do this not by using explicit recommendations, instructions, or even reasonable arguments, but by showing the results of such actions.[378]

---

[377] For the historiographic literature on Grags pa rgya mtsho, see Schwieger and Dagyab 1989.

[378] Cf. Straub 1998:157, 159, 165.

The way a peripheral people is described in this *lo rgyus* may function even more strictly than a mere guide for promising behavior.[379] It is generally known that the way people are classified interacts with the people so classified.[380] Each of us "inhabits" certain historical stories,[381] and each of us is a construct of such stories— about our people, our culture, nation, region, family, and so on. Due to such stories, the people of Brag g.yab see themselves as something particular, and simultaneously as having certain characteristics. Telling simple stories like these helps a social group to define and maintain a distinct unity.

At the beginning, right after the setting, the narrator tells a kind of foundation legend or origin myth, the fairy tale-like story of a raven who guides the first lama to the place where he founds the first Dge lugs pa monastery. In the next chapter he goes on to relate how this lama established the Ma ni bum bsgrub ceremony. When all this happened is not specified; somehow it was in the beginning, before the time remembered through personal and communicated experience of the living. This alone is sufficient. More detailed historical knowledge is merely knowledge of the recent past or part of a more elaborated written literature. Thus it seems quite natural that the only detailed portion of the *lo rgyus* is the passage describing the the Ma ni bum bsgrub ceremony, an event which clearly belongs to the personal experience of the narrator.

Nevertheless this short origin story expresses historical awareness, a fixed presence of the knowledge that a people and all their institutions exist in time, that they have an origin and also a future. In general, social groups base a consciousness of their unity and particularity on past events. Societies need the past especially to define their identities and selves. Strictly speaking there is no common history but only a variety of experiences. Memory is always a partial reconstruction of the past which takes into account and combines the

---

[379] Generally, this used to be one of the essential motives for the interest in history, regarded as a kind of "Orientierungsrahmen" (Konersmann 1996:339).

[380] Hacking 1999:31: "Ways of classifying human beings interact with the human beings who are classified. There are all sorts of reasons for this. People think of themselves as of a kind, perhaps, or reject the classification. All our acts are under descriptions, and the acts that are open to us depend, in a purely formal way, on the descriptions available to us." See also *ibid.*:103ff.

[381] Assmann 1999:17, 142.

tracks of the past according to present needs and interpretations.[382] The oral text at hand provides a form through which collective memory may be precipitated into individual consciousness. History can be distorted beyond recognition, with all but some prominent key events abridged. In historiographical literature, the events of the past have been selected as well, but they are reconstructed and combined into a plot that give meaning to contingency. The master plot in Tibetan historiographical literature, as I have pointed out elsewhere,[383] consists of incarnate Buddhas and Bodhisattvas acting for the welfare of Tibet and its people. In the oral *lo rgyus* recorded here, no plot governs the entire text unit. In some chapters the lama is also a pro-minent figure, but he does not act to save living beings from *saṃ-sāra*. He functions instead as a culture hero connected with the ori-gins and maintenance of Brag g.yab. Such figures function as signs to which memory is fastened, and as symbols for collective identity.

When a social group wants to consolidate itself as such, it creates certain places, feasts and customs as symbols of identity and cues for memory. In traditional, premodern societies such symbols were mostly taken from the sphere of religion, which functioned as the core of culture. It is therefore hardly surprising that monasteries and religious feasts were especially regarded as specific symbols of Brag g.yab identity. However the fairy tale-like stories about gold tax-paying ants, grass tax-paying wind, and a tax-collecting mule dem-onstrate that more secular topics can also help compose a special picture of local identity. Such stories serve also as explanations for specific phenomena to be found in Brag g.yab. For instance, circum-ambulating a specific heap of *ma ṇi* stones works as a medicine against tooth ache in the story about the tax-collecting mule, in whose memory these stones were laid down. The story is a sufficient explanation; rational argument over what a mule has to do with a tooth ache is unnecessary.

---

[382] Polkinghorne 1998:24. What is selected by the collective memory for transmission does not necessarily have to be correct, but important or meaningful. Cf. Röhrich 1988:90, 99.

[383] Schwieger 2001:960.

Conclusion

We can observe even in this modest oral text how the concept of Brag g.yab is constructed and its identity constituted. It is achieved through the conjunction of different prefabricated parts or concepts, such as: the succession of lamas, the first establishment of a religious and cultural center around which the social unit develops, the culture hero who patterns social behavior, special feasts, customs and wondrous phenomena. These give the whole unit a specific color, how monasteries structure social space, and so on. But we are also able to observe the fleeting nature of such a construct. Especially when the original conditions for its maintenance fade away, its single parts tend to become pale and rudimentary. Thus what we see is a genuine snapshot of the conditions of everyday culture in an oral economy.

Translation of the Lo rgyus

The following translation reflects the original oral speech as far as possible, including breaks, contradictions and confused sentences. It avoids literary and stylistic "improvements," corrections and elaborated explanations. The numbers follow the "parole sentences" of the speaker. An original linking particle is sometimes represented by a punctuation mark. My comments are added within brackets. Names are given in their common modern written form.[384]

I. Setting
  1. The first incarnations of the Brag g.yab bla ma are Grags pa rgya mtsho, Ngag dbang bsod nams lhun grub, Sprul sku Ngag dbang tshul khrims, Bla ma Blo bzang rnam rgyal, Dpal ldan bstan pa'i rgyal mtshan, Lung rigs mkhas btsun rgyal mtshan.[385]
  2. Up to the sixth incarnation I can list their names.
  3. Then the names of the next three incarnations I don't know very well.
  4. This is the ninth incarnation, the present one.
II. The Temporal Beginning

---

[384] I wish to thank Brag g.yab Rin po che for his assistance in identifying the place names.

[385] The last name actually refers to the seventh incarnation. The sixth was named Blo bzang thub bstan 'jigs med chos kyi rgya mtsho.

5. First this one, the one called *bka' bcu* Grags pa rgya mtsho, (also) called Bu gdugs dkar. He was born into a poor family. This Brag g.yab monastery was (at that time) called Brag g.yab Monastery.

6. Then meditating in a cave, when he was making *gtor ma* and so on, there came a raven. The raven carried the *gtor ma* molds away, carried them to a so-called open place.

7. At that place where the *gtor ma* are thrown, the open place, (there is a) s*e 'bru* (pomegranate tree); well, what shall I say?

8. Many different names are given to this s*e 'bru.*

9. In Tibet we say *se 'bru.*

10. S*e 'bru* is something which has seeds inside. On the outside it is red, something which you can eat.

11. Under such a tree he carried them, and Bu gdugs dkar followed him.

12. After having followed the raven he said, "If I construct a monastery here I probably would become a hermit king, but the monastery won't exist for a long time."

13. After having said this he built a monastery on that open place. Later, when the Chinese came, this monastery got destroyed.

14. So it happened.

15. Then Brag g.yab Ma dgon was built down there.

16. Then Brag g.yab Ma dgon, the place which is called the center (of Brag g.yab), was built down there.

17. Then he went to the monastery (*grwa sa*).

18. Living in that very monastery he gave teachings. This was the first, the first incarnation, the so-called *bka' bcu* Grags pa rgya mtsho.

19. Now, when I say, "What is his lineage?" it is said, "It is the lineage of *grub thob* Nyag smyon."

20. The lineage of *grub thob* Nyag smyon in the past in Tibet— those who were known as the ones from Ra ma rdzong—what is meant by native region, his birthplace, what is meant by his birthplace, it is the place called Ra ma rdzong in Tibet. It is said that he was from there.

21. Being born there, (this is) then his native place.

III. Religious Feasts, Religious Customs

22. Then his Ma ṇi bum bsgrub (ceremony), the one which lasts one month: the central government (*sde pa gzhung*) granted a kind of permission to establish it.

23. There was this. Then this Ma ṇi bum bsgrub was entrusted to the 'Bras spungs Nyag re khang tshan.

24. Oh, this is it.

25. Because in 'Bras spungs were those who study books of Buddhist philosophy, he thought, "If they assemble to (recite) the *ma ṇi* for about one month, the books of Buddhist philosophy can be neglected a bit."

26. He kept this in mind. "Over there I have the two monasteries Ma- and Bu dgon. They are very poor. Now in those two I will carry out the Ma ṇi bum bsgrub," he said. Then they used to carry out the Ma ṇi bum bsgrub in Brag g.yab—in Brag g.yab Ma- and Bu dgon, those two, starting from the twelfth calendar day of the eleventh month until the thirteenth calendar day of the twelfth—in those months.

27. Early in the dawn of the thirteenth calendar day, about three o'clock, if the recitation isn't yet finished, they have to count *ma ṇis* for two days and nights, the whole day and the whole night.

28. Now there were about 1500 monks.

29. These were divided up into four departments (*dum bu*) now.

30. When they were divided up into four departments, they made four departments for the daytime and four departments for the night time; then they had to recite the *ma ṇis*.

31. Then on the thirteenth calendar day the initiation was granted.

32. After the initiation has been granted, then on the following day, then on the fourteenth calendar day—on the thirteenth calendar day (!)—the Brag g.yab bla ma grants the initiation to the public.

33. If we pour about one *pāti* [a Nepalese measure, approximately 3.5 kgs.] of *ma ṇi* pills in [the speaker demonstrates], they will increase up to three *pāti* (coming) out of the bottle.

34. After countless *ma ṇis* have been accumulated the monks finish (the ceremony).

35. They present these *ma ṇis* in the monastery.

36. Then he confers the initiation.

37. The initiation is conferred by giving the *ma ṇi* pills to the families.

38. The day after...[break]. After the initiation has been granted, at the end, they perform the *'cham* dance.

39. They perform the *'cham* dance.

40. On that day the monks wear their best robes, their upper and lower garment, and perform the *'cham* dance.
41. Afterwards, on the next day, they wear the boots and the other, the good (costumes).
42. If there are no other good ones to wear, it can also be done.
43. When they wear the *'cham* costumes, the *'cham* costumes are made of brocade, aren't they?
44. They wear these *'cham* costumes and masks and black hats and so on. In the morning they perform the *'cham* dance.
45. Later they throw the *gtor ma*.
46. Regarding the so-called exhibition of the *gos sku* (*i.e.*, the large *thang ka*) on the fifteenth, the large *thang ka* must be cleaned.
47. In the past, that big *thang ka* was burned by the Chinese; later this place (!), this *thang ka*, couldn't be produced once more.
48. Cleaning the many small *thang kas* we wash and consecrate them.
49. Apart from this the earlier large *thang ka* does not exist anymore because it was burned by the Chinese.
50. Now (the small ones) are washed and consecrated.
51. Now regarding the so-called *gos sku:* now on the fifteenth the big assembly is finished.
52. Now on the sixteenth there is nothing at all.
53. On the seventeenth calendar day...[break]. There is now a monastic community of that Brag g.yab bla ma.
54. If this monastic community were in Tibet [*i.e.*, Central Tibet, Bod] it would be similar to the Rnam rgyal ra ba [*i.e.*, Rnam rgyal grwa tshang].
55. What is called the big *'cham* of that monastic community is this:
56. On that day they wear the monk robes and perform the *'cham*.
57. On the eighteenth calendar day they have to rest.
58. Now on the nineteenth the performance called *dgu 'cham:* performing the excellent *'cham* in that monastic community in an extraordinary way there are such good *'cham* costumes [the speaker underlines it with a gesture].
59. Then this evening they throw the *gtor ma*.
60. Starting with the twenty-third they prepare the *lo gsar dgu thug* [soup for the Tibetan New Year containing nine special ingredients] until the beginning of the New Year festival.
61. For one week starting with the twenty-third they make *gtor ma*.

62. The production of *gtor ma* is now done by all large assemblies, by all those monastic communities, by many different ones at the same time.
63. It is so. [break]
64. What has to be said now?
65. If I may say "the lama lineage," if I may say "the way they came," it is like that. [This statement refers to section II.]

IV. Spatial Structure

66. Now regarding how Brag g.yab Ma- and Bu dgon are situated, so it is like this: In that Ma dgon (area) there are thirty-two big monasteries. Including the great assembly (of all monastic communities) there are thirty-three, including Pasong.[386] It is said there are prostrations and offerings for thirty-three gods.
67. In the past the old people used to tell it this way.
68. In Bu dgon are twelve monasteries.
69. Adding the great assembly to the twelve monasteries there are thirteen.
70. Normally it is said that including Dpal rdo rje there are prostrations and offerings for thirteen gods.
71. Normally it is said like this but (further) there are the branch monasteries of the thirty-two head monasteries, the branches, the small ones scattered around. So today some monasteries are called the Gro shug monasteries.
72. Asking how it came that they were called Gro shug monasteries so it is like this: The so-called Gro ba monastery (and) the so-called Shug cog monastery became two components [syllables] within one word.
73. In this way down there two monasteries became one.
74. However there might be (altogether) seventy monasteries in Ma dgon.
75. It is similar in Bu dgon but they are summed up to twelve monasteries.
76. They are summed up.
77. Regarding the hermitages it is similar.
78. There are three Sa skya monasteries: Gtsang sar dgon pa, Tsher chung dgon pa and the other are a place in Sde gsum.
79. Apart from these three places I can't say it clearly.

---

[386] Not identified. It may be a small monastery.

80. Scattered all over are the hermitages of the Rnying ma, for those who practice individually. Apart from this I cannot say whether there are many.

81. I cannot say it.

82. Regarding the hermitages they are countless.

83. If now in such a family someone becomes old, when father and mother become old, they come down home in summer, look after the children, help to prepare the meal and so on.

84. When it becomes winter they store meat, butter, *rtsam pa*, wheat flour, everything including firewood in the hermitage and stay there counting *ma ṇis*.

85. Such abodes, hermitages, such hermitages—every family has such a small hermitage. There is hardly anyone who does not have such a one.

86. It is like this.

87. Apart from this, the big monasteries are all mixed but most of them are Dge lugs monasteries.

88. It is like this.

V. Wondrous, Astonishing Stories

89. Then at the place called Rang grub, as I have told—Rang grub stod ma, Rang grub—ants paid gold tax.

90. The breeze paid grass tax.

91. Inside there is a cave, there is a large cave.

92. By putting many loads of grass into it every day the wind used to pay grass tax.

93. At a place where the river falls down into a great lake called Sheep's Head Whirlpool, wood and carcasses of wild animals were carried (by the water). By this, it was said, venison tax was paid.

94. First it was like that, it is said: The ants paid gold tax.

95. Then there was a white mule called Dung bu ("son of a conch-shell" because it was so white).

96. There was a white mule.

97. Now regarding this white mule. . . [break].

98. In the past in Tibet we used to have a *srang ma* (scales).

99. Here now (in Nepal) it is the balance scale which has to be lifted up, isn't it?

100. First the scales, (then) the measuring jug to measure the grains, and further there usually is the so-called *dung* (a kind of sack).

101. In Central Tibet one calls it *phad* (sack), isn't it?

102. It is said that loading this on the mule and sending it away, the mule, without being accompanied by a man, went to collect taxes.

103. It is said that the mule didn't leave before being satisfied.

104. Lying down at the door it could not be persuaded to leave, it is said.

105. Later this mule died, it is said.

106. Regarding the white mule called Dung bu, there were a lot of *ma ṇi* inscriptions—what shall I say?—something like a *mchod rten*, a great commemorative column.

107. It is said if one has toothaches and walks around it, it will help.

108. Then in Brag g.yab Bu dgon there is an incredible spontaneously formed statue of the *jina* Maitreya.

109. Well, including the golden throne the size is like this [the speaker shows it with his hand].

110. Apart from the golden throne it is not more than about (the size of) myself.

111. Now the Chinese destroyed it totally. They destroyed it from here upwards, it is said. [The speaker roughly marks a diagonal line over the upper part of his body.]

112. It is said they destroyed it from here upwards. Whatever might be done, it is impossible to take (the rest of the statue) out of the house, it is said.

113. The door got stuck.

114. There was such a spontaneously formed statue of the *jina* Maitreya.

115. Then at the place called Ri mda' there is an incredible monastery of the Three Victorious Ones. Its three stories jut out of the front side of the rock.

116. At the place called Blang [or Glang] rung there was also (a monastery of) the Three Victorious Ones.

117. On the stone there were, well, silver and gold ribbons, ornaments, reliefs. There were such incredible reliefs that the sculptors from Lhasa never would be able to make them out of clay.

VI. Metaphor for Spatial Structure

118. What shall I say next?

119. If I now may talk about the description of Brag g.yab, according to the monasteries so the people, the eighteen clans, are the belly of the white (snow) lion.

120. The knowledge of Bu dgon alone is the head of the white lion.

121. Ma dgon Bkra shis chos rdzong is the tail of the white lion.

122. First Kye ne Lhun grub bstan and second Chu bar Bsam dkar (?) bstan and Dpal ri Dge 'dun bstan and—what shall I say?—also a temple [i.e., Spyi stod dgon pa]—what shall I say?—such a one is the fourth. These are the limbs of the white lion, it is said.

123. Counting the four big monasteries, if I may say the way both Ma- and Bu dgon are situated, these monasteries are situated like this.

124. If I may say the way they are situated, now the way my country is situated, if I may say it approximately, it is like this. Apart from this, as someone who already went to Ma- and Bu dgon, I reach less than the half, just a little bit (of what actually could be told).

VII. The People

125. Only nomads...[break]. 'O 'bom, 'Khor ra, Sdom gzhung, Lha gsum, Rtsal bzang, actually all places where there are no fields at all, are filled with the cattle of the nomads.

126. Actually only yurts, actually such big yurts for the summer and the winter, actually they live having only yurts.

127. Such ones living like this are countless!

128. Actually it is less populated than nowadays here (in Nepal). One gets yields twice (a year). Those, for example, on both sides of the Zla chu (the river resulting from the confluence of) the Ngom chu and the Rdza chu,[387] those kinds (of people) get yields twice.

129. The owner of the two yields...[break]. Their fruits (shing tog) are so many [he demonstrates it vaguely], their food...[break]. There are even lower places than here (Nepal) [explaining the many fruits].

130. Then on the higher places, well, where the nomads are, actually, well, the semi-nomads, mostly there are semi-nomads in my country.

---

[387] Generally today the river is also called Rdza chu after the confluence of the Ngom chu and the Rdza chu (Mekong).

131. There is no water to irrigate fields.

132. When it rains (there is fieldwork)....

133. When the snow falls there in wintertime the (wild) animals (even) come on top of three-storied (houses) making sounds of "*thab thab.*"

134. When the snow falls...[break].

VIII. The Relationship Between Periphery and Center

135. Well, in the past regarding the so-called Mgron gnyer khri chen [a title], having a famous name and being very capable—well, this Brag g.yab bla ma, the first one called *bka' bcu* Grags pa rgya mtsho, apart from his (title) *bka' bcu*, had a high rank.

136. Later then the Brag g.yab bla ma was invited (to Lhasa).

137. When he was invited...[break]. Well, this what is called a se-dan-chair—well, I have forgotten (the name)—the Dalai Lama has such a one.

138. The sedan-chair was made of *'go snam* (broadcloth).

139. Regarding the so-called sedan-bearer, regarding the best among the sedan-chairs, there were dancers, those who go like this [he demonstrates].

140. Regarding such a sedan-chair: unless for the Dalai Lama no one was allowed to carry such a yellow one, isn't it—this *'go snam* (sedan-chair)?

141. Well, such a yellow one was made for the Brag g.yab bla ma, the Mgron gnyer khri chen.

142. There were the seams of the yellow sedan-chair, weren't there?

143. Well, below these seams there was applied blue dye like this [he demonstrates].

144. There was applied blue dye like this.

145. Then the sedan-chair was made of yellow *'go snam* and he was invited to Central Tibet (Bod), it is said.

146. When he was invited the central government (*sde pa gzhung*) said, "You are not allowed to be received with such a yellow se-dan-chair."

147. When we received the strict order...[break]. In our Brag g.yab even good wool is not available, leave alone *'go snam*.

148. We bought this *'go snam* from abroad.

149. In the beginning it was blue.

150. It was blue.

151. Then it faded by the sun, the rain soaked it, it faded. Like this it was carried for many days and months on the road (to Central Tibet). "Therefore come and see whether it is like that or not!" they said.

152. Coming closer (and seeing the blue color below the seams) they [the government officials] said: "It is really blue!"

153. It is said they got no chance to make objections.

154. Being like this, if I may say so, the way they got the sedan-chair was like this.

155. Then, once in the past—which successor of the Dalai Lama?—(who however) one died, it is said.

156. Once during that period they went with the ceremonial peacock-umbrella and all the ritual objects in Central Tibet, with the ceremonial umbrellas.

157. In my native country they also would have peacock-umbrellas and all this.

158. It was (in Brag g.yab) just as if the Dalai Lama would come.

159. In our native country (the Brag g.yab bla ma) is called Skyabs mgon Rin po che.

160. Apart from this one does not say Brag g.yab bla ma.

161. One speaks of the Skyabs mgon Rin po che, Skyabs mgon Rin po che.

162. Well, however for Central Tibet, for the whole world the Skyabs mgon Rin po che of all Tibet is the Rgyal ba Rin po che (the Dalai Lama). Therefore it is not appropriate to call the Brag g.yab bla ma anything else but Brag g.yab bla ma, isn't it?

163. It is not appropriate to say.

164. If I may say "his rank," so it is like this, it is said.

165. Well, today there are both the (Mongolian) No yon Hu thug thu and the (Tibetan) Hu thug thu, it is said.

166. Their history is the story of the old people.

167. Apart from this, if I may say "the origin," I cannot tell it clearly.

168. Well, actually there were the *hu thug thu* of China and the *hu thug thu* of Tibet, these two, it is said.

169. Like this it used to be told.

170. Unlike other lamas, this one had the highest rank, and (also) 'Phags pa lha from Chab mdo, these two.

171. Well, in the region of Khams, among all the lama names, these two had the highest status.

172. Now he was received in Central Tibet like this.

173. At that time this so-called Mgron gnyer khri chen (*i.e.*, the Brag g.yab bla ma) submitted this petition to the government: "Please give me a place (the size) of an animal skin!

174. Then I will construct a house on this place (the size) of an animal skin."

175. When he said this (the government) said, "It's possible to give you a place (the size) of an animal skin. Well, (the size of) an animal skin is all right."

176. They gave him a place (the size) of an animal skin.

177. Well, they cut the skin into a small strip (as one peels an apple so that they could cover a larger piece of land). Then there was the place called Thal phung sgang in Lhasa. In the past at that place there were thirty envoys from Brag g.yab.

178. Regarding the hats of these thirty, today people wearing such hats are not to be seen at all. But it used to be the so-called Mongolian hat.

179. This hat was similar to this (cup) turned upside down [he demonstrates]. From here downwards [he points to the cup] it is red. On top is the red of the silk, inside hanging down is the silk cap, to wear it on the head like this [he demonstrates]. Wearing such a hat, the thirty people who wear this, in all Tibet there is no one else who was allowed to wear these Brag g.yab hats.

180. There was no one to wear them.

181. It was said when the summer teachings and the winter teachings were held, this place was a place to look after [this functions as an explanation why so many envoys were needed in Lhasa]. There (also) the dance was performed.

182. (Those thirty people) performed the dance and wore the hats. During the summer teachings and the winter teachings and the new year festival this place had to be taken care of, it was said.

183. Regarding the stories of the house...[break]. The house was not very good.

184. Once in the past the Chinese—how were they called?—set this house on fire, it is said. It was impossible to rebuild it.

185. (Just) one story—such is the place to live for common people. Apart from this it was not such a rich house.

186. In the past the Mgron gnyer khri chen received such a place and constructed a spacious house (*i.e.*, the first, original building).

187. When the central government had an objection to make, saying "It is not allowed to build such a house," he said, "If it is not allowed to build such a spacious house, I just asked for a place (the size) of an animal skin.

188. That which I asked for I have received.

189. (Even) if I pitch a beggar's tent on an animal skin, it does not fit on an animal skin.

190. Then I cut it into strips and created this place."

191. For this they got no reason to raise objections.

192. Then regarding what is called the copper gutter, except for temples, big assembly halls of monastic communities and then government buildings, it is not allowed to install them.

193. If it would be here (in Kathmandu) one would construct the gutter with the cement over there [he points to it out of the window], isn't it?

194. Regarding the copper gutters of Tibet, such ones were on government buildings.

195. Well, a copper gutter must have been hammered and set up, isn't it?

196. (When the government officials) said, "You have installed such a copper gutter," (he replied,) "That I must ask to be allowed to set up a gutter at the house…[break]. That I ask to be allowed to set up a copper gutter…[break]. It won't give any gutter, unless there is a house.

197. That I had to hand a petition to the government indicates (the question) whether it is permitted to set up a copper gutter or not. Doing this I have (already) asked for it."

198. Regarding this they got no chance, if I may say so, to have any objections, it is said.

199. Later, (after the fire) about one length of the copper gutter was still there.

200. One piece, a rotten piece, was left on the roof after the Chinese had set the house on fire.

201. Well, from the old times, what shall I say, something like a propitious keepsake transferring the property laws from one leader of the people, it was entrusted to the next one.

202. It was like this.

203. (The government officials said,) "The one called Mgron gnyer khri chen...[break].

204. This incredible Mgron gnyer khri chen down there must be arrested. Otherwise this man is an incredible one."

205. When this was said, well, when (the Mgron gnyer khri chen) said, "What (to do) now?" he thought long, day and night.

206. Then he faked a letter.

207. He wrote a letter, wrote (another) letter, wrote (another) letter and so on.

208. Well, in our native country there are (place-)names like Watermaker (Chu bzo ba), Enemy Chief (Dgra mgo ba), Four Horse Corrals (Rta ba bzhi ba), Like a Spear (Mdung 'dra ba). There are many places like these ones.

209. He mentioned the so-called twelve villages of Brag g.yab as if there would be 1000 times twelve.

210. Among these 1000 times twelve (villages)...[break]. Villages, villages, villages...[break]. (Based on the place-names) he made like this (inventing names of military brigades): "Unafraid of Water," (originally the place-name) Watermaker, now functioned as one thousand soldiers.

211. "Unafraid of Spears," (originally) Like a Spear, functioned as another brigade.

212. "Unafraid of Enemies," (originally) Enemy Chief, he took as another brigade and so on.

213. He said (like this),

214. "Well, the time has come to set up the military camp for the winter.

215. Regarding this, make the preparations—food, firewood, etc., everything!" he said (in his false letter). He pretended a messenger would be sent to the heads of the people. Making such a false letter, making a messenger, a person, he slowly created such a lie pretending that a messenger arrived from Brag g.yab.

216. The messenger went fast and straight to the cabinet meeting of the government, to the cabinet and asked, "Where is the residence of the Mgron gnyer khri chen of Brag g.yab?"

217. "We do not know any Mgron gnyer khri chen. This is cabinet of the government."

218. "I have to find the Brag g.yab Mgron gnyer sku mdun," (the messenger) said.

219. "Why?

220. Seize him!"

221. When they snatched his bag and when they looked into the bag, it was written in the letters (they found), "Because of the winter such brigades will arrive the day after tomorrow.

222. Please make preparations and precautions!" Because this was written there the cabinet called the Mgron gnyer khri chen and negotiated with him.

223. "If you pull back the army, it is all right.

224. Such ones don't have to come!

225. We can talk about it," they said.

226. Well, if I may say "the discussion"...[break].

IX. Conclusion

227. What now? It is more like a legend (*sgrung*), isn't it?

228. In the past it used to be told like this.

229. Nowadays the old generations have to tell it this way.

230. Well, the details like in the books, without omissions, I do not know how to tell them.

231. If I may say "the origin (of Brag g.yab)," usually it was told this way, isn't it?

232. Well, except this there is nothing to tell.

BIBLIOGRAPHY

Adamzik, Kirsten. *Sprache: Wege zum Verstehen.* Tübingen, Basel: A. Francke, 2001

Assmann, Jan. *Das kulturelle Gedächtnis. Schrift, Erinnerung und politische Identität in frühen Hochkulturen.* München: C.H. Beck, 1999.

Brinker, Klaus. *Linguistische Textanalyse. Eine Einführung in Grundbegriffe und Methoden.* Fourth edition. Berlin: Erich Schmidt, 1997 (1985).

Gergen, Kenneth J. "Erzählung, moralische Identität und historisches Bewußtsein. Eine sozialkonstruktivistische Darstellung." In Jürgen Straub, ed. *Erzählung, Identität und historisches Bewußtsein. Die psychologische Konstruktion von Zeit und Geschichte* (Erinnerung, Geschichte, Identität 1). Frankfurt/M: Suhrkamp, 1998, pp.170-202.

Goetz, Hans-Werner. *Proseminar Geschichte: Mittelalter.* Stuttgart: Eugen Ulmer, 1993.

Hacking, Ian. *The Social Construction of What?.* Cambridge, Mass.: Harvard University Press, 1999.

Konersmann, Ralf. "Kultur als Metapher." In Ralf Konersmann, ed. *Kulturphilosophie.* Leipzig: Reclam, 1996.

Kretschmer, Monika. "Volkserzählungen aus Mustang. Ein erster Überblick." In Bernhard Kölver, ed. *Formen kulturellen Wandels und andere Beiträge zur Erforschung des Himalaya.* Colloquium des Schwerpunktes Nepal, Heidelberg, 1-4 February, 1984. (Nepalica, H. 2). Sankt Augustin: VGH Wissenschaftsverlag, 1986, pp.417-429.

Lüthi, Max. *Märchen.* Seventh edition. Stuttgart: Metzler, 1979 (1962).

Ong, Walter J. *Orality & Literacy. The Technologizing of the World.* London, New York: Routledge, 1982.

Parry, Adam, ed. *The Making of Homeric Verse: The Collected Papers of Milman Parry.* Oxford: Clarendon Press, 1971.

Phukhang, J.K. and P. Schwieger. *Erzählgut aus A-mdo und Brag-g.yab.* (Märchen, Sagen und Schwänke vom Dach der Welt, Vol. 4). Sankt Augustin: VGH Wissenschaftsverlag, 1982.

Polkinghorne, Donald E. "Narrative Psychologie und Geschichtsbewußtsein. Beziehungen und Perspektiven." In Jürgen Straub, ed. *Erzählung, Identität und historisches Bewußtsein. Die psychologische Konstruktion von Zeit und Geschichte* (Erinnerung, Geschichte, Identität 1). Frankfurt/M: Suhrkamp, 1998, pp.12-45.

Röhrich, Lutz. "Orale Traditionen als historische Quelle. Einige Gedanken zur deutschsprachigen mündlichen Volkserzählung." In Jürgen von Ungern-Sternberg and Hansjörg Reinau, eds. *Vergangenheit in mündlicher Überlieferung.* (Colloquium Rauricum Band 1). Stuttgart: B.G. Teubner, 1988, pp.79-99.

Rüsen, Jörn. Einleitung: "Für eine interkulturelle Kommunikation in der Geschichte. Die Herausforderungen des Ethnozentrismus in der Moderne und die Antwort der Kulturwissenschaften." In Jörn Rüsen, Michael Gottlob, and Achim Mittag, eds. *Die Vielfalt der Kulturen* (Erinnerung, Geschichte, Identität 4). Frankfurt/M: Suhrkamp, 1998, pp.12-36.

Schuh, Dieter, in Collaboration with Wangdu Lama, Monika Kretschmar and M.L. Karmacharya. "Investigations in the History of the Muktinath Valley and Adjacent Areas, Part I." In *Ancient Nepal. Journal of the Department of Archeology*. No.137. Kathmandu: Ministry of Education, Culture & Social Welfare, The Department of Archeology, 1994, pp.9-91.

Schwieger, Peter. *Tibetisches Erzählgut aus Brag-g.yab*. Sankt Augustin: VGH Wissenschaftsverlag, 1989

——"Geschichte als Mythos—zur Aneignung der Vergangenheit in der tibetischen Kultur, ein kulturwissenschaftlicher Essay." *Asiatische Studien (Études Asiatiques), Zeitschrift der Schweizerischen Asiengesellschaft* 54(4):945-973, 2001.

——and L. S. Dagyab. *Die ersten dGe-lugs-pa-Hierarchen von Brag-g.yab (1572-1692)*. Monumenta Tibetica Historica, Abteilung II, Vol. 2. Bonn: VGH Wissenschaftsverlag, 1989.

Straub, Jürgen. "Geschichte erzählen, Geschichte bilden. Grundzüge einer narrativen Psychologie historischer Sinnbildung." In Jürgen Straub, ed. *Erzählung, Identität und historisches Bewußtsein. Die psychologische Konstruktion von Zeit und Geschichte* (Erinnerung, Geschichte, Identität 1). Frankfurt/M: Suhrkamp, 1998, pp.81-169.

Ungern-Sternberg, Jürgen von, and Hansjörg Reinau. "Introduction." In Jürgen von Ungern-Sternberg and Hansjörg Reinau, eds. *Vergangenheit in mündlicher Überlieferung*. Colloquium Rauricum Band 1. Stuttgart: B.G. Teubner, 1988, pp.1-5.

Vansina, Jan. *Oral Tradition as History*. Madison, Wisconsin: 1985.

Vater, Heinz. *Einführung in die Textlinguistik*. Second edition. München: Wilhelm Fink, 1994 (1992).

Vorländer, Herwart. "Mündliches Erfragen von Geschichte." In Herwart Vorländer, ed. *Oral History, Mündlich erfragte Geschichte*. Göttingen: Vandenhoeck & Ruprecht, 1990, pp.7-28.

Wagner, Peter. "Fest-Stellungen. Beobachtungen zur sozialwissenschaftlichen Diskussion über Identität." In Aleida Assmann and Heidrun Friese, eds. *Identitäten* (Erinnerung, Geschichte, Identität 3). Frankfurt/M: Suhrkamp, 1998, pp.44-72.

Wilpert, Gero von. *Sachwörterbuch der Literatur*. Stuttgart: Kröner, 1969.

SHAR RDZA HERMITAGE:
A NEW BONPO CENTER IN KHAMS

TSERING THAR (CHINA CENTER FOR TIBETAN STUDIES, BEIJING)

Shar rdza Bkra shis rgyal mtshan (1859-1934) was the greatest master and the most remarkable scholar of the Bon religion in the last century. His great works in eighteen volumes are laudable contributions to Tibetan culture. The manner of his death, the rainbow body ('ja' lus), became a model for his followers, especially for disciples who practiced Bon *rdzogs chen* and tantra. But in the present paper, I focus more on the life of Shar Rdza Bkra shis rgyal mtshan, the Shar Rdza Hermitage, his main residence, and his influence upon the Bonpo community in the Kham and Amdo regions.

As the hermitage is located in the eastern part of the Rdza khog area of Sde dge in Kham, it is called Shar rdza, 'eastern Rdza khog'. The hermitage is located at 32°06.10' north latitude and 99°25.90' east longitude, on the side of Gyer za che ba mountain on the eastern bank of the Rdza chu River. There are three mountains in the Gyer za group—Gyer za che ba 'Big Gyer za', Gyer za chung ba 'Small Gyer za', and Gyer za 'bring ba 'Middle Gyer za'. Gyer za che ba is located on the eastern bank of the Rdza chu River, Gyer za chung ba on the western bank opposite Gyer za che ba, and Gyer za 'bring ba is located north of the other two. Gyer za che ba, on which the hermitage is located, is also considered important and sacred by Bonpos. This mountain was named Shar rdza G.yung drung lhun po or Rdza Khra ldom wer snying mi 'gyur.[388] Shar rdza Bkra shis rgyal mtshan mentions in the colophons of many of the texts he wrote that this was the place he composed them. Of special note is a panegyric on Shar rdza G.yung drung lhun po and Bde chen Hermitage written by Dbra ston Skal bzang bstan pa'i rgyal mtshan (1897-1959).[389]

---

[388] ShKShGN:39.

[389] *Shar rdza g.yung drung lhun po'i gnas bstod tshangs pa'i nga ro*, and *Kun bzang bde chen gling gi dben pa'i 'dus sde la bsngags pa rab dga'i dbyangs snyan*, the collected works of Dbra ston Bskal bzang bstan pa'i rgyal mtshan, the xylograph edition. The author was one of the most important disciples of Shar rdza Bkra shis rgyal mtshan and the author of his biography.

The hermitage is divided into two parts: Ri khrod gong ma, the 'higher hermitage' (also called Bde chen ri khrod), and Ri khrod zhol ma, the 'lower hermitage'. In 1892, the first seat at Shar rdza Hermitage was the Bde chen Hermitage, opened by Shar rdza Bkra shis rgyal mtshan when he was thirty-four years old. It became his main residence throughout his life. The lower hermitage was established by his followers during his lifetime. Blo gros rgyal mtshan, one of his most important disciples, who later took his place after his death, was especially key in founding the lower hermitage. Therefore his name, Rgyal tshab Blo gros rgyal mtshan, appears frequently in several texts and is recorded in oral history.

Shar rdza Bkra shis rgyal mtshan was born on the eighth day of the eighth month in the Earth-Sheep Year of the fourteenth *rab byung* (1859).[390] He is descended from the family of a tribe, said to have been the original population of the Rdza khog area, called Pha bzhi bu drug which belonged to Hor. His father was named Bkra shis dga' and his mother Bo legs. He took *dge bsnyen* vows at the age of nine and *rab byung* vows at age nineteen at Steng chen Monastery from Bskal bzang nyi ma tog gi rgyal mtshan, an abbot of G.yung drung gling Monastery. Soon after he became a monk at Steng chen, Bde chen gling pa, a great Khampa Bonpo master, came to Steng chen and prophesied that Bkra shis rgyal mtshan would attain great achievements if he established a hermitage instead of remaining in the monastery.

When he was twenty-one years old, he became fed up with general affairs at the monastery. At that time, he took three oaths from Dbra sprul Bstan 'dzin dbang rgyal, a master in the Dbra lineage of Steng chen. First, he vowed never to perform religious practices for families in order to make a living. Second, he vowed not to use the aid of a horse for travel until he reached the age of fifty. Third, he vowed to establish a hermitage during his lifetime. However, because of a disagreement with Nyi ma 'od zer, a reincarnate who was then a *khri pa* at Steng chen, he had to delay his plan.[391] In 1892, at the age of thirty-four, he was able to realize his promise to open a hermitage on Gyer za Mountain. At first, he pitched a black yak hair tent at the site of Bde chen Hermitage for his practices, then later built a small cell to replace it. The full name of the hermitage was Bde chen ri

---

[390] ShKShGN:41-42.
[391] ShKShGN:159.

khrod drang srong dgyes pa'i skyed tshal, abbreviated to Bde chen ri khrod. With the arrival of Pad ma blo gros and Tshul khrims mchog rgyal from Nyag rong the following year, he started to receive students at the hermitage.

Because he was extremely bright and made great efforts in his studies, he became a very learned master at a young age. Gradually his knowledge and strict observance of religious principles won him a fine reputation not only within the Bonpo community of the Rdza khog area, but also among some monasteries of the Rnying ma pa, Bka' brgyud pa and Sa skya pa Buddhist sects in Kham. Monks from Steng chen Monastery went to Bde chen Hermitage so often for his instruction, that the monastery asked Bkra shis rgyal mtshan to return in order to keep the monks in the monastery. However, Gsang sngags gling pa (1864-?) was able to convince the monastic authorities to keep him at the hermitage. Except for his religious journeys, he spent the rest of his life at the hermitage until the age of seventy-six. Throughout his life he accomplished great achievements in study, practice, and transmission of the Bon religion.

In addition to his work in the Rdza khog area, he made several important journeys during his life. His first journey was also his longest. In 1882, when he was twenty-five years old, he went to Central Tibet on pilgrimage with twenty-five monks from Rdza khog, visiting Khyung po, Kong po, Sman ri, Dben sa kha, Mkhar sna, G.yung drung gling and Lhasa.

His second journey was instigated by a conflict between Dgon gsar Monastery and Steng chen Monastery, when monks from Dgon gsar burned down Steng chen in 1902.[392] As a result, the monks from Steng chen had to escape into exile.[393] Nyi ma 'od zer went to Nag chu kha and the older monks went to Gser thar.[394] Shar rdza Bkra shis rgyal mtshan was allowed by the monks of Dgon gsar to remain at the hermitage, but the intensity of the conflict later made him leave for Nyag rong. In 1903, he visited many monasteries in Nyag rong, such as Rgyal zhing, Gong rgyal, Dbal khyung, Ye shes, La kha, Klu

---

[392] Dgon gsar is a Dge lugs pa monastery in the Rdza khog area. It was founded by Hor chos rje Ngag dbang phun tshogs during the time of the Fifth Dalai Lama. See KhKGL:643-645.

[393] ShKShGN:172-176.

[394] Gser thar is in Dkar mdzes Prefecture, Sichuan Province. At the present time it is a county and traditionally a part of Mgo log. It appears sometimes as Bswe thar. See ShKShGN:175.

'bum and Brag g.yab. During these visits, he gave a number of lectures in the Bonpo monasteries of Nyag rong and became more and more famous in the Bonpo community there. After his time in Nyag rong, he taught the concepts of the *bon chos dgongs pa gcig sgrub* at the 'Gro mgon Monastery in Bzhag gsar.[395]

He also gathered monks from Brag ra, Dbu gur and Smin char Monasteries for teachings on the *Bka' lung rgya mtsho*[396] at the Chu mig Monastery in 'Dra.[397] He had long discussions on the differences between the old and the new Bon treasures (*gter gsar* and *gter rnying*) with several *dge bshes* of Sman ri in Rgyal gtso Monastery.[398] He went on a pilgrimage to Rgyal mo Dmu rdo,[399] visited the monasteries of Khro chen rgyal po, Brag steng rgyal po, Dge bshes rgyal po,[400] and those belonging to some small kingdoms, such as Mtsho mtho,[401] Phu dud, Nyi shu, Khyung lung and Bya dor Bde chen gling in Rgyal rong. He spent about five years in those monasteries, especially in Nyag rong, before returning to Rdza khog at the age of fifty. It was at that time, 1908, that Steng chen Monastery started to rebuild.[402]

His third journey started three years later. He had been invited by the Bonpo monasteries of Brag mgo and Nyag rong for many years. So in 1911, he departed for Nyag rong via Brag mgo, later returning to his hermitage in the same year.

---

[395] Bzhag gsar or Bzhag pa is a place name in Li thang. 'Gro mgon is the only Bon-po monastery in Li thang today.

[396] The *Bka' lung rgya mtsho* is a text written by Shar rdza Bkra shis rgyal mtshan himself.

[397] The 'Dra area is in modern Rta'u County, Dkar mdzes Prefecture. Among those four monasteries, only Chu mig Monastery is still active in the 'Dra area today.

[398] Rgyal gtso Monastery was located in modern Brag mgo County, Dkar mdzes Prefecture.

[399] A mountain in Rgyal rong sacred to the Bonpos, located in modern Rong brag County, Dkar mdzes Prefecture.

[400] Khro chen, Brag steng and Dge bshes are three of the traditional Eighteen Kingdoms of Rgyal rong. Khro chen or Khro skyabs is located in modern Kyo mo Township, Chu chen County, Rnga pa Prefecture. Brag steng is located in Brag steng Township, Rong brag County, Dkar mdzes Prefecture. Dge bshes is located in modern Dge bshes rtsa Township, Rong brag County, Dkar mdzes Prefecture.

[401] The monastery of the royal family of Khro chen rgyal po. Dbra ston Bskal bzang bstan pa'i rgyal mtshan records its name as Mtshams tho. See ShKShGN, p.224.

[402] ShKShGN:236.

His fourth journey was in 1914, when he was fifty-six years old. He was invited by the Bonpo monasteries of 'Dzin khog[403] to give teachings there, after which he returned to the hermitage in the same year.

His fifth journey was in 1920. He was invited to teach at Rtogs ldan Monastery in Rnga pa, where he stayed for seven months. During that time he also visited the Dga' mal[404] and Rin spungs[405] Monasteries in Zung chu. After returning to Rtogs ldan Monastery from Zung chu, he was invited again to visit by the Khro chen king, who then asked him to write a long statement of counsel.[406] On the way back, he re-visited Brag steng and Dge bshes rtsa, fulfilling the hopes of the people there.

The journeys mentioned above are only the journeys he took out-side Rdza khog. Many times he went to visit the monasteries in the Rdza khog region, such as Khro tshang, Smon rgyal and 'Bum rmad. Aside from giving *dbang, lung* and *khrid,* his main activities were teachings on Bon, as well as several texts written by himself, such as the *Sde snod mdzod,* the *Dbying rig mdzod* and the *Nam mkha' mdzod.*

We learn from his biography that he was seemingly a very ordinary boy when he first became a monk. It was only due to his intelligence and diligent study that he became a great master and a distinguished Bon scholar of the twentieth century. His hermitage also became a new and influential center for the practices of Bon tantra and *rdzog chen* due to his growing renown, especially in Kham and Amdo areas. There are several reasons for these achievements and his widespread influence.

First, of course, his scholarship has made him a renowned figure. There are eighteen volumes in his collected works. His five *mdzod* ('Treasuries') in particular became very famous in the Bonpo com-

---

[403] 'Dzin khog is a long valley in Kham, traditionally belonging to the Sde dge area, located in today's 'Dzin khog Township, Dpal yul County, Dkar mdzes Prefecture. *'Dzin* appears sometimes as *'dzing.* See ShKShGN:254.

[404] Dga' mal was the largest Bonpo monastery in the Zung chu area. It appears in ShKShGN:286 as Dga' me. About ten years ago it was divided into two monasteries, Bya dur Dga' mal dgon chen and Dga' mal G.yung drung dar rgyas gling, at the same site. It is located in Gsal chu Township, Zung chu County, Rnga pa Prefecture.

[405] Rin spungs Monastery is located in Gtso tshang Township, Zung chu County, Rnga pa Prefecture.

[406] ShKShGN:297-307.

munity and even in certain Buddhist arenas.[407] The five *mdzod* were published in a xylograph edition at the hermitage and spread throughout Rdza khog, Nyag rong, 'Dzin khog, 'Dra yul, Rgyal rong and Rnga pa. Today, prints can be found in almost all the Bonpo monasteries of Tibet.

Second, his point of view regarding the unification of Bon and Buddhism was largely accepted in Kham and Amdo and even more so today. Because of emerging Buddhist influence at that time, a Bonpo creed developed which sought to the utmost to integrate Buddhism, especially in theory. It was called the 'New Treasure' (*gter gsar*).[408] Of course, this tradition was active in Kham much before Bkra shis rgyal mtshan, but he inherited and developed it as part of his great academic achievement. Later, one of his disciples even wrote a special text to explain it.[409] Sectarianism has accompanied the whole history of Tibetan religion, but it has been much less evident in Kham than in Central Tibet (Dbus-Gtsang) and Amdo. I am not familiar with the history of Steng chen Monastery where Bkra shis rgyal mtshan received his basic Bonpo education when he was young. However, Dbra ston records that a statue of Avalokiteśvara and many Buddhist texts used to be kept at Steng chen.[410] This clearly indicates that the monks there were quite aware of and receptive to Buddhism. Because of this tradition, Shar rdza Bkra shis rgyal mtshan's development of the unification doctrine was

---

[407] The five mdzod are the *Nam mkha' mdzod*, *Dbying rig mdzod*, *Sde snod mdzod*, *Lung rig mdzod* and *Legs bshad mdzod*. The *Legs bshad mdzod* is the brief title of *Legs bshad rin po che'i gter mdzod dpyod ldan dga' ba'i char*. It was translated into English by Karmay 1972, and republished in Tibetan under the same title by Mi rigs dpe skrun khang in Beijing, 1985.

[408] Tibetans generally recognize two traditions of Bon: *bon dkar* and *bon nag*, 'White' and 'Black' Bon. The former is a tradition somewhat closer to Buddhism, and the latter somewhat different from it, but Bonpos themselves neither agree with this apperception nor the appellations mentioned above. They call these traditions the *bka' gsar* and *bka' rnying*, the new and old teachings. Since these categories and names indicate a point of view over the difference between the two traditions, neither did Shar rdza Bkra shis rgyal mtshan agree with it. He considered calling them *gter gsar* and *gter rnying*, the new and old treasures, because he attri-buted the difference between the two traditions to the times when early and later Bonpo *gter ma* emerged.

[409] *Bstan gnyis dgongs pa gcig tu sgrub pa thar 'dod yid kyi mdzes rgyan* by Dbra ston Bskal bzang bstan pa'i rgyal mtshan, the xylograph edition of his collected works. ShKShGN:344.

[410] ShKShGN:173.

neither exceptional for nor confined to the Bonpo community, but it engaged the interests of the area's Buddhists as well.

In 1902, Rdza rgyal 'phags pa,[411] a master of Bka' gdams pa sect, came to the hermitage to visit Bkra shis rgyal mtshan. He had been asked by Bla ma Ye shes rdo rje of the Rnying ma pa Pho ba khug Monastery to give *rdzogs chen* teachings at his monastery during Shar rdza Bkra shis rgyal mtshan's journey to Dbal khyung Monastery in Nyag rong in 1904.[412] Another Rnying ma pa monastery, Rang shar sde pa, officially invited him to give teachings to all the monks in the monastery while on his second journey to Nyag rong in 1911.[413] When he was at Rdzong gsar, a Sa skya pa monastery in Sde dge, the reincarnate of the monastery, "Gser pa mchog sprul,"[414] asked him for a copy of his collected works. He said that he understood from Bkra shis rgyal mtshan's *Dbyings rig mdzod* that though there existed differences of time and space between Bon and Buddhism, in the end there was no significant difference between the two religions.[415]

Since the introduction of Buddhism into Tibet in the seventh century, there has been an ongoing struggle between Bon and Buddhism. However, a qualitative change took place after the later development of Buddhism. At that time, Buddhists began to assume a dominant position in Tibet and the Bon religion was banished from Central Tibet. It was allowed to exist only in some remote, out-of-the-way places. Bon's position in Tibet suffered a disastrous social decline. Therefore, with many Buddhist doctrines and concepts having been completely accepted by Tibetans, most places in Tibet abandoned Bon. In fact, this indigenous religion of Tibet became a heresy in its own home, and many Bonpos lacked the courage even to acknowledge their own beliefs in public.

Under such oppressive social stress, many Bonpo scholars tried to absorb aspects of Buddhist doctrine. Furthermore, Bonpo monks be-

---

[411] ShKShGN:160-161 refers to him only as a disciple of Rdzogs chen Dpal sprul rin po che, but there is no further reference to the latter. It could be Dpal sprul 'Jigs med chos kyi dbang po (1808-1887), the author of *Kun bzang bla ma'i zhal lung*.

[412] ShKShGN:181.

[413] ShKShGN:247.

[414] "Gser pa mchog sprul" refers to Chos kyi blo gros (1893-1959), the reincarnation of 'Jam dbyangs mkhyen brtse dbang po (1820-1892) of Rdzong gsar Monastery. See KhKGL:478-479.

[415] ShKShGN:259.

gan changing almost every doctrine and practice to be similar, if not identical to, Buddhist ones in order to become more socially acceptable. This movement reflected a growing tendency toward religious assimilation due both to a wish to coexist in peace and to satisfy the people's expectations. The Bonpos never perceived that this movement would cause the Bon religion to lose many of aspects of its own tradition. But while they did succeed in integrating it with Buddhism, Bon lost many of its own characteristics and it is still losing them. Shar rdza Bkra shis rgyal mtshan was the outstanding scholar of this movement, the reason his texts were so welcomed in Bonpo and even Buddhist society. With eighteen volumes of works, his name had already become renowned in the Bonpo community even in his own time. In the 1980s, his works were reprinted again in Tibet and now many monasteries have several volumes of them. Today, Shar rdza Bkra shis rgyal mtshan's works, and even statues of him, appear in Buddhist monasteries in Kham, such as Dga' lang steng in Sde dge and Khams mdo sgar in Go 'jo.

Third, his strict adherence to monastic vows was another reason for his fame. Many Bonpo monasteries laid down very strict rules for their monks. However, most, commonly even all, clergy, in many of Kham's Bonpo monasteries, were lay people, who went to the monasteries only on some fixed ritual occasions. Indeed, they had to work the land alongside their families and keep animals as well. Therefore, this dual lifestyle became one of the reasons why Bonpo monasteries and their monks were much less socially respected. In stark contrast, Shar rdza Bkra shis rgyal mtshan kept his vows very strictly throughout his life. He also vowed neither to eat meat nor to wear any animal skin.[416] He left Steng chen and hid at Bde chen Hermitage for peace and quiet. He tried many times to escape the bustle of the people who gathered in response to his fame, and hid himself in a small cell covering himself up with clay at the hermitage.[417] He spent all the offerings he received on his journeys to publish texts at the hermitage and offered them to the monasteries in the Rdza khog area, even Kha rag Monastery in 'Dzin khog.[418] However, he himself spent his life as a very poor and simple monk. Finally, his life became a model for Bon-po monks.

---

[416] ShKShGN:122.
[417] ShKShGN:140-141, 153,178.
[418] ShKShGN:328.

Fourth, his rainbow-body death became an example of great achievement for Bonpo *rdzogs chen* practices. As a result, he is also called 'Ja' lus pa Shar rdza Bkra shis rgyal mtshan.

Fifth, there were two cultural contexts for Shar rdza Hermitage, a macro-context and a micro-context.

The Macro-context

The macro-context was the cultural environment of the Kham regions. History and geographical proximity impacted the relationship between Bon and Buddhist monasteries. In fact, there was little disparity in number between them, and this led to their relative balance. Therefore, many monasteries and communities of the Bon and Buddhist sects lived in peace with each other. This situation reduced the amount of prejudice and discrimination among the people as well. For this reason, religious prejudice and discrimination among the Bonpo and Buddhist sects in Kham was much less evident than in the Central Tibetan and Amdo regions. Furthermore, the position of the Bon religion was much better in Kham than in Central Tibet and Amdo. In fact, many monasteries, even though they belonged to different religions and sects, had very close relationships, *e.g.*, Rdzong gsar Monastery in Sde dge which was historically separated from Ri spun Monastery.[419] Both been Bonpo monasteries in the past, yet still influenced by Buddhism. The former was converted into a Sa skya pa monastery at a later time. Despite all these factors, both monasteries still maintain a very close relationship until today.

Over the years Rdzong gsar monastery developed much more than Ri spun. Yet, even today, the relationship is still good and Rdzong gsar has been helping and looking after Ri spun. Rig 'dzin Nyi ma was recognized as the reincarnation of Seng ge dbang phyug of the Sa skya pa E wam Monastery in Nyag rong.[420] Yet, because he had an earlier acquaintance with Bon, it was no problem for him to stay at Ye shes, a Bonpo monastery. One can see together in some monasteries statues of Padmasambhava, the five great masters of the

---

[419] KhKGL:472-484, 631-632; *Ri spun dgon gyi lo rgyus* by Blo gros phun tshogs, MS.

[420] KhKGL:363-366.

Sa skya pa,[421] the Bka' brgyud pa Mar mi dwags gsum,[422] the Dge lugs pa Tshong kha pa[423] and the Bonpo Shar rdza Bkra shis rgyal mtshan. In the libraries of various monasteries and in the homes of individuals in Kham are texts from several religions and sects. One can hear many such stories and examples familiar to people living in areas of Kham. But it is difficult to find a similarly cooperative religious environment in other places. The Khampa context allowed Shar rdza Hermitage a lenient atmosphere within which it could develop and increase Bkra shis rgyal mtshan's reputation.

The Micro-context

The micro-context was, and is, the cultural environment of Rdza khog, which is geographically a very isolated place. From Nya 'gug Village, about one kilometer away from 'Bum rmad Monastery, to Bsam 'grub Monastery[424] takes about twelve hours by horse via a small footpath along the Rdza chu River. The serpentine Rdza chu flows from north to south through a deep gorge between the mountains. The region lacks both electricity and a motorable road. Villages are scattered at valley mouths and upon the hillsides on both sides of the river. There are neither motorized vehicles for agricultural work nor transportation even now. Radio is the only modern convenience for the village people.

The total area of Rdza khog is about 400 square kilometers. This isolation has kept local culture and activities relatively stable against the encroachment of modern culture. There are six Bonpo monasteries distributed along the Rdza chu River from A phyug Pasture to Gshis pa Village. The monastery nearest the hermitage is Steng chen. The close relationship between Steng chen and the hermitage is not only because of their proximity, but because Shar

---

[421] The *Sa skya gong ma rnam lnga*, to wit, Kun dga' snying po (1092-1158), Bsod nams rtse mo (1142-1182), Grags pa rgyal mtshan (1147-1216), Kun dga' rgyal mtshan (1182-1251) and Blo gros rgyal mtshan (1235-1280).

[422] Mar pa Lo tsa ba Chos kyi blo gros (1012-1097), Mi la ras pa (1040-1123) and Dwags po lha rje Bsod nams rin chen (1079-1153).

[423] Tsong kha pa Blo bzang grags pa (1357-1419).

[424] Bsam 'grub is a Dge lugs pa monastery on the bank of the Rdza chu River, in Middle Rdza khog Township, Dkar mdzes County. It was founded by Ba brtse Kun dga' rgyal mtshan, Khyung rtse Kun dga' 'od zer and A sang 'Jam dbyangs kun dga' in the fifteenth century.

rdza Bkra shis rgyal mtshan himself was a monk from Steng chen. In fact, the hermitage belongs to Steng chen Monastery.

Shar rdza Bkra shis rgyal mtshan is known for his great efforts in rebuilding Steng chen Monastery after it was burnt down by the monks of Dgon gsar Monastery.[425] Now many years later, Steng chen Monastery still looks after his hermitage. After Steng chen, Zer 'phro and 'Phen zhol are the monasteries nearest the hermitage. Historically they were branch monasteries of Smon rgyal Monastery. However, because they are located too far from Smon rgyal and much closer to Steng chen, they no longer keep any relationship of *ma dgon* and *bu dgon* with Smon rgyal, but have become much closer to Steng chen. Zer 'phro especially, which is too small to arrange all of its religious activities independently, needs help from a bigger monastery. Hence, Steng chen is the only choice for it in the area. As a result, the monks of Zer 'phro join in all the regular rituals at Steng chen. In addition, the 'Bum rmad, 'Phen zhol, Smon rgyal and Khro tshang Monasteries are farther away from Steng chen and Zer 'phro. These six Bonpo monasteries surround the hermitage on the banks of the Rdza chu River in Rdza khog. Together they form a group of Bonpo monasteries and all of them have their own *lha sde*, the offering tribes.[426] This surrounding Bonpo community was the micro-context which gave birth and growth to Shar rdza Hermitage.

Unfortunately, I have only been able to gather exact information on the population in the *lha sde* of 'Bum rmad Monastery, where there is an average of 5.8 people in each family. Multiplied by 608 (the total number of the families), today's Bonpo community in Rdza khog numbers approximately 3500 people (see chart, below).

Before Shar rdza Bkra shis rgyal mtshan, Gyer za was already said to be a sacred mountain (*gnas ri*). However, because of his reputation, the hermitage became a gathering place for his disciples and Bonpo tantrics. After his death, and especially because of the way of his death—the rainbow body, his hermitage became much

---

[425] ShKShGN:201, 265, 273-278, 328.

[426] *Lha sde* are tribes or villages which, to a certain extent, are disciples of and belong to a monastery. They offer labor, money, material and monks to a monastery, and the monastery also performs rituals for the health, deaths, crops, riddance of calamities and blessings for the people in the *lha sde*. *Lha sde* are called *yul pa* or *mtha' ba* in different places.

more sacred than before. People have been going there not only for
practice, but also for pilgrimage.

Monasteries	Monks	Tribes	Families	Population
Khro tshang	120	3	93	
Smon rgyal	98	8	105	
'Bum rmad	60	3	94	546
Steng chen	63	5	213	
Zer 'phro	20	7	66	
'Phen zhol	21	7	37	
Total	382	33	608	

At the end of his lifetime, Shar rdza Bkra shis rgyal mtshan
appointed his nephew Blo gros rgyal mtshan (1915-1952) as his
rgyal tshab at the hermitage. However, the latter died when he was
forty years old. Yet prior to his death, he made a journey to Central
Tibet, appointing Zer 'phro Tshul khrims dbang phyug as his *rgyal
tshab* at the hermitage before his departure for Lhasa. Rgyal tshab
Zer 'phro Tshul khrims dbang phyug died in 1960. In 1985, Mthu
stobs rnam rgyal (b.1926) was selected as the *rgyal tshab* of Shar
rdza Bkra shis rgyal mtshan at the hermitage. After about twelve
years, some problems at Steng chen Monastery caused the *rgyal
tshab* to leave the hermitage and return to 'Bum rmad, his original
monastery. After he left, A 'jigs, a monk from Ye shes Monastery in
Nyag rong, took responsibility for the hermitage. Obviously he is not
the official *rgyal tshab* of the hermitage although the monks there
call him *mkhan chung*, 'younger abbot'.

As part of a Japanese project on Bonpo culture under the guidance
of Professor Yasuhiko Nagano, I visited Shar rdza Hermitage in the
autumn of 1997. Since the hillside upon which the hermitage is located is too precipitous for taking photos, I had to cross the Rdza chu
River by raft and climb the mountain side of Gyer za chung ba, exactly opposite the hermitage, to photograph it with the help of A 'jigs.
Fortunately, I had met both Mthu stobs rnam rgyal and A 'jigs at that
time, the former at 'Bum rmad and the latter at the hermitage. Mthu
stobs rnam rgyal, the present *rgyal tshab*, was born in the Fire-Tiger
Year of the fifteenth *rab byung* (1926) in 'Bum mda' village in Shar
rdza. He received his first teachings from Shar rdza Bkra shis rgyal
mtshan when he was nine years old. Soon after that, he became a
monk at 'Bum rmad Monastery in the Rdza khog area. He started to

receive teachings from Rgyal tshab Blo gros rgyal mtshan when he was eighteen years old. When he was twenty, he went to Central Tibet on pilgrimage to Bonpo sacred places. After his return, he was invited by Kun grol hum chen (1901-1956), the sixth Kun grol grags pa, to be a teacher of his son Smon rgyal Lha sras. A few years after the cultural revolution, A g.yung Rinpoche (1922-1996)[427] restarted Bonpo religious activities at the hermitage. Mthu stobs rnam rgyal assumed his position as *rgyal tshab* in 1985.[428]

There are more than fifty monasteries in Sde dge consisting mainly of Bonpo monasteries and three sects of Tibetan Buddhism, the Rnying ma pa, Sa skya pa and Dge lugs pa. The authorities of Sde dge County founded four religious schools to train monks from the smaller monasteries of the same religion or sect. Shar rdza Hermitage was selected to be the Bonpo school. At that time, A g.yung was again at the hermitage and, as representative of the local government, was given permission to found the school in 1993. Although there are no funds to start the school, the permission to do so gave it official sanction to exist.

When I visited Bde chen Hermitage four years later in 1997, the practice cell of Shar rdza Bkra shis rgyal mtshan had been rebuilt,

---

[427] A g.yung is the abbreviated name of G.yung drung bstan pa'i rgyal mtshan, or Gshen bstan mtha' rgyas. He was born in the Water-Dog Year of the fifteenth *rab byung* (1922) in Rgya ra gshis in Nyag rong. When he was five years old, he was recognized by Bstan pa'i nyi ma as a reincarnation of Bya btang Dri med 'od zer of Gong rgyal Monastery in Nyag rong. However, his uncle, Tshul khrims mchog rgyal, a hermit, disagreed, and A g.yung stayed in Ye shes Monastery instead of going to Gong rgyal Monastery to be their master. He received monastic (*rab byung*) vows from Dbra ston Bskal bzang bstan pa'i rgyal mtshan (1897-1959), after which he and Khyung po G.yung drung bdud 'dul (1923-1996) became the two masters of Ye shes Monastery. He became a vice-chairman of the Chinese Political Consultative Conference of Dkar mdzes Prefecture. He went to Shar rdza Hermitage when was sixty-two years old to restart religious activities and officially reopen the hermitage as a Bonpo center. In the next year, he went to work at the Nationalities Institute of Sichuan Province in Chengdu, and soon after that started to reprint the Bonpo *Bka' 'gyur* for the first time. He had been to most Bonpo monasteries in Dkar mdzes Prefecture during his active service and helped them to retrain young monks. He made great contributions to the development of the Bon religion in Kham for two decades, from the end of the 1970s on. He passed away in the Fire-Rat year of the sixteenth *rab byung* (1996). See *Sprul sku g.yung drung bstan pa'i rgyal mtshan gyi rnam thar lha chab 'khyil ba* by Rig 'dzin Nyi ma, MS., and a short untitled autobiography of Mkhan po Mthu stobs rnam rgyal, MS.

[428] A short and untitled autobiography of Mkhan po Mthu stobs rnam rgyal, MS.:3.

and a young monk from Khyung po Steng chen[429] was in retreat in
the cell. A very old stupa in the forest on the hillside below Bde chen
also still remained. At the lower hermitage, in addition to the stupa,
one can find the cell in which Shar rdza ba is said to have
disappeared by the rainbow body. Nearby a new printing house and a
row of cells for monks at the lower hermitage have already been
built. A 'jigs from Ye shes Monastery is the contemporary leader of
the hermitage. At the time of my visit, he was more than thirty years
old and is called Mkhan chung, 'younger abbot', by the monks of the
hermitage. Currently there are fourteen monks from different
monasteries living there, but none of them will become a permanent
resident. Monks and lay tantrics have always come and gone. The
Shar rdza Hermitage is usually a place for practicing various rituals.
Most monks and lay tantrics come there for their own practices,
usually for three years. Of course, they also receive Bonpo teachings
from the *mkhan po* and other important masters, and in particular
some tantric empowerment ceremonies.

Before Shar rdza Bkra shis rgyal mtshan, Bonpo monasteries sent
their monks only to Sman ri Monastery to take their monastic vows,
meditate and improve their level of knowledge in the Bon religion.[430]
Because of Mnyam med Shes rab rgyal mtshan (1356-1415),[431] Sman
ri Monastery was able to take the place of Dben sa kha[432] and became
a very important institution of the highest learning for Bon in Tibet.
Furthermore, Sman ri Monastery had an even more important religious function than Dben sa kha. It effectively developed the Bonpo
vinaya (*'dul ba*) tradition in Tibet. Since Shes rab rgyal mtshan
founded Sman ri as a pure monastic institution, his reputation made it
the monastic center for Bonpos in Tibet. Many monasteries, even
from very remote places like Amdo and Kham, sent their monks to
Sman ri to take monastic vows and study there, a practice which
became a tradition for Bonpos in Tibet for centuries.

---

[429] Khyung po Steng chen Monastery is in Steng chen County, TAR.

[430] Sman ri Monastery was founded by Mnyam med Shes rab rgyal mtshan in
1405.

[431] *Rje rin po che'i rnam thar mdor bsdus skal ldan dang ba 'dren byed ngo
mtshar pad mo stong ldan* by Nyi ri shel zhin, MS.

[432] A Bonpo monastery founded by Bru chen Nam mkha' g.yung drung, a disciple
of Gshen chen Klu dga' (996-1035) in Gtsang G.yas ru in 1072, "which became the
great seat of learning for the Bonpo until it was destroyed by a flood in 1386"
(Karmay 1998:119).

In several monasteries, only the monks who had been trained at Sman ri could become an abbot or gain higher positions. Monks who studied at Sman ri often became more powerful and honored in their own monasteries and in local Bonpo communities. Sman ri Monastery was called *grwa sa,* 'the place for monks'. Furthermore, this indicates that the *grwa sa* Sman ri was the only important place for taking monastic vows throughout a period in Bonpo history. However, the majority of the Tibetan populations in Dbus and Gtsang converted to Buddhism. Since the shrinking Bonpo population could no longer provide sufficient economic support to Sman ri Monastery, its power and influence suffered seriously and atrophied within the whole Tibetan cultural area.

For the Bonpo population in the Kham and Amdo regions, Sman ri was also geographically very far away. It was therefore difficult to transport goods to take care of the monastery's needs. Nag chu kha was nearer than Kham and Amdo, so Bonpos there became Sman ri's main sponsors. Shar rdza Hermitage, however, has had a different historical course.

Unlike Sman ri, it has steadily increased its influence over the years. Even now, its fame is increasing, and it has become such a sacred place that monks from the Kham and Amdo areas prefer to go to Shar rdza Hermitage to take monastic vows instead of going to the *grwa sa* as in the past.

Of course, there have also been other Bonpo centers for philosophic studies over the past two centuries, such as G.yung drung gling Monastery near Sman ri, but their function and position in Bonpo history were different from Sman ri's. Correspondingly, there were also two places for philosophic studies for Bonpo monks in the Amdo and Kham areas: Snang zhig and Rtogs ldan Monasteries in Rnga pa.[433] Many monks went to the hermitage for pilgrimage and practices and to Snang zhig and Rtogs ldan for study. The majority of monks going to the hermitage were from monasteries in Kham rather than Amdo. From developmental trends at Snang zhig Monastery, it is apparent that Snang zhig will become the most important monastic institution for Bonpos, particularly for the tradition of the old treasure. At the same time, Shar rdza Hermitage has already become

---

[433] "There are several Bonpo monasteries in rNga-ba. The two largest are sNang-zhig dgon-pa and rTogs-ldan dgon-pa, situated a short distance from each other a few kilometres outside the modern administrative centre" (Kvaerne 1990:207-221).

a new center for Bonpos from Kham and Amdo, and in particular for those following the *Rdzogs chen* and the new treasure traditions.

Shar rdza Hermitage cannot replace Sman ri Monastery completely. Sman ri was historically a very important monastic institution and it produced many very learned scholars. However, Shar rdza Hermitage has become mainly a sacred place for pilgrimage and the practices of Bonpo *rdzogs chen* and tantra. There are also significant differences between the two traditions within the Bon religion. Except for some empowerment ceremonies, when some high masters come to the hermitage, the tantrics always practice individually. They do not even have the kind of gathering place, such as a *'du khang*, found in all monasteries. At the same time, Snang zhig Monastery, as the largest Bonpo monastic institution in Tibet, does have this function. Snang zhig receives Bonpo monks from many monasteries in Kham and Amdo, and it even produces Bonpo *dge bshes* every year.

Not all Bonpos agreed with Shar rdza Bkra shis rgyal mtshan's unification approach. For example, Snang zhig Monastery did not invite him to visit when he stayed at the nearby Rtogs ldan Monastery for seven months in 1920. Dbra ston Bskal bzang bstan pa'i rgyal mtshan also criticized people who considered the works of Bkra shis rgyal mtshan to be new Bon (*bon gsar ma*), and that he was a new lama (*bla ma gsar ba*).[434] Apparently people started to criticize him even during his lifetime for integrating and unifying Bon and Buddhism. Even today, some Bonpo monasteries strictly keep the tradition of the old treasure in Tibet. They still do not accept Shar rdza ba's main religious ideas. It is evident that the extent of his influence is much less in Central Tibet than in Kham and Amdo.

---

[434] ShKShGN:376-377.

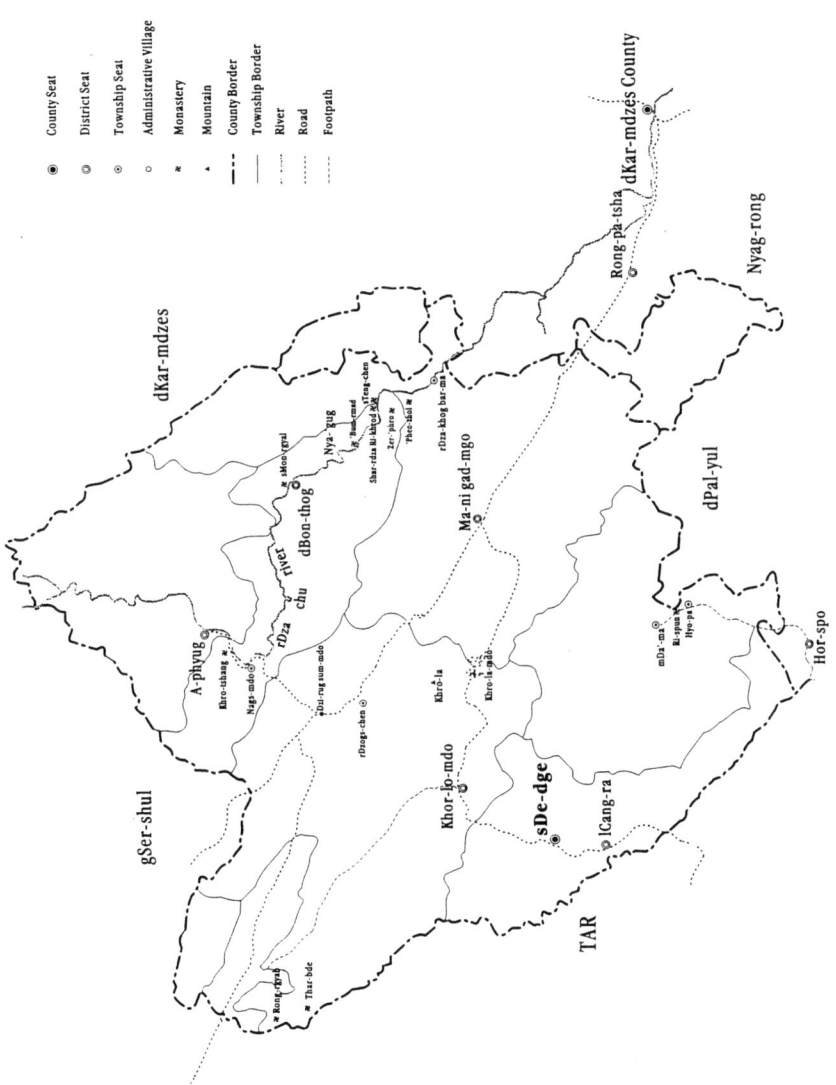

Derge County and the Area around Shar rdza Hermitage

BIBLIOGRAPHY

KhKGL = *Khams phyogs dkar mdzes khul gyi dgon sde so so'i lo rgyus gsal bar bshad pa nang bstan gsal ba'i me long. Krung go'i bod kyi shes rig zhib 'jug lte gnas kyi chos lugs lo rgyus zhib 'jug so'o, Krung go bod brgyud nang bstan mtho rim slob gling bod brgyud nang bstan zhib 'jug khang, Zi khron zhing chen dkar mdzes khul chos lugs cud & Dkar mdzes khul yig bsgyur cud.* Vol. 1 (Nang chen khul gyi rgyu cha). Beijing: Krung go bod kyi shes rig dpe skrun khang, 1999.

Karmay, Samten G. *The Treasury of Good Sayings: A Tibetan History of* Bon. London: Oxford University Press, 1972.

——"A general introduction to the history and doctrines of Bon." *The Arrow and the Spindle, Studies in History, Myths, Rituals and Beliefs in Tibet.* Kantipath, Kathmandu: Mandala Book Point, 1998.

Kvaerne, Per. "The Monastery of sNang-zhig of the Bon Religion in the rNga-ba District of Amdo." *Rivista degli Studi Orientali* 63, 1990.

ShKShGN = Dbra ston Bskal bzang bstan pa'i rgyal mtshan. *Shar rdza bkra shis rgyal mtshan gyi rnam thar. (Full Title: Rje btsun bla ma dam pa nges pa don gyi g.yung drung 'chang dbang dpal shar rdza chen po bkra shis rgyal mtshan dpal bzang po'i rnam par thar pa ngo mtshar nor bu'i phreng ba thar 'dod mkhas pa'i mgul rgyan).* Tsering Thar, ed. Beijing: Krung go'i bod kyi shes rig dpe khrun khang, 1990.

LIST OF CONTRIBUTORS

WILLIAM COLEMAN is a Ph.D. candidate in the Department of History at Columbia University. He is currently working on his dissertation, which focuses on social history in Khams in the eighteenth and nineteenth centuries.

FABIENNE JAGOU is a research scholar at the French Institute of East Asian Studies (École française d'extrême-orient). Her Ph.D. in History, May 1999, at the École des hautes études en sciences sociales at Paris, is entitled "The 6th Panchen Lama (1883-1937): Traitor or Visionary?"

CAROLE MCGRANAHAN is Assistant Professor of Anthropology at the University of Colorado. Her doctoral dissertation is on Khampa histories of twentieth century Tibet.

PENG WENBIN is a Ph.D. candidate in Anthropology at the University of Washington, Seattle. His fields of interest cover ethnicity, regionalism and cultural nationalism in southwest China..

PETER SCHWIEGER studied Tibetology, Comparative Religious Science and Philosophy at the University of Bonn. He is currently a professor at Bonn University. He has done research on language, literature, religion and history of the Tibetan cultural area.

WIM VAN SPENGEN holds a Ph.D. in Human Geography from the University of Amsterdam. His main research interests are in the historical geography of Tibet and the Himalayan region. Currently he is a member of staff at the Social-Geographical Institute, University of Amsterdam.

TSERING THAR holds an MA in Tibetan Language and Literature from Qinghai Nationalities University in Xining. He conducts research in Tibetan religion at the China Center for Tibetan Studies, Beijing.